Virginia

K. M. Kostyal

Revised by Conrad Little Paulus
Photography by David M. Doody

COMPASS AMERICAN GUIDES
An imprint of Fodor's Travel Publications

Compass American Guides: Virginia
Editors: Bland Crowder, Kristin Moehlmann
Designer: Siobhan O'Hare
Compass Editorial Director: Daniel Mangin
Editorial Production: Stacey Kulig
Photo Editor: Jolie Novak
Archival Research: Melanie Marin
Map Design: Mark Stroud, Moon Street Cartography (Civil War map by Eureka Cartography)
Cover photo by David M. Doody: A surveyor at Colonial Williamsburg

Fourth Edition
ISBN 1–4000–1241–4
ISSN 1542–328X
Compass American Guides, 1745 Broadway, New York, NY 10019
PRINTED IN SINGAPORE
10 9 8 7 6 5 4 3 2 1

To my parents, Dick and Helen Kostyal,
who bred me with Bay water in my veins
and Virginia on my mind.

C O N T E N T S

Sidebars and Topical Essays

Literary Extracts

Maps

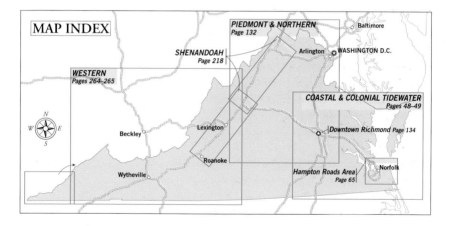

VIRGINIA FACTS

Nickname: Old Dominion
Capital: Richmond
State motto: *Sic Semper Tyrannis* (Thus Always to Tyrants)
State flower: Dogwood
State tree: Dogwood
State dog: Foxhound
State bird: Cardinal
Entered the Union: June 25, 1788 (the 10th state to do so)

■ POPULATION 7,078,515 (2000 U.S. CENSUS)

LARGEST CITIES BY POPULATION

Virginia Beach:	425,257
Norfolk:	234,403
Chesapeake:	199,184
Richmond:	197,790
Arlington:	189,453
Newport News:	180,150
Hampton:	146,437
Alexandria:	128,283

■ VIRGINIA'S PRESIDENTS

1st	George Washington	9th	William Henry Harrison
3rd	Thomas Jefferson	10th	John Tyler
4th	James Madison	12th	Zachary Taylor
5th	James Monroe	28th	Woodrow Wilson

■ OTHER FAMOUS VIRGINIANS

Arthur Ashe, Pearl Bailey, Richard E. Byrd, Mother Maybelle Carter, Willa Cather, Patsy Cline, Ella Fitzgerald, Patrick Henry, Thomas J. "Stonewall" Jackson, Robert E. Lee, Meriwether Lewis and William Clark, Pocahontas, Edgar Allan Poe, Walter Reed, Maggie Walker, Booker T. Washington, Tom Wolfe

■ CLIMATE

Highest recorded temperature: Balcony Falls, 110 degrees F, July 15, 1954
Lowest recorded temperature: Mountain Lake Bio Station, minus-30 degrees F, Jan. 22, 1985
Highest annual rainfall: Wallaceton, Norfolk County, 54.39 inches
Lowest annual rainfall: Woodstock, Shenandoah County, 33.89 inches

■ INTERESTING FACTS

- Virginia is officially a commonwealth rather than a state, and has been since independence from Britain. Kentucky, Massachusetts, and Pennsylvania are also commonwealths, but Virginia was the first to have that status.
- Virginia has 95 counties, plus 40 independent cities separate from their surrounding counties.
- Thomas Jefferson died at Monticello on July 4, 1826, the 50th anniversary of the signing of the Declaration of Independence. A few hours later, another of the nation's founding fathers and the only other ex-president, John Adams, died in Massachusetts, whispering on his deathbed, "Thomas Jefferson survives."
- The surrenders ending both the American Revolution and the Civil War took place in Virginia, at Yorktown and Appomattox.
- The first female member of the British Parliament was a Virginian, Nancy Astor, née Langhorne, elected in 1919.
- The longest-running film in American history is *Williamsburg: The Story of a Patriot,* directed by George Seaton (who won an Oscar for *Miracle on 34th Street)* and starring Jack Lord. Shot in VistaVision, the first ultra-wide-screen film format, and using Todd-AO six-channel stereo, an early form of "surround sound," it has been shown daily at Colonial Williamsburg since March 31, 1957.

VIRGINIA

0   5   10 Miles

0   5   10   15 Kilometers

Elevation
in feet

5,729
3,000
2,500
2,000
1,500
1,000
500
250
0

MARYLAND

DELAWARE

MARYLAND

Baltimore

Winchester

Berryville

Front Royal

Leesburg

Reston

Arlington

Annapolis

WASHINGTON D.C.

Centreville

Fairfax

Alexandria

Warrenton

Manassas

Opal

Dale City

Woodbridge

Culpeper

Skyline Drive

Gordonsville

Fredericksburg

George Washington Birthplace National Monument

Stratford Hall

Port Royal

Cuckoo

Warsaw

Tappahannock

Scotland

Pocomoke City

Chincoteague

PIEDMONT

Central Garage

Saluda

Reedville

Kilmarnock

Onancock

Chesapeake Bay

RICHMOND

Bon Air

Exmore

Farmville

Chester Colonial Heights Petersburg

Hopewell

Williamsburg

Jamestown

Gloucester

Cape Charles

Yorktown

Poquoson

Hampton

Blackstone

Waverly

McKenney

Smithfield

Newport News

CAPE HENRY

Virginia Beach

Lawrenceville

Windsor

Suffolk

Norfolk

Portsmouth

outh Hill

Franklin

Chesapeake

Emporia

Dismal Swamp National Wildlife Refuge

Currituck

Roanoke Rapids

NORTH CAROLINA

TIDEWATER

Atlantic Ocean

OVERVIEW

■ COASTAL VIRGINIA

The vast Chesapeake Bay is known for its harbor towns, blue crabs, and seafood restaurants; the Eastern Shore's Assateague Island has pristine beaches, a famous candy-striped lighthouse, and wild ponies, which are auctioned off once a year on nearby Chincoteague Island. Virginia Beach is one of the mid-Atlantic's most famous summer resorts, and across Hampton Roads the vibrant port of Norfolk and old Portsmouth hold hands with Newport News and historic Hampton.

■ COLONIAL TIDEWATER

Between the York and James Rivers lie three of the most significant sites in colonial American history: Jamestown, where the first English settlement was established; Williamsburg, the colonial capital; and Yorktown, site of the final battle of the American Revolution. Along the banks of the James stand historic plantations; on the Middle Peninsula, between the York and the Rappahannock, colonial churches and courthouses are preserved; and on the Northern Neck, Washington and Lee, Virginia's two greatest heroes, were born.

■ PIEDMONT

The rolling hills of the Piedmont sweep across central Virginia, gathering in their folds Richmond, capital of the Confederacy, and the historic towns of Petersburg, Charlottesville, and Fredericksburg. Thomas Jefferson's splendid architectural achievements are here, including his home, Monticello, and the original buildings of the University of Virginia.

■ NORTHERN VIRGINIA

The hillsides and towns of Northern Virginia are rich in American history. Robert E. Lee's mansion overlooks Arlington National Cemetery; Old Town Alexandria with its small shops and cobblestone streets is not far from Mount Vernon, George Washington's home. To the west lie Manassas National Battlefield Park, site of two great Civil War battles, and Loudoun County, full of old towns and celebrities.

■ SHENANDOAH VALLEY

The Shenandoah Valley, bordered by the Blue Ridge on the east and the Allegheny Mountains on the west, is an exceptionally beautiful place, easily explored via scenic highways. The Skyline Drive runs the length of lush Shenandoah National Park and continues south as the Blue Ridge Parkway, snaking its way past mountain peaks. During the Civil War, this serene countryside suffered more battles than any other region in the country, and poignant reminders are scattered throughout the valley.

■ WEST BY SOUTHWEST

The Blue Ridge Highlands of the state's southwest corner provide a compelling setting for such pleasures as hiking through and around the Cumberland Gap or listening to country music in Floyd. Pretty Abingdon, one of the region's many small towns, is noted for its arts and architecture and the legendary Barter Theatre.

INTRODUCTION

Planning a vacation and wondering where to go? To tell you the truth, Virginia's rounded old mountains are mole hills beside the Rockies, or even compared to the Adirondacks. If it's beaches you want, there are wider and whiter ones farther south along the Atlantic. And the Old Dominion's countryside, as beautiful as it may be, is matched by New England's and surpassed by that of many states out West.

But though Virginia isn't the most exotic of destinations, there's a mystique about the place, perhaps because everybody loves the antique—old houses and furniture, the tales and songs of long ago, folklore and history. Virginia condenses all of these into a heady, hearty stew, one with an ingredient or two for everyone, all of it flavored by the disparate souls who have streamed into this area over the centuries: on those small brave ships that landed at Jamestown, down the Great Wagon Road from the North, in floating hellholes on the Middle Passage. Cavaliers, convicts, and captives, fortune seekers and farmers, patriots and politicians—the ghosts of our nation's history congregate here, lending glamour to the ordinary.

I was born and raised in Virginia, and though I now live "up north," I return several times a year. As I traveled throughout Virginia revising K. M. Kostyal's delightful, evocative book, I stayed with friends and relatives, visiting my old haunts: the gray-shingled cottage line at "the Beach," the Fan in Richmond where I grew up, "the University" in Charlottesville, where I'd misspent some of my youth. I expected to wallow in Virginia's near-obsession with the past, and I figured the food would be unadventurous, but I hoped to explore places I'd never seen and find a new openness and spirit of adventure.

I searched out the old and the new—one friend told me about Occoquan, a tiny 18th-century town near Alexandria, and another pointed me to Floyd, an up-and-coming country music town in the Valley of Virginia. Everywhere I went I met busy people (but not too busy to be friendly and polite) doing interesting things: starting a new Shakespeare theater in Staunton, establishing a black history museum in Hampton, hosting elderly hunters and steeplechasers at a historic B&B. I visited stately homes and mansions and found not shrines to the past, but active places being used in innovative ways as part of working lives.

I learned that these days the antique stew is evolving into an altogether new dish as old notions yield to 21st-century reality. In early 2003, a respected Harvard lawyer was sworn in as Virginia's first African-American Chief Justice in the court's 224 years. Young women are now integrating Virginia Military Institute. And some folks hereabouts are even ready to concede that country hams from nameless farms are the equals of those labeled Smithfield. And speaking of that food I'd assumed would be lackluster, I found delicious unwashed oysters in shucking sheds on the Eastern Shore, ate divine soul food in Richmond, and sampled many wines from old and new wineries—even ordered some bottles to take home. In restaurants and bistros, dives and diners, from the D.C. border to Petersburg and out to the Cumberland Gap, I discovered that chefs are expanding their horizons, growing their own produce and preparing splendid meals informed by the cuisines of the world.

In other words, the Old Dominion is full of surprises. The arts are flourishing, rampant development is being kept at bay, and the Revolutionary and Confederate heroes and their houses are being pressed into serving the people of today. Forget the highest mountains or the whitest beaches—catch them on another trip. Come to Virginia for the history, the art, the music, the food, and the fun.

I had such a ball on my trip, I'd do it again for no pay.

—Conrad Little Paulus

H I S T O R Y

History haunts Virginia like a lost lover. Images, mementos, echoes of the past float along its rivers, get tangled in the thick press of its forests, stand beside the gallant statues that pose in its courthouse squares.

So much history; so many histories. Native American and European, male and female, black and white. After all, Virginians trace their lines back to the first settlers, to major players in the Revolution, to founding fathers of the nation. And Richmond was a capital of the Confederacy and the state a primary battleground of the Civil War. For older Virginians—and younger ones who cleave to the Commonwealth's past—that war, regardless of its cost, was a moment of glory.

Glory clearly colors the Old Dominion's past, sometimes to its detriment. Virginians have had a deserved reputation for courting old traditions, for looking backward more often than forward. But that old-line conservatism seems to be receding. Virginia may not be one of America's most progressive states, but with the past as a sort of patina, it has made significant strides in recent decades, particularly in the area of race relations.

■ FRUITFULLEST VIRGINIA

The Virginia saga began somewhere in the vaguest past, when bands of nomads drifted out of Asia across the Bering land bridge into what is now Alaska, eventually reaching virtually every part of the Americas. When they reached the Atlantic Ocean they could go no farther, so they settled along the rivers and bays that empty into it, making their homes in the endless coastal forests, slowly resolving themselves into tribes and kingdoms. Most of these coastal tribes belonged to the large group that spoke Algonquian languages. In the inner coastal plain lived Iroquoian tribes, and the Piedmont was home to members of the Sioux nation.

In the 16th century another band of wanderers, the European explorers, entered their world, intent on a migration of their own, but in a direction opposite that of the Asian nomads' dispersal: they had been pushing west toward the riches of India—until North America got in their way.

Robertson's Windmill at Colonial Williamsburg is a reproduction of one owned there in the early 18th century by William Robertson, a lawyer with a custom mill business.

HISTORY TIME LINE

A.D. 1500s Native peoples of the Algonquian language group inhabit present-day Virginia, from the Chesapeake Bay area to the mountains. When the first English settlers arrive, the eastern tribes are led by paramount chief Powhatan.

1584 Expedition sent by Sir Walter Raleigh to explore North America for Queen Elizabeth I names newly discovered land Virginia in honor of the Virgin Queen. The land in question is Roanoke Island, in present-day North Carolina, and efforts to colonize it in subsequent years fail.

1607 After a journey of 18 weeks, 105 English settlers reach Cape Henry. They sail upriver and establish the Jamestown settlement. By the end of the year, more than two-thirds of the group have died.

1609 Reinforced by new arrivals, settlers number nearly 500. Capt. John Smith, leader of the Jamestown settlement, is wounded and returns to England. Relations with the Powhatan become hostile.

1610 Jamestown reduced to 60 survivors after winter famine; saved by the arrival of Gov. Thomas West (Lord De La Warr) who brings new settlers, needed supplies, and strong leadership.

1612 Captain John Smith's book *A Map of Virginia: With a Description of the Countary, the Commodities, People, Government and Religion* published in England.

1614 Pocahontas, converted to Christianity, marries John Rolfe, tobacco planter; first shipment of settler-grown tobacco exported to England.

1619 First democratically elected legislative body in New World, the House of Burgesses, is formed. First Africans arrive on a Dutch man-o'-war, to be sold as indentured servants.

1622 The Powhatan, under new paramount chief Opechancanough, massacre hundreds of settlers along the James; colonists retaliate.

1624 Captain John Smith's *General History of Virginia, the Summer Isles and New England* published in England; includes his story of rescue by Pocahontas.

1675 Nathaniel Bacon leads unauthorized attacks against Indians. He and his adherents end in open rebellion, the next year driving British governor William Berkeley out of Jamestown and burning the town.

1693 The College of William and Mary is chartered in Williamsburg; after Harvard, it is the second-oldest institution of higher learning in the United States.

1699 Capital moved to Williamsburg.

1722 New York, Pennsylvania, and Virginia governors enact peace treaty with the Iroquois; in Virginia, they are restricted to west of the Blue Ridge Mountains.

1774 House of Burgesses dissolved by British governor John Murray. Patriots convene at nearby Raleigh Tavern.

1775 Patrick Henry delivers his "Give me liberty or give me death" speech, predicting the start of violence. On April 19, Revolutionary War begins in Massachusetts.

1776 Last Revolutionary convention in Williamsburg unanimously carries a resolution calling for independence. Motion passes on July 2. Declaration of Independence, written by Virginian Thomas Jefferson, signed in Philadelphia.

1781 On October 19, Lord Cornwallis surrenders British army to Gen. George Washington at Yorktown.

1789 George Washington becomes the first president of the United States.

1801 Thomas Jefferson of Monticello is elected the nation's third president, defeating incumbent John Adams.

1809 James Madison becomes the nation's fourth president, the third from Virginia.

1817 James Monroe becomes the fifth president of the United States, the fourth (and the third in a row) from Virginia.

1841 William Henry Harrison, born at Berkeley plantation, dies after only one month as the nation's ninth president and is succeeded by John Tyler, of Charles City County, who serves a full term as the 10th.

1849 Zachary Taylor, born near Barboursville, becomes the 12th U.S. president, the seventh from Virginia.

1861 Virginia secedes from the Union and joins the Confederacy, causing the western counties to separate from the state. Col. Robert E. Lee becomes commander of Virginia's forces.

The Algonquin village of Pomieooc was sketched in the 1580s by John White, a member of Sir Walter Raleigh's Roanoke Island colonizing expedition. An engraving based on the sketch appeared in a volume on Virginia published in Frankfurt in 1590.

1865   On April 9, Lee surrenders the Confederate army to Gen. Ulysses S.Grant at Appomattox.

1870   Virginia is readmitted to the Union, having accepted the Fifteenth Amendment guaranteeing that the right to vote cannot be denied because of "race, color, or previous condition of servitude."

1913   Staunton-born Woodrow Wilson becomes 28th president; leads the country during World War I and, for his efforts at the Paris Peace Conference, wins Nobel Prize for Peace in 1919.

1932   Tomb of the Unknown Soldier—an unidentified American killed in World War I—opens to the public at Arlington National Cemetery.

1941–1945   More than 215,000 Virginians serve in World War II; 185 warships are built at Newport News shipyard.

1954   Supreme Court, in *Brown v. Board of Education* (Kansas), finds racial segregation in public schools unconstitutional. (The NAACP had filed a similar lawsuit in Richmond in 1951.)

1957   Queen Elizabeth II and Prince Philip visit Jamestown on the 350th anniversary of its founding.

1964   Passage of the U.S. Civil Rights Act, followed the next year by the Voting Rights Act, forces progress in Virginia.

1970   State elects its first Republican governor since 1886, and its third constitution is approved.

1990   L. Douglas Wilder, the first elected African-American governor in the United States, begins his term as head of the Commonwealth.

2001   On September 11, terrorists hijack American Airlines Flight 77 and crash it into the Pentagon, killing 182 people.

2002   Congress approves bill to spend $50 million over five years to preserve Civil War battlefields, thus saving the Mullins Farm at Chancellorsville from development.

2003   Statue of Abraham Lincoln and his son, Tab, unveiled at Richmond National Battlefield Park. The statue commemorates Lincoln's visit in 1865, just after the fall of Richmond.

In the 1560s, Spanish adventurers captured a native chief from what is now Virginia, named him Don Luis de Valasco, and took him back to Madrid to be educated. When Spanish Jesuits returned him to the Virginia coast in 1570, he reasserted his rights as a chief, and when the Jesuits built a mission, hoping to convert the Indians to Christianity, Don Luis, instead, killed the Jesuits. Little was heard from Europeans until 1585, when an English expedition sent by Sir Walter Raleigh tried to colonize Roanoke Island, in what is now North Carolina but was then the newly discovered territory the English had named Virginia, after Elizabeth, their Virgin Queen. By 1590 that colony had vanished. Indeed, the story of the mysterious Lost Colony is reenacted every summer in an outdoor drama on Roanoke Island.

Then, in December 1606, when James I occupied the throne of England, another band of aspiring English settlers, aboard three small ships—the 100-ton *Susan Constant,* the 40-ton *Godspeed,* and the 20-ton *Discovery*—sailed down the Thames. Backed by the newly formed Virginia Company, this expedition was a business venture. Its members had been instructed to do four things in the strange, wild land that the poet Edmund Spenser called "fruitfullest Virginia": locate a sea passage through it to the Orient; search out its wealth; convert its "heathens"; and, along the way, bring glory to themselves and their sovereign. They accomplished none of these, but they did manage to establish what would be the first permanent English settlement in the New World.

■ JAMESTOWN ESTABLISHED

About half of the 105 settlers who survived the trip were younger sons of gentry who had nothing to gain by staying in 17th-century England, where they would inherit neither land nor wealth. This exotic Virginia held the promise of untold riches. That they would have to work for any of this might not have crossed their minds as they set sail with high hopes but few skills.

The rest of the settlers were mostly artisans weary of England's entrenched class structure and lack of opportunity. Unfortunately, their particular crafts and experiences weren't what was needed to tame a wilderness—but who knew what was needed? Only one man among those on board seems to have been suited by temperament and experience for the business of establishing a new world. This seasoned mercenary and adventurer, John Smith, would prove to be a godsend. But his chronic braggadocio managed to get him arrested before the ships had crossed the Atlantic.

"He that will not worke shall not eat," proclaimed Capt. John Smith in order to cajole the gentry into doing their share of the work at Jamestown.

The crossing was plagued from the start. Before setting off down the Thames, they were cursed with the ill omen of Halley's Comet streaking across the night sky. Then they spent six weeks floundering in contrary winds and wicked weather off the British coast, depleting their precious provisions.

Finally, after four and a half months en route, with stops in the Canary Islands and the West Indies, they sighted the low, wooded coastline of Virginia. Reaching the capes at the mouth of the broad and benevolent Chesapeake Bay, they stopped to erect a cross in gratitude at what would be named Cape Henry. They then proceeded up a wide river that they called James, for their king.

It was late April, and white dogwood blossoms dappled Virginia's new-green forests. The newcomers reconnoitered the shoreline, gorging on wild strawberries and on the clams and mussels that paved the shoals. After exploring the lower James for a few weeks, they chose a small peninsula 60 miles upstream on which to build a fort. This "island," as it has always been called, seemed easy to defend against French or Spanish warships or hostile half-clothed natives such as those that had assaulted them when they landed at Cape Henry.

In high spirits, the small band set about transforming the island they had named Jamestown into a facsimile of rural England. They built a stockaded fort and planted crops, working communally as the Virginia Company had prescribed. They also searched voraciously for gold, optimistic that the very river sands were spangled with its glint. And very soon they began to die. By autumn, malnutrition, malaria, dysentery, and typhoid fever, a disease they had unwittingly brought with them from England, had carried away half their members. Recounting the grisly scene, one of them described "men night and day groaning in every corner of the fort…some departing three or four in a night…their bodies trailed out of their cabins like dogges to be buried."

Only John Smith, who was not released from his bondage until a month after the arrival at Jamestown, seemed to understand the potential—and the requirements—of this new wilderness. By September he had been made president of the governing council, and he was quick to push every man, even the cosseted gentry, into action. Smith's first commandment was simple: "He that will not worke shall not eat." For a year his determination, his ability to deal effectively with the natives, who were sometimes helpful and sometimes hostile, and his sheer zeal for adventure kept the struggling band alive against all odds.

In the fall of 1609, Smith was badly wounded when a musket accidentally discharged into his leg. Afraid the injury might be the end of him, he sailed for England. He never returned. Ironically, the man who, more than any other, had grafted England onto the Virginia soil, spent less than a year and a half in the New World.

Disaster followed Smith's departure. Winter was coming on, and new settlers had arrived, so that the population now numbered 500. The drought of 1609 was the worst Virginia had suffered in 700 years, recent research has shown, so the harvest had been negligible. Although new stores had been laid in, the settlers couldn't reach livestock corralled outside the fortress because of unrelenting Powhatan aggression. That grim winter of 1609–10 is remembered as the "Starving Time." When spring came again, only 60 souls, half-dead, remained to greet it.

They also greeted a new problem: a fresh contingent of English settlers who had been delayed by shipwreck in the Bermudas and, expecting to find a thriving settlement, had brought only scant provisions. Their leader, Governor Gates, took a long look at the forlorn survivors of drought and devastation and at the destroyed fortress, whose wood had been pulled down for fires during the winter, and decided that Jamestown could not be saved. The English would have abandoned

CAPTAIN SMITH AND POCAHONTAS

When John Smith was born in Lincolnshire, England, in 1580, the Elizabethan "age of wonder and delight" was in full cry, with Asia, Africa, and the West Indies only recently discovered by Europeans. A soldier of fortune, Smith proved a formidable fighter. In the Balkans he had become something of a legend, particularly after he took the heads of two Turkish noblemen in successive hand-to-hand duels. Soon after that, though, young John found himself a captive of the Turks, then sold as a slave to a pasha. The wily Smith managed an almost impossible escape and made his way slowly across Europe to England.

He returned home just as fever for the New World was sweeping London. At 27, Smith set sail with the first band of settlers—and found himself arrested before ever setting foot in Virginia. There was even talk on board of hanging the outspoken braggart.

Once in Virginia, the expedition opened sealed orders from the King's Council, which named seven men to head up the settlement. John Smith was one of them. Still, at first he had little say in how things were run. Instead, he watched disdainfully as the settlers grappled ineffectively with the frontier and occupied himself by exploring the region. From these expeditions, he created remarkably accurate maps and charts of coastal Virginia.

On one such trip Smith met Matoaka, the Powhatan chief's favored daughter, known to posterity by her nickname, Pocahontas—"playful one." Smith had been taken prisoner by a Powhatan hunting party and at first avoided execution by enthralling his captors with the "magic" of his compass. The Indians eventually presented him to their chief, also called Powhatan, and, according to Smith (in his memoir, written years later, the facts most assuredly embellished), the Indians were "ready with their clubs, to beat out his braines," when Pocahontas "got his head in her armes, and laid her owne upon his to save him from death: whereat the Emperour was contented he should live...." After that encounter, Pocahontas apparently developed a devotion to Smith and visited Jamestown a number of times. She even saved him—and the settlers—a second time when she warned them of a Powhatan plot to attack the fort.

Smith may have had a strong ally in the Indian princess, but his colleagues did not hold him in such high esteem. One detractor described him as "an ambityous, unworthy, and vayneglorious fellowe." Ambitious, yes; vainglorious, oh, yes; but unworthy? No. John Smith's "worthiness" kept Virginia alive through its first struggling year.

If Smith saved Jamestown through stamina and vision, Pocahontas saved it through devotion and charm. She seems to have been captivated by English ways. Though the settlers kidnapped her after Smith left for England, she still chose to wed a colonist, John Rolfe (who was chiefly responsible for introducing the settlers to a palatable tobacco), and their union resulted in the "Pocahontas Peace"—almost eight years of good relations between the Powhatan and the English.

The couple and their infant son, Thomas, sailed for England in 1616, where the exotic Lady Rebecca, as Pocahontas had been christened, soon became a London celebrity. When she was presented at court, her regal bearing induced English gentlewomen to curtsy before her and, when leaving a room she was in, to back out. She also had a brief reunion with her friend John Smith, who by then was devoting all his time and energy to promoting Virginia.

This engraving of Pocahontas, in the National Portrait Gallery, was made during her visit to London in 1616 by Dutch engraver Simon van de Passe. It shows her dressed as she probably was when presented at the court of James I and is the only life portrait of her known to exist.

After 10 months in England, Lady Rebecca reluctantly left Britain behind and set sail with her husband for Virginia. But a short distance down the Thames, she became ill, and very soon, Pocahontas—favored lady at both the Powhatan and English courts—was dead at age 21. Her son returned to prospering Virginia as a young man and married a well-placed colonial woman.

their only foothold in America had another group of English, a well-provisioned relief expedition of some 300 men and women under Lord De La Warr, not arrived in the nick of time.

John Smith had considered the 1,500-acre island of Jamestown "a verie fit place for the erecting of a great cittie," although it was little more than a low-lying malarial swamp. In the settlement's first dozen years, aspiring settlers faced a one-in-seven chance of survival. Inexplicably, they poured out of England anyway, many apparently ignorant of the hardships ahead and others willing to stake their lives on the chance of a new beginning. Also inexplicable was their inability to adapt to or make use of the resources of this rich land. In the face of woods teeming with game and rivers full of fish and shellfish, they starved, though that can be somewhat explained by the almost constant threat of Indian attack.

Finally, in 1611, they founded a new settlement, Henricus, upriver on higher ground near what would become Richmond. Jamestown remained the hub of colonization, but this second settlement, although it did not last, gave the settlers new hope. At about the same time, the Virginia Company halted its misbegotten experiment in communalism and issued the settlers their own plots of land from which to reap their own profits. Sooner than they could have predicted, they began to produce gold—not the yellow metal but Virginia gold: tobacco.

Like many 17th-century Europeans, the Powhatan were devotees of the "esteemed weed," but the variety that grew in Virginia was too harsh for European tastes. Then the enterprising John Rolfe found that he could cultivate a milder type of West Indian tobacco that was popular in Europe. Soon, even the streets of Jamestown were patched with tobacco plants, as Europe clamored for what King James, an early and ardent nonsmoker, called "the horrible Stygian smoke of the pit that is bottomless."

Although disease, attacks by the natives, and the hardships of the wilderness still plagued the early Virginians, they could now smell success in that smoke. They pushed the frontier westward, establishing small tobacco farms along the James and York Rivers. In 1622, many of the families on those scattered farms were slaughtered in a violent massacre plotted by the Powhatan chieftain Opechancanough. Still the settlers persisted, and two years later, King James officially declared Virginia a colony, taking it out of the private Virginia Company's hands.

(following pages) Map of Virginia, with north to the right. William Hole's engraving of 1624 was based on Capt. John Smith's original, published in 1612.

Even in those early years, the idea of self-determination was becoming the backbone of the colonial esprit. Virginia already had its own elected assembly of representatives—and a growing sense of inalienable rights. The entrenched oligarchy of England wasn't the way of Virginia. A man could arrive in the colony as an indentured servant, pay off his seven years' indenture, then go on to become a prospering and prominent colonist.

■ VIRGINIA LEAVES THE CROWN

The colonists' growing sense of independence from English authority came to an unexpected head in 1676, when Virginians staged a short-lived but portentous rebellion against the king's arrogant governor, William Berkeley. A virtual war had been raging between the Powhatan and the colonists, but Berkeley had refused to organize a force against the Powhatan. A charismatic newcomer named Nathaniel Bacon took matters into his own hands, and with a band of followers, attacked a Powhatan village. Berkeley was enraged by this upstart behavior and labeled Bacon a traitor.

Throughout the summer and early fall of 1676, Bacon's growing army of rebels fought surprisingly well against the governor's forces and at times seemed about to win. But Virginia was not yet ripe to overcome her British overlords. By October, Bacon was dead, and Berkeley had reclaimed his authority. The governor spent the rest of his rule bludgeoning the colonists and avenging himself on the rebels. He had 23 of them killed, leading King Charles II to comment that "that old fool has hanged more men in that naked country than I did for the murder of my father." In Bacon's Rebellion, English authority had won a round. But the fight had just begun.

As Virginia's first century came to a close, the untrammeled wilderness and its opportunities were already passing. Tobacco had an insatiable appetite for both land, which it quickly exhausted, and labor, which it demanded in quantities high enough to mire the colony in the horrors of slavery. By the early 18th century, a gentry had seeded itself across Virginia. In the east, yeoman farmers became an increasingly rare breed, as wealthy tobacco planters, backed by legions of African slaves, claimed the countryside. The wealthy also became serious land speculators, buying up northern and western lands, then reselling smaller plots to those willing to face the hardships of a new frontier. Virginia's landed aristocracy had been born.

Jamestown, malarial and star-crossed, was finally abandoned as the capital in 1699, and a new town—Williamsburg—took its role as the hub of colonial culture and politics; it even had its own college, named after the beneficent monarchs William and Mary. But while Tidewater society had became entrenched and gentrified, the western reaches of the known frontier were home to industrious owners of small farms. In the 1730s a flood of Scots-Irish, Germans, Quakers, and Mennonites streamed out of Pennsylvania and into the grassy, open Shenandoah Valley. The coastal Virginians were happy to have them there as a buffer against the Indians—and against the French, who were inching ever south and east into British-claimed territory.

In 1752 war broke out, and the Crown called up the Virginia militia to fight against the French and Indians along the western front. When the fighting ended with a British colonial victory, the courageous young commander-in-chief of the colony's militia emerged a hero. His name was George Washington.

Having just supplied the British with men and equipment for the French and Indian War, the colonists were less than pleased when, in 1765, Parliament imposed a new tax on them. The infamous Stamp Act, which levied a tax on

When you visit Colonial Williamsburg, you put the present behind you.

nearly all printed documents, from calendars to licenses, raised the hackles of liberal Virginians, who were tired of the mother country's demands. A firebrand orator named Patrick Henry stood in the Virginia House of Burgesses and admonished the Crown in shocking terms: " …Caesar had his Brutus, Charles the Third his Cromwell, and George the Third may profit by their example. If this be treason, make the most of it."

In less than a decade, Virginia and the other colonies would definitely be making the most of it. The Boston Tea Party, an outburst against British taxation in 1773, was followed in 1774 by the convening of the First Continental Congress, in Philadelphia. By the time the Second Continental Congress met a year later, British and colonial forces had exchanged fire at Lexington and Concord in Massachusetts. The Revolution was on. To lead its forces, the congress unanimously elected one of the colonies' few proven military heroes—George Washington.

While Washington struggled to turn ill-equipped and untrained colonial farmers, merchants, and artisans into fighters, another Virginian was distinguishing himself in the Philadelphia corridors. Thirty-three-year-old delegate Thomas Jefferson had been charged by his colleagues to draft a paper that would explain the colonists' position to King George. On July 4, 1776, the congress adopted the Declaration of Independence. Written over the course of only a couple of weeks, the document reflects Jeffersonian clarity and humanism:

> We hold these truths to be self-evident: that all men are created
> equal; that they are endowed by their Creator with certain
> unalienable rights; that among these are life, liberty and the pursuit
> of happiness….

For its first half-dozen years, the Revolution raged largely in the colonies to the north and south of Virginia, though the British did harass its easily accessible coastline. In the midst of the war, Virginia's capital was moved out of Williamsburg to the more centrally located village of Richmond. By 1781, though, the war was driving deep into Virginia, as the turncoat Benedict Arnold led his troops against Richmond. Jefferson, governor at the time, ordered the General Assembly out of the defenseless town and west into Charlottesville. Looking to corral the impudent author of the Declaration of Independence, the brilliant British commander Lord Cornwallis sent troops in pursuit. But a farmer named John Jouett spotted the redcoats moving along the moonlit roads and, suspecting their intent, mounted his

A Britisher Reflects on Washington

He undoubtedly pants for military fame, and, considering the little military knowledge and experience he had before he was made a general, he has performed wonders. He was generally unfortunate (indeed I may with propriety say always) in every action where he was immediately concerned until the affair at Trenton in the Jerseys. Since that unlucky period (for us) he has only been too successful.

His education is not very great nor his parts shining, his disposition is rather heavy than volatile, much given to silence…. His person is tall and genteel, age between forty and fifty, his behavior and deportment is easy, genteel, and obliging, with a certain something about him which pleases everyone who has anything to do with him. There cannot be a greater proof of his particular address and good conduct than his keeping such a number of refractory, headstrong people together in any tolerable degree of decorum.

His house is at a place called Mount Vernon, about twelve miles below Alexandria on the banks of the Potomac River in Virginia, where he has a very fine plantation and farm, but, by the best accounts I could get, his estate, altogether, before these troubles did not amount to more than £300 a year in Virginia currency. But estates in this country are seldom valued by the year; it is some difficulty to know exactly what they are worth where they keep great numbers of Negroes and make large crops of tobacco. His friends and acquaintances reckon him a just man, exceedingly honest, but not very generous. Perhaps they may give him this character because he manages his estate with industry and economy, and very seldom enters into those foolish, giddy, and expensive frolics natural to a Virginian.

He keeps an excellent table, and a stranger, let him be of what country or nation, he will always meet with a most hospitable reception at it. His entertainments were always conducted with the most regularity and in the genteelest manner of any I ever was at on the continent (and I have been at several of them, that is, before he was made a general). Temperance he always observed, was always cool-headed and exceedingly cautious himself, but took great pleasure in seeing his friends entertained in the way most agreeable to themselves. His lady is of a hospitable disposition, always good-humored and cheerful, and seems to be actuated by the same motives with himself, but she is rather of a more lively disposition. They are to all appearances a happy pair.

—*The Journal of Nicholas Cresswell, 1774–1777*

horse and dashed through the night to warn Jefferson and the others in Charlottesville that the British were coming.

Defeated in this little foray, Cornwallis settled his forces in the Virginia port of Yorktown, about 25 miles from the mouth of the Chesapeake Bay. Washington, who was fighting in New York, saw a chance to do the British irreparable harm, particularly with the aid of the French, now his allies. Sneaking out of New York with his troops—16,000 war-weary Colonials and French reinforcements—he marched relentlessly south into Virginia. By early September he had Cornwallis cornered at Yorktown, and French warships at the mouth of the bay cut off a British escape by sea. Washington's army laid siege, as Cornwallis, vastly outnumbered, pulled back and waited for British reinforcements. They never came. The British fleet, sailing to the rescue, was engaged in battle and turned back by the French fleet, and after several weeks, Lord Cornwallis admitted defeat. But with characteristic disdain, he refused to appear in person for the surrender ceremonies. The opposing forces gathered in an open field, and as the Redcoat fifes and drums played "The World Turned Upside-Down," British Brig. Gen. Charles O'Hara surrendered what turned out to be almost a quarter of a continent to Washington. Although the war dragged on for another year and a half in New York, Yorktown marked America's decisive moment.

■ From Colonialism to Modernism

With peace came all the freedoms and problems of independence. Under the loosely knit Articles of Confederation, each of the new states operated virtually on its own. After a decade of fumbling along in 13 often contentious directions, the barely united states recognized the need for some central authority, particularly to manage commerce, banking, and foreign affairs. A Constitutional Convention was held in Philadelphia in 1787, and after much wrangling, the United States Constitution emerged. The newly formed union also voted unanimously to make the hero of the Revolution, George Washington, the country's first president. After more wrangling, the Congress empowered Washington to establish a new "federal city" somewhere in the southern precinct. He chose a spot on the Potomac River about 15 miles upstream from his beloved Mount Vernon. A slice of Virginia, including the thriving port town of Alexandria, was included in the federal tract.

George Washington as a young man. Washington, whose great-grandfather emigrated from England in the mid-1600s, was the third-generation of the family in Virginia.

During the country's first decades under the Constitution, Virginia retained its prominence, contributing seven of the nation's first 12 presidents. Although the state remained rural and agrarian, the first pockets of industrialization were located in Tidewater and in cities near the fall line—Fredericksburg on the Rappahannock River; Petersburg on the Appomattox, a tributary of the James; and Alexandria on the Potomac. The capital, Richmond, on the fall line of the James, had likewise put water power to good use, becoming a major tobacco-processing and flour-milling center as well as the home of the Tredegar Ironworks, a major producer of cannons and other military hardware before the Civil War and the South's most important arsenal during it.

In western Virginia, coal, iron, and salt mining were burgeoning, as was a growing disaffection with the eastern "Tuckahoes"—the Tidewater gentry that still relied on slave labor and had a disproportionate hold on the reins of Virginia's political power. The western "Cohees" (from "Quoth he") of the Shenandoah Valley and surrounding mountains lived in another world, and the state did nothing constructive to knit its two halves together. When the age of railroads arrived in the mid-1800s, Virginia might have taken better advantage of the technology and built rails linking the goods of the west with its ports and markets in the east. But rivalry between cities like Richmond, Petersburg, and Norfolk resulted in small "short lines" that went only from one point to another, with no real intrastate network.

Then there was the question of slavery. It hung ominously over the state—and over the 19th century—just as Jefferson had predicted it would. He had called it "a firebell in the night" that "awakened and filled me with terror. I consider it at once a knell of the Union." By mid-century, many other Virginians had come to share Jefferson's terror. In 1859, abolitionist John Brown launched his famous raid on the Federal arsenal at Harpers Ferry (now in West Virginia, but then in Virginia), intent on stealing weapons to carry out an armed uprising of slaves. Though hanged for treason for his effort, the event had riveted the nation's attention.

With Lincoln's election in 1860, the moment that Jefferson had dreaded was at hand. In quick succession the seven "cotton states"—South Carolina, Alabama, Georgia, Florida, Mississippi, Louisiana, and Texas—seceded from the Union. Ironically, in Virginia, the state that would suffer most from the war, only a quarter of the white population owned slaves, and the state waited three more months to

Coal trains at Roanoke, in western Virginia.

GRANT MEETS LEE AT APPOMATTOX

On April 9, 1865, Gen. Ulysses S. Grant met with Gen. Robert E. Lee at Appomattox to accept the surrender of the Confederate army. Brig. Gen. Horace Porter, Grant's aide-de-camp, wrote the following account of the meeting.

The contrast between the two commanders was striking and could not fail to attract marked attention as they sat ten feet apart facing each other. General Grant, then nearly forty-three years of age, was five feet eight inches in height, with shoulders slightly stooped. His hair and full beard were a nutbrown, without a trace of gray in them. He had on a single-breasted blouse, made of dark-blue flannel, unbuttoned in front, and showing a waistcoat underneath. He wore an ordinary pair of top boots, with his trousers inside, and was without spurs. The boots and portions of his clothes were spattered with mud. He had had on a pair of thread gloves, of a dark-yellow color, which he had taken off on entering the room. His felt, "sugarloaf," stiff-brimmed hat was thrown on the table beside him. He had no sword, and a pair of shoulder straps was all there was about him to designate his rank. In fact, aside from these, his uniform was that of a private soldier.

Lee, on the other hand, was fully six feet in height and quite erect for one of his age, for he was Grant's senior by sixteen years. His hair and full beard were a silver-gray, and quite thick, except that the hair had become a little thin in front. He wore a new uniform of Confederate gray, buttoned up to the throat, and at his side he carried a long sword of exceedingly fine workmanship, the hilt studded with jewels. It was said to be the sword that had been presented to him by the state of Virginia. His top boots were comparatively new and seemed to have on them some ornamental stitching of red silk. Like his uniform, they were singularly clean and but little travel stained. On the boots were handsome spurs, with large rowels. A felt hat, which in color matched pretty closely that of his uniform, and a pair of long buckskin gauntlets lay beside him on the table. We asked Colonel Marshall afterward how it was that both he and his chief wore such fine toggery and looked so much as if they had turned out to go to church, while with us our outward garb scarcely rose to the dignity even of the "shabby genteel." He enlightened us regarding the contrast by explaining that when their headquarters wagons had been pressed so closely by our cavalry a few days before and it was found they would have to destroy all their baggage except the clothes they carried on their backs, each one, naturally, selected the newest suit he had, and sought to propitiate the god of destruction by a sacrifice of his second-best.

A contemporary Currier & Ives lithograph of Robert E. Lee's surrender to Ulysses S. Grant at Appomattox.

General Grant began the conversation by saying: "I met you once before, General Lee, while we were serving in Mexico, when you came over from General Scott's headquarters to visit Garland's brigade, to which I then belonged. I have always remembered your appearance, and I think I should have recognized you anywhere." "Yes," replied General Lee, "I know I met you on that occasion, and I have often thought of it and tried to recollect how you looked, but I have never been able to recall a single feature."

—Brig. Gen. Horace Porter, 1865

secede. Not until Lincoln ordered up local militia to fight on the side of the North did Virginia leave the Union, refusing to do battle against the states to the south. Richmond soon became capital of the Confederacy, and the state chose a brilliant military careerist, Robert E. Lee, to lead its forces. The war had been under way a year before the Confederate president, Jefferson Davis, made Lee commander of the Army of Northern Virginia.

Almost from the beginning of the war, the fighting took place in Virginia. Yankee forces quickly moved on Norfolk, burning buildings and scuttling several of the South's precious few ships. In July, members of Congress packed their picnic baskets and drove south to Manassas to watch their northern troops whomp the southern upstarts. Soon, they jested, they would all be dancing in Richmond. And it looked as though the battle was going to be a northern rout when suddenly an eccentric professor from the Virginia Military Institute, Thomas Jonathan Jackson, turned it around by managing to hold on to an impossible position on Henry House Hill. Seeing him and his men there, South Carolina's General Bee rallied his retreating troops by calling, "There stands Jackson like a stone wall! Rally behind the Virginians!" The southern forces took Manassas against all odds, and the war dug deeper into the soul of Virginia.

After Manassas, Stonewall Jackson went on to wage his legendary Valley Campaign. For three weeks his band of 6,000 to 19,000 men outfought and out-witted the 65,000-strong Union forces, making fools of the northerners up and down the Shenandoah Valley—and keeping them away from already beleaguered Richmond. By now Lee was in command of his Army of Northern Virginia, and he was intent on shoving the Yankees that were crawling across the Old Dominion back across the Potomac and into Washington. By August he had managed to do just that, but to little avail. The North could simply regroup, resupply, and come at the South again. But every battle cost Lee men and supplies he couldn't replace. In late August 1862, when the North and South squared off in Maryland at Antietam, the Confederacy suffered a serious blow.

The next year, the South's fortunes turned up again, with stunning victories at Fredericksburg and Chancellorsville, sites within 10 miles of each other and within 50 miles of Washington. But Chancellorsville was bought at an immense cost, because it was there that the seemingly invincible Stonewall fell. Riding out at dusk after a victorious day, Jackson was mistakenly shot by southern sentries. Part of his wounded arm was amputated, and he seemed to be recovering when he took ill with pneumonia. He was dead within a week.

If Jackson had lived, perhaps the devastation of Confederate forces at Gettysburg could have been avoided, or at least lessened. In any case, the human cataclysm that occurred in that small Pennsylvania crossroads claimed 28,000 southern casualties and 23,000 northern ones. After Gettysburg, Lee and his generals knew the war was lost, but they fought on. By the summer of 1864, Petersburg was under siege and nearby Richmond in jeopardy. On a fine April morning in 1865, the Confederate capital was abandoned and much of it put to the torch by its own people. There was nothing left to fight with, or for. On April 9, Lee met with Grant in a small house in the central Virginia crossroads of Appomattox, and the two generals worked out the terms of a surrender.

The war was over, the Union restored, and the Old Dominion a vast wasteland. Its farmlands were ruined, a seventh of its white men were either dead or disabled, its currency was utterly worthless, and it had no capital with which to rebuild. What Virginia did seem to have in abundance was a tough and inordinately proud people who began adapting to a new age. Ex-slaveholders in southeast Virginia slowly turned their farms over to sharecroppers, parceling out small plots in return for a portion of the harvested crop. While the system helped get the state back on its feet, it was only a step above the slavery that blacks had suffered.

In the western part of the state, however, farmers wisely diversified, turning to wheat, vegetables, and livestock. Mining also slowly recovered, and by the turn of the century, partly because Virginia had finally built a network of rails to bring its western products east, the James River ports led the world in coal exports.

Still, most of the state remained rural and also deeply attached to traditions, not all of them benign. Through the first decades of the 20th century, Virginia adhered to the discriminatory Jim Crow laws commonplace in the South. The result was a dual culture—whites and blacks had separate schools, separate stores, separate neighborhoods, and separate colleges (several black Virginia colleges earned a national reputation for excellence). In spite of, or maybe because of, the state's segregationist policies, in some parts of Virginia—notably Richmond and Tidewater—African-American businesses and culture flourished. Black Virginians who gained national prominence include educator Booker T. Washington, basketball player Moses Malone, dancer and actor Bill "Bojangles" Robinson, jazz great Ella Fitzgerald, singer and actress Pearl Bailey, opera star Camilla Williams, tennis champion Arthur Ashe, and television weatherman Spencer Christian.

Getting ready for a big bang—interpreters of the past at Colonial Williamsburg play their part in the American Revolution.

Like their white counterparts, African-American Virginians suffered with the Depression and prospered with the World Wars. World War II created a major boom in northern Virginia, where proximity to Washington has always fueled the local economy. For the first time, blacks and whites, and even women, worked side by side for the war effort. Tidewater, with its strong military and shipbuilding tradition, became a national focus of incoming and outgoing men and matériel. At war's end, those areas continued to thrive, and in the 1950s, the Chesapeake Bay Bridge-Tunnel, an engineering milestone connecting mainland Virginia with the Eastern Shore, opened another corridor from the populous north. The state as a whole began slowly but inexorably to shed its antebellum identity.

When the issue of segregation came to a head with the Supreme Court's 1954 *Brown v. Board of Education* decision, Virginia reacted much as it had during Civil War secession. Always more Virginian than strictly southern, the state and its schools never became armed battlegrounds over the issue. Still, the governor postured like a diehard segregationist, and the General Assembly enacted a law that withheld state funds from any school honoring integration. During the next five years, some public schools closed, along with parks and other public facilities. Then in 1959, a handful of black children were admitted to white schools in Norfolk and Arlington, heralding the beginning of the end of a racial system whose roots went back 300 years. Meaningful change did not, however, occur overnight. The Virginia legislature adopted nearly two dozen laws—part of what became known as the Massive Resistance plan—to thwart desegregation, and it was only after court decisions in the early 1970s that Virginia's public schools became fully integrated.

■ PAST, PRESENT, FUTURE

Virginia today is proud of its past. Its residents carefully tend colonial houses and honor their Civil War heroes, of which, in both cases, there are many. When developers proposed building a Wal-Mart on the site of George Washington's boyhood farm, they were met with furious opposition, as were those who proposed to build a colonial-themed amusement park near Williamsburg, plans that were eventually scuttled. However, the state no longer "makes the painful impression," as British historian Arnold Toynbee wrote in 1940, "of a country living under a spell, in which time has stood still."

Time is moving more rapidly here now. In 1990, Virginia inaugurated the first elected African-American governor in U.S. history, L. Douglas Wilder. And perhaps just as meaningful, in Richmond, Virginians have erected a statue of Arthur Ashe, a black native-son athlete who died of AIDS, along a boulevard that commemorates Civil War heroes, and unveiled a statue of Abraham Lincoln at Richmond National Battlefield Park.

As in the past, the shipbuilding industry and the military are huge economic forces—and an anchor to windward against the shaky economics of the early 21st century. And the state's influential Golden Crescent—the urban corridor that stretches from northern Virginia south to Richmond, then east to Hampton, Norfolk, and environs—has become a major component of the eastern megalopolis. There are significant migrations out of rural areas to the cities, which are burgeoning (and sprawling), and people are settling outlying areas as far as 75 miles away, commuting to urban jobs.

Thus the melting pot boils. The last 50 years have brought as much change to the Old Dominion as did the previous 300. The civility remains, praise be, but time-hardened attitudes are softening as diversity increases. Certainly, there are still areas of never-say-die traditionalism, but they only add to the state's divinely eccentric personality. Pinch most any of Virginia's natives, whether liberal or conservative, and they'd probably agree with former governor J. Lindsay Almond: "The only sane and constructive course to follow is to remain in the house of our fathers—even though the roof leaks, and there be bats in the belfry, rats in the pantry, a cockroach waltz in the kitchen and skunks in the parlor."

COASTAL VIRGINIA

The huge, pulsing heart of Coastal Virginia is the Chesapeake Bay. Its tributaries web the land in a network of estuarine rivers, creeks, and marshlands that flow back and forth to the bay's tidal beat. This vast shallow inland water, named for a Native American tribe, is encompassed by several thousand miles of coastline and has an average depth of only 20 feet. It connects to the Atlantic Ocean, which in turn defines the eastern extreme of Virginia, blessing it with some fine ocean beaches. But the ocean is enormous, somewhat overwhelming, and the property of so many. The bay—or at least its broad southern expanse—belongs to the Old Dominion. (Maryland claims ownership of its upper half.) If you explore its waters and shoreline and wander around the enormous historic harbor of Hampton Roads, you'll soon discover the simplicity, and complexity, of life along the Virginia coast.

■ EASTERN SHORE   *map pages 48–49, E/F-1/4*

Bounded by the Chesapeake on the west and the Atlantic on the east, this alluring tongue of land best preserves the old coastal style of Virginia. Its prairie-flat fields of corn and vegetables never lie fallow: in winter they seem to grow flocks of Canada geese and other wintering birds. As elsewhere in rural Virginia, small towns with long histories appear out of nowhere, and here watermen still work the bay's creeks and inlets. Towns on the coast, bayside and seaside, provide fishing of all kinds—charter boats, small boats with or without a guide, and guide service for duck or game bird hunting are easily available.

Virginia's Eastern Shore was explored before Jamestown was settled, when in 1603 Sir Walter Raleigh sent his nephew, a Captain Gilbert, and six others in search of traces of the Lost Colony of Roanoke Island. An Indian ambush left only two survivors of the expedition. One of them, Thomas Canner, wrote the earliest account of this visit to the Eastern Shore, and another made drawings and paintings depicting the Indians' way of life. In 1608 Capt. John Smith came across the bay from his base at Jamestown, exploring and map making, and in 1614 the first permanent English settlers arrived.

On the beach at Virginia Beach.

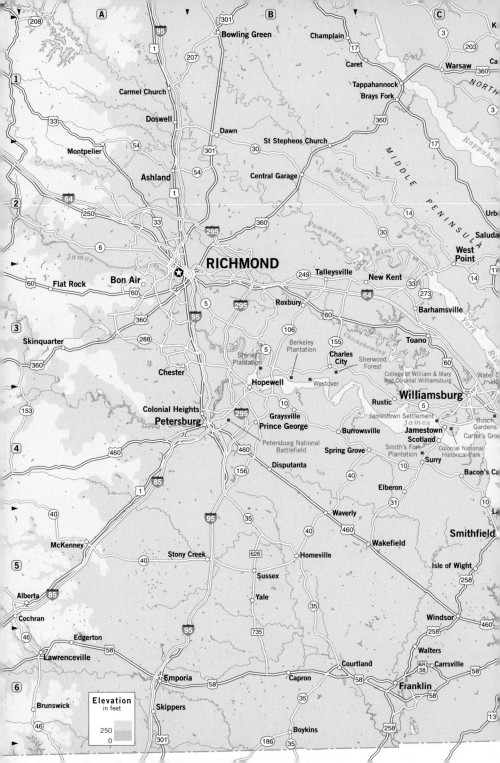

COASTAL VIRGINIA & COLONIAL TIDEWATER

MARYLAND

D **E** **F**

Potomac River

Heathsville
Burgess 360
201
Reedville 200

NECK

Lancaster 3

Christ Church
354
Kilmarnock
Irvington
White Stone 3

River

198
Dutton 3
14
Mathews
Gloucester 14
Ware Church
White Marsh
Abingdon Church
Mobjack Bay
Bavon
17
Severn
Achilles
Gloucester Point
Yorktown
173
Lee Hall
Tabb
134 117
Poquoson
Langley Air Force Base
Virginia Living Museum
60
64
Hampton
Mariners' Museum

Newport News
664
Norfolk
Portsmouth 264
337
464
58
165
190
Suffolk
165
Chesapeake
Dismal Swamp National Wildlife Refuge
17
168
Lake Drummond

NORTH CAROLINA

413
Crisfield

Ferry

New Church 13
NASA Wallops Flight Facility
Temperanceville
Wattsville
175
Chincoteague

Pocomoke Sound

Bloxom
Nelsonia
Wallops Island

Tangier Island
Ferry
Tangier
Parksley
Assawoman Island

Ferry

316
Metompkin Island

Onancock
Accomac
Onley
Melfa
Cedar Island

13
Pungoteague
180
Wachapreague
178
182
Quinby
Belle Haven
Exmore
183
Willis Wharf
Parramore Island
Jamesville

Hog Island Bay

Machipongo
Hog Island

600
Great Machipongo Inlet

Eastville
Cobb Island

Oyster
Wreck Island

Cape Charles
South Bay
Ship Shoal Island

13
Myrtle Island
Capeville

Smith Island

Kiptopeke
Fishermans Island
Cape Charles Lighthouse

Chesapeake Bay Bridge-Tunnel
Cape Charles

13
See Hampton Roads map page 65 for sites in this area

Cape Henry
60
Virginia Beach
279
Camp Pendleton
149
Back Bay National Wildlife Refuge

False Cape State Park

Yorktown Victory Center
Colonial National Historical Park

Assateague Island National Seashore
Chincoteague Island
Chincoteague National Wildli Refuge
Assateague Island

Atlantic Ocean

N
W E
S

COASTAL VIRGINIA & COLONIAL TIDEWATER

0   4   8 Miles

0   4   8   12 Kilometers

You could make a collection of the marvelous town names: Modest Town, Melfa, and Bloxom; Birdsnest, Horsey, and Oyster; Accomac, Nassawadox, and Wachapreague. Part of what some call the Delmarva (Delaware, Maryland, Virginia) Peninsula, the Eastern Shore is simply its own place—blessedly provincial and still remarkably pure. If you can manage to visit during Historic Garden Week in April, you'll be able to see many of the privately owned early houses that are open only then.

■ CHINCOTEAGUE ISLAND   *map pages 48–49, F-1*

Chincoteague Island is this area's best-known attraction, made famous by its oysters, its cowboys, and a pony called Misty. For almost 80 years now, the Chincoteague Volunteer Fire Department has been minding a herd of wild ponies on adjacent Assateague Island. Once a year, on the last consecutive Wednesday and Thursday in July, the young ponies are rounded up and made to swim across the inlet that separates the islands. They're then sold at a lively auction. What seems like half the East Coast gathers on Chincoteague for the pony penning, which keeps the herd at a sustainable level and also raises funds for the fire department.

Chincoteague ponies, a recognized breed, live wild on Assateague Island.

Assateague Island.

Local legend holds that ponies first arrived on Assateague in the 16th century, when a group of horses swam ashore from a shipwrecked Spanish galleon. Howe's *History of Virginia* (1845) states that the pony penning was so popular that it had made Chincoteague "the marriage market of the Eastern Shore." In the 1940s, writer Marguerite Henry spent some time here and made the island's ponies famous with her classic *Misty of Chincoteague.* The book was later turned into a movie, and the pony swim and penning have been a popular affair ever since. Misty's hoof prints are enshrined in cement, à la Hollywood's Grauman's Chinese Theatre, in front of the local movie house. You can even stay in the house where Henry wrote the book, just down Main Street from the theater. **Miss Molly's Inn** (4141 Main Street; 757-336-6686 or 800-221-5620), an 1896 Victorian with porches, pergolas, and a screened gazebo, seems frozen in time—you might fancy you see Miss Molly herself, who lived there all her life, descending the fretwork walnut staircase with the globe light.

The area is worth a visit any time of year. Chincoteague charms with its weathered but tidy houses and abundant seafood restaurants. Try **Etta's Channel Side** (East Side Drive; 757-336-5644), on the water, for some of the best. To learn how your meal got to the table, check out the **Oyster & Maritime Museum** (7125 Maddox Boulevard; 757-336-6117), just before the bridge to Assateague, the only museum of its kind in the country. Among the wonderful decoys on exhibit at the **Refuge Waterfowl Museum** (7059 Maddox Boulevard; 757-336-5800) are examples by the island's many well-respected carvers.

■ ASSATEAGUE ISLAND *map pages 48–49, F-1*
Beyond Chincoteague, a short causeway leads to Assateague Island, which provides Maryland and Virginia with a magnificent 37-mile stretch of unsullied, undeveloped beach, a rare find on Virginia's Atlantic coast. The Maryland part, **Assateague Island National Seashore,** and the Virginia part, **Chincoteague National Wildlife Refuge,** support migratory birds, white-tailed and sika deer, and graceful year-round residents such as egrets and herons—not to mention the herds of wild ponies. You can take a wildlife tour bus through the refuge, or, after 3 P.M., drive yourself on a 3-mile loop tour.

The candy-striped **Assateague Lighthouse** (757-336-2873 or 757-336-5917) warns mariners of the shoals, as it has since 1857, and it's open to the public one weekend per month from May through October. Because these islands sided with the Union in the Civil War, this was one of the few Virginia lighthouses that operated throughout the war.

As you drive away from Chincoteague, you might stop on Wallops Island to visit NASA's **Wallops Flight Facility** (757-824-2298) a research center, test range, and orbital tracking station. The visitors center has fascinating exhibits, interactive displays, and demonstration programs.

■ SHORT STOPS AND DRIVE-BYS
As you meander down (or up) the Eastern Shore, poking along the bay side and taking quick detours from U.S. 13 into appealing small towns, keep your eyes open for examples of the typical Eastern Shore dwelling in the "big house, little house, colonnade and kitchen" style. These comfortable farmhouses, often built over several generations, have sprung up all over.

Accomac *map pages 48–49, F-2*

Don't miss this nicely shaded old town, which has a slew of pre-Revolutionary houses. Their friendly owners are pleased that people appreciate them, so wander around—and you might still find an antique or two. The **Debtor's Prison** (Route 764, across the street from the county building), built in 1782 as the residence of the county jailer and converted into a prison in the 1820s, is a wonderful example of an 18th-century tradesman's house. Another noteworthy structure is **St. James Church** (Drummondtown Road; 757-787-4892). Built in 1838, with fluted columns in Greek Revival style, the church has box pews and trompe l'oeil painting decorating the altar wall and the ceiling.

Onancock *map pages 48–49, E-2*

This lively little town on the bay side was founded in 1680, when a courthouse began to operate, and it had a militia barracks during the Revolution. Today it has old houses, plenty of good food, many artists at work, the famous Corner Bakery, and the 155-year-old **Hopkins & Bro. Store** (2 Market Street; 757-787-3100). Still in business as a general store and restaurant, the weathered building sits on the wharf from which sailing vessels once departed with passengers and cargo bound for Baltimore and beyond, and from which ferries today take you to Tangier Island.

A real 18th-century treasure is **Kerr Place** (1799–1803), once the stately brick home of an Onancock merchant, now the Eastern Shore of Virginia Historical Society's museum. The changing exhibits of local artifacts and decorative arts are meticulously researched. *69 Market Street; 757-787-8012.*

If you'd like to stay overnight here, try **Montrose House Bed and Breakfast,** an Eastern Shore house that dates back to 1804. The furnishings are spectacular—the best of English and American antiques put together with an artist's eye. *20494 Market Street; 757-787-7088.*

■ TANGIER ISLAND *map pages 48–49, E-1*

Seemingly floating in the gray-green flatness of the Chesapeake Bay, Tangier Island barely raises its head above the level of the sea. Yet this 2.5-mile-long strip of land manages persistently to survive against time, weather, and the bay. Life moves slowly here, the watermen in their white deadrises—typical Chesapeake Bay workboats—still plying the island's reed-lined channels. Neat houses stand crammed into narrow lanes, and soft-crab "plantations," little sheds raised on stilts above the

water, present a picturesque image along the main Tangier boat channel. Most visitors arrive by boat and spend a few hours poking around the local gift shops and eating exceptional seafood, particularly at **Hilda Crockett's Chesapeake House** (757-891-2331). From mid-April to mid-October, this island landmark sets guests down at long family-style tables to feast from platter after platter of crab cakes, ham, potato salad, clam fritters, cole slaw, and homemade bread.

When you arrive on the island you'll be met by a local guide who will fill you full of interesting facts about Tangier and show you where you can rent a bike or a moped or a golf cart for your stay (you can't bring a car). You can walk the narrow lanes and do the place once over lightly before your boat departs, but you might be tempted to stay the night at a B&B and go back the next day.

The *Capt. Eulice* (757-891-2552), once the mail boat, leaves Onancock daily for Tangier between Memorial Day and October. You can also get here in season by larger cruise boat from Reedville (804-453-2628) or Crisfield, Maryland (410-968-2338), and year-round by mail boat from Crisfield.

■ **MORE SHORT STOPS** *map pages 48–49, E/F-2*
Between **Onley** and **Melfa,** on the west side of U.S. 13, you can visit the **Turner Sculpture Gallery, Foundry, and Studios,** to admire the variety of animal and bird bronzes. At **Wachapreague,** there's the **Island House Restaurant** (17 Atlantic Avenue; 757-787-2105), a big place on stilts, looking out over the barrier islands. It was made to resemble a Coast Guard station, complete with the cupola, and you can climb up for a good look.

Farther south, at **Machipongo,** the **Barrier Islands Center** has exhibits about the lifesavers, fishermen, and others who lived or worked on the islands until the sea reclaimed too much of them and drove the people out. The center is housed in the white clapboard buildings of the restored **Almshouse Farm.** The main house, a poorhouse for whites, dates from around 1840; a small building for African-Americans dates from 1910 and a third, possibly a kitchen, dates from about 1710. *U.S. 13; 757-678-5550.*

If you're feeling peckish about now, you have a couple of good choices. You can stop in **Exmore,** on the east side of U.S. 13, at the **Trawler Restaurant** (757-442-2092), in what was once an oyster-shucking shed, for fried oysters and crab cakes.

Tangier Island.

Or you can make a short detour seaward from U.S. 13 to **Willis Wharf,** one of the seaside jumping-off places for ocean fishing. In spring and fall you can visit an oyster house and watch the shucking firsthand, and any old time you can visit the **E. L. Willis & Co. Restaurant** (4456 Willis Wharf Road; 757-442-4225). An old country store that now has a catering business, E. L. Willis was and is the center of social life here.

Eastville *map pages 48–49, E-3*

About 5 miles farther yet you come to Eastville, whose courthouse and clerk's office (both 1731) and debtors' prison have the oldest continuous legal records in the United States, begun in 1632. Just inside the door of the clerk's office is installed a sliding wood rod (rather like that on a doctor's scale), with a typed card that reads: "Eastville: the Ancient Measuring Rod. By this rod slaves were measured, and then sold from the door of this old clerk's office."

The Eastern Shore was once called Accawmacke, which derives from an Indian word meaning "over the water place," and the Algonquins here were a part of Powhatan's empire. Being over the water from Powhatan seems to have disinclined them to toe the line, though. Against orders they befriended colonists. A monument on the courthouse lawn at Eastville commemorates Debdeavon, the "Laughing King of Accawmacke," for warning the colonists about an uprising in 1621.

Two or three miles south of Eastville on the bay side of U.S. 13 is Eyre Road and a long alley of trees leading to **Eyre Hall** (1735), a magnificent mansion and gardens on Cherrystone Creek. You can see the house and its distinguished furnishings and paintings only during Historic Garden Week in April, but the gardens are open to the public year-round and well worth the detour. The house has been occupied by 11 generations of the Eyre family. How's that for continuity?

Cape Charles *map pages 48–49, E-3*

This town on the bay side began life in 1884 when the railroad came, connecting with a passenger steamer–freight barge line to Norfolk. Between then and 1920, many large Victorian houses were built on a well-planned grid, which today is a historic district on the Virginia and the National Registers. The Colonial Revival Wilson-Lee House is run as a B&B, with eclectic furnishings and every possible amenity. *403 Tazewell Avenue; 757-331-1954.*

In the mid-20th century the transportation systems changed, everything bypassed Cape Charles, and the town began to die. But today, it seems to be holding its own, as evidenced by **Arts Enter Cape Charles** (10 Strawberry Street; 757-331-2787), a new performing arts center in the restored art deco Palace Theater, and the huge Bay Creek project, a 1,700-acre golf and marina community, with two 18-hole courses (one already in use), home sites, apartment complexes, and deepwater slips for yachts or rowboats. Bay Creek shows all signs of success, and it will probably take Cape Charles with it well into the 21st century.

Off U.S. 13 toward the bay on Route 644 (Arlington Road) are the ornate Custis tombs and the site of the **Arlington Plantation,** where in 1670 John Custis II built a splendid mansion at a time when most people lived in small wooden houses. For a short time in 1676 the plantation became the seat of the colonial government, when, during Bacon's Rebellion, Royal Governor William Berkeley fled Jamestown and took refuge here. Archaeologists have discovered the foundation of the building, which has been outlined in the lawn, and there are signs explaining the site for the public.

Looking at the ornate tombs of John Custis II and his grandson John Custis IV might lead you to consider the convolutions of this branch of Virginia's family tree. Another grandson, Daniel Parke Custis, married a young lady named Martha Dandridge, and after he died she married a Virginia farmer and soldier named George Washington. Many years later Martha's grandson, George Washington Parke Custis, built a neoclassical mansion across the Potomac from the new capital of the country and named it Arlington, after his ancestral home. His daughter Mary Ann Randolph Custis later inherited that house, in which she spent happy years with her husband, Robert E. Lee. *Arlington Chase Road off Custis Tomb Road.*

A few miles before you reach the Chesapeake Bay Bridge-Tunnel, keep a lookout on your left for the Cape Center Exxon gas station. Inside is **Sting-Ray's** (757-331-2505)—"Chez Exxon" to the locals—a mandatory stop for wonderful fresh seafood, barbecue, and really homemade desserts.

■ CHESAPEAKE BAY BRIDGE-TUNNEL *map pages 48–49, E-4/5*
More than just a transportation corridor, this 17.6-mile engineering marvel connecting the Eastern Shore with the city of Virginia Beach cuts out the 95 miles it once took to go around the bay and allows you to drive onto—and into—the bay,

with gulls wheeling overhead and maybe an enormous oceangoing ship passing in front of your car.

Officially called the Lucius J. Kellam Jr. Bridge-Tunnel (757-331-2960), the elaborate complex of four man-made islands connected by 12 miles of trestled roadway, two mile-long tunnels, two bridges, and 2 miles of causeway opened in 1964. During the 1990s, to accommodate 21st-century traffic, it was doubled, becoming a twin-span, four-lane route. Unfortunately, the tunnels are still the originals, one lane in either direction, so that traffic must merge before entering, which sometimes creates a gigantic bottleneck.

Jutting out from one of the four islands is a 625-foot-long fishing pier, the only spot where you can get out of your car to savor the experience of being on the bay. Bird-watching is popular here, and you can dine with a view at the **Sea Gull Pier Restaurant** (757-464-4641).

■ **VIRGINIA BEACH** *map page 65, C/D-2/3*

Virginia Beach is just that—miles of Atlantic beach, boardwalk, and high-rise resort hotels. It is the state's most populous city, because years ago it annexed all of Princess Anne County west to the Norfolk city limit, thus becoming "the largest resort city in the world." And it's still growing. The *Wall Street Journal* declared it a "boom town of the '90s." To visitors, it is first and foremost a beach, a place to come to watch dolphins frolic just offshore, to loll in the sand, to beachcomb, Rollerblade, bar-hop, or take in yet more of Virginia's history.

The resort area, stretched along Atlantic and Pacific Avenues between Rudee Inlet and 39th Street, includes a 3-mile boardwalk (or so it's called—it is actually a concrete sidewalk), with lanes for pedestrians, bicycles, and canopied multicycles, flanked by pleasantly planted grassy strips. You'll encounter whimsical, bigger-than-life sculptures, a fishing pier, an oceanfront entertainment stage, shops, out-door cafes, and blocks and blocks of new sand, added in an ongoing effort to maintain a wide beach in the face of erosion. It's tan rather than white, but the strand is impressively wide.

(opposite, top) On the boardwalk at Virginia Beach in 1939.
(opposite, bottom) Virginia Beach today.

Summer fun lingers off-season in Virginia Beach.

■ BREAK FROM THE WAVES

Away from the built-up bustle and typical beach shops, there are plenty of unexpected finds to check out when the sun and sand get to be too much.

The excellent **Virginia Marine Science Museum** occupies two buildings. You can see river otters and harbor seals do their underwater dances, get a chance to tickle a stingray, tong oysters like a waterman, and watch an IMAX movie. An outdoor boardwalk and nature trail cross a pristine salt marsh. The museum sponsors whale- and dolphin-watching trips and pontoon-boat excursions into the marsh. *717 General Booth Boulevard; 757-425-3474.*

The elegantly designed **Contemporary Art Center of Virginia** mounts changing exhibits and sponsors art events in its vaulted atrium, galleries, studio space, and auditorium. *2200 Parks Avenue; 757-425-0000.*

New Age types know the **Association for Research and Enlightenment** as the house that Edgar Cayce built. Sometimes called the father of holistic medicine, Cayce was an early-20th-century psychic who, while in a self-induced sleep, could diagnose and treat the ailments of people who sought his help. This center, founded in 1931 on Cayce's spiritual principles, helps visitors explore such topics as dreams, ESP, reincarnation, and health. A day spa offers massage and other holistic services, and you can wander through a meditation garden with a Japanese bridge over a lily pond, a waterfall, and a bamboo grove. *67th Street and Atlantic Avenue; 757-428-3588.*

The beautifully preserved **Old Coast Guard Station** has exhibits about Virginia shipwrecks and U.S. lifesaving history. An interactive touch-screen in the upper gallery lets you see what the "tower cam" is shooting from the tower's summit. You can identify ships preparing to enter Hampton Roads, zoom in on people on the beach, and even see the Bridge-Tunnel. *24th Street and Boardwalk; 757-422-1587.*

The oceanfront de Witt Cottage, built in 1895 and occupied by the family until 1988, now houses the **Atlantic Wildfowl Heritage Museum.** Exhibits here focus on Virginia Beach history, including old hunting clubs, and on the art of decoy carving, with demonstrations and many decoys on loan from well-known collectors. Admission is free, and there's a fascinating gift shop. *Atlantic Avenue and 12th Street; 757-437-8432.*

■ CAPE HENRY   *map page 65, D-2*

Cape Henry defines the northern end of Virginia Beach, its windswept tip now safely surrounded by well-guarded Fort Story. It is well worth showing your driver's license to the gatehouse guard so that you can drive through the base to the historic hub of Virginia's coast.

The buff-brick **Old Cape Henry Lighthouse,** built in the early 1790s under orders from George Washington, is the oldest government-built lighthouse in the country. (In 1881 its functions were taken over by the "new" Cape Henry Lighthouse just across the road.) You can climb first its 76-step hill and 13-step entrance stair, then the 84-step circular staircase, then a nine-step ladder and another nine spiral steps to the top, to gaze out across the Atlantic. *583 Atlantic Avenue; 757-422-9421.*

A short distance north of the lighthouse in a grassy clearing stands a simple stone monument, the **First Landing Cross,** marking the first place that band of Englishmen, the Jamestown settlers, landed on Virginia soil, in 1607. Across the grass, gazing south toward a plaque commemorating the Battle of the Capes, stands a statue of Admiral Joseph Paul de Grasse. In that critical Revolutionary sea battle in 1781, de Grasse, commanding the French fleet, managed to prevent the

British fleet, under Admiral Thomas Graves, from sailing to reinforce Cornwallis at Yorktown. Because the British ships never made it, Washington and his allies won the battle that turned the British Empire upside down.

■ **FIRST LANDING STATE PARK** *map page 65, D-2*

If you exit from Fort Story onto Shore Drive and turn right, you'll soon see signs for First Landing State Park (formerly Seashore State Park), Virginia's most visited state park. To the right, on the Chesapeake Bay, are the camping area and the beach, and south of Shore Drive are hiking and bicycle trails and about 20 rental cabins. Some of the trails are on boardwalks over marshes, where silent cypresses are reflected and Spanish moss has found a home. At the east end of the park there's another entrance, from 64th Street at the oceanfront, with a boat ramp. Botanists have long been interested in the diversity of plant species here, and the park seems to be the place where palm really does meet pine. Take a guided tour or just spend a day exploring. *2500 Shore Drive; 757-412-2300.*

■ **HISTORIC HOMES**

Virginia Beach also has several historic houses that offer public tours; among the oldest brick houses in America, the first two of the three described below reflect a lifestyle common in the colonies before the tobacco barons began to build their palaces. In addition, the privately owned **Upper Wolfsnare** (757-491-3490) is sometimes open to the public.

The **Adam Thoroughgood House,** built around 1680 on the Lynnhaven River, has a wonderful stair hall flanked by kitchen and parlor, with bedchambers above. The period furnishings, which illustrate 17th- and 18th-century domesticity, are on loan from the Chrysler Museum in Norfolk. A 17th-century garden is on the Historic Garden Week tour each spring and in early summer is awash in the scent of magnolias. *1636 Parish Road; 757-431-4000.*

Like the earlier Thoroughgood House, **Lynnhaven House** (1724), with its steeply pitched roof and double exterior chimneys, is a wonderful example of late-Jacobean architecture, its leaded casement windows looking out on what is still a peaceful rural setting. As at other dwellings in Princess Anne County, the bricks were probably made on the site, along with the oyster-shell mortar that has lasted so well. You can wander in the garden and peer at the gravestones in the Revolutionary War cemetery. *4405 Wishart Road; 757-460-1688.*

Low, Sorrowful Beauty

Riding down to Port Warwick from Richmond, the train begins to pick up speed on the outskirts of the city, past the tobacco factories with their ever-present haze of acrid, sweetish dust and past the rows of uniformly brown clapboard houses which stretch down the hilly streets for miles, the hundreds of rooftops all reflecting the pale light of dawn; past the suburban roads still sluggish and sleepy with early morning traffic, and rattling swiftly now over the bridge which separates the last two hills where in the valley below you can see the James River winding beneath its acid-green crust of scum out beside the chemical plants and more rows of clapboard houses and into the woods beyond.

Suddenly the train is burrowing through the pinewoods, and the conductor, who looks middle-aged and respectable like someone's favorite uncle, lurches through the car asking for tickets... and when you ask him how far it is to Port Warwick and he says, "Ab*oot* eighty miles," you know for sure that you're in the Tidewater....

You look out once more at the late summer landscape and the low, sorrowful beauty of tideland streams winding through marshes full of small, darting, frightened noises and glistening and dead silent at noon, except for a whistle, far off, and a distant rumble on the rails.

—William Styron, *Lie Down in Darkness,* 1951

Though the Francis Land family immigrated in the first half of the 17th century, the present gambrel-roofed **Francis Land House** was built (probably by the fifth or sixth Francis Land) late in the 18th. It has been much remodeled over the years, but most of the building is authentic, and it is charmingly, if sparsely, furnished. The gardens are shady, and a 3-acre history park and trail nearby were opened in 1999. *3131 Virginia Beach Boulevard; 757-431-4000.*

■ **NATURAL AREAS** *map pages 48–49, E-6*
The barrier island at the southern end of Virginia Beach comprises two natural areas. The **Back Bay National Wildlife Refuge** is an 8,000-acre playground for winter waterfowl, summer-nesting osprey and songbirds, and fall and spring migratory flocks following the Atlantic flyway. It has dunes, maritime forests, freshwater marshes, ponds, and beaches. You can fish and bike or hike or take a

canoe or kayak, and also explore by tram or the Terra-Gator people mover. Maybe you'll see deer, red fox, otters, or even the recently reestablished bald eagle. *4005 Sandpiper Road, south of Sandbridge; 757-721-2412.*

Continue south from the wildlife refuge on foot, by bike, boat, tram, or Terra-Gator (and they're the only ways to get there) to enter the 4,320-acre **False Cape State Park.** One of the few really undeveloped areas on the Atlantic coast, it has 6 miles of deserted beaches, blinds for birding and photography, an education center, and the remains of Wash Woods, once a village of 300 people. You might even see wild boar here, or the endangered glass lizard, thought to exist nowhere else. You can camp here if you're willing to hike in and carry your own water. *4001 Sandpiper Road; 757-426-7128.*

■ HAMPTON ROADS   *map page 65*

The term "Hampton Roads" can be confusing. Strictly speaking, it refers to the large natural harbor into which the James, Elizabeth, Hampton, Nansemond, and Lafayette Rivers flow. But Hampton Roads has also come to mean the lands surrounding this body of water. That's where lines begin to blur. Some people call only the area on the south side of the James River Hampton Roads, referring to the north side by its traditional name, the Peninsula. Other people call the south side simply that, the south side. However the regions are labeled, they have in common a mutual regard for the military-industrial complex, a long history, and, except for up-and-coming Norfolk, a similar conservative character.

As to the history, the Powhatan were here long before that first band of Englishmen arrived in the spring of 1607. Though the English did not linger long before continuing upriver to Jamestown, they returned and established a fort at Old Point Comfort within three years. Shortly after that, they attacked a Kecoughtan village, drove out the natives, and "opened up" the general terrain for settlement. Soon a smattering of colonists had located in what is now Hampton. Situated near the James River's entrance to the Chesapeake, the region quickly developed as a shipping and maritime hub.

But war more than anything sealed the fate of this area. When the Revolution broke out, Hampton Roads' strategic position was not lost on the British. Norfolk, Portsmouth, and Hampton were ravaged. Even the traitor Benedict Arnold stopped in the area on his way up the James to attack Richmond. Not long after him, the British Lord Cornwallis arrived in Portsmouth with his entire force, planning to set sail from here to New York. But his superiors ordered him to establish a post somewhere on the Virginia coast, and after some thought he chose Yorktown. History has recorded what happened there.

The Civil War, as well, struck Hampton Roads hard, tearing the area in two. From the beginning, the Union held onto Fort Monroe, using it as a stronghold in the midst of Confederate territory. Soon, much of the rest of the region was in Federal hands.

Ironically, recent wars have brought only prosperity to this area, as servicemen and servicewomen, matériel, and money have flooded in. Even in these post–Cold War days, the Navy, Air Force, Army, and NATO are all well-represented, and Hampton Roads remains home to one of the greatest concentrations of military might on earth.

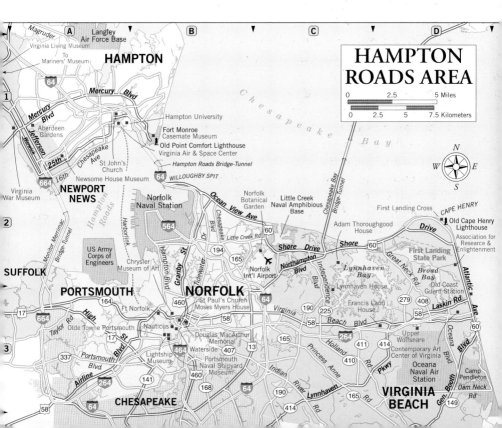

BATTLE OF THE IRONCLADS

In 1861 Portsmouth sat safely in the middle of the Confederacy, and the Union troops stationed in its federal shipyard were essentially surrounded. Given their situation, they judiciously decided to jump ship, but before they did, they torched everything of worth, including several ships in for repairs. One of those, the unremarkable steam frigate *Merrimac,* was to rise phoenix-like from the ashes.

The secretary of the Confederacy's nonexistent navy ordered that an "unsinkable" ship be built, reasoning that "inequality of numbers may be compensated by invulnerability." So, the half-burned *Merrimac* was raised and resurrected as something her re-creators called an ironclad. Though she made less than 6 knots and drew 22 feet, she did seem unsinkable, with her iron-plated hull. She was duly christened the CSS *Virginia.*

Word of this indomitable threat reached Northern ears, and soon the Union too was at work on an unsinkable warship, the *Monitor.* The *Virginia* struck first. On March 8, 1862, the ironclad ran out of the Elizabeth River and into Hampton Roads, making for the five federal warships that had blockaded Virginia's most important ports. At battle's end she had effectively destroyed or run off all five of them.

Two days earlier the *Monitor* had left New York under tow. As she rounded Cape Henry, her men could hear the cannon booming in Hampton Roads, but they arrived too late to join the fray. The *Monitor* got her chance, though, the following day. Spectators lined the shores as the two ironclads took to the ring. For four hours the ships stalked and sparred with each other, but apparently they were fairly evenly matched, because their duel ended in a draw. The *Monitor* crept back to Union-held Fort Monroe, in Hampton, while the *Virginia* returned to Portsmouth. Though both ships stayed in Hampton Roads for two more months, they never engaged again, mostly because President Lincoln had ordered that the *Monitor* "be not too much exposed."

When Norfolk fell to the Union in May 1862, the *Virginia*'s commander wanted to take her upriver to safety in Richmond, but he was warned that her draft was too great to get past the flats at Jamestown. On May 11, the legendary ironclad was blown up by her own forces. The *Monitor* survived until the following December, when she went down in a storm off North Carolina's Cape Hatteras. She lay undisturbed until she was discovered in 1973, when her anchor and other artifacts were brought to the surface. In the summer of 2002, after a major, multimillion-dollar effort, the *Monitor*'s turret was salvaged and brought to rest at the Mariners' Museum in Newport News.

The Battleship Wisconsin *is permanently berthed at Nauticus in Norfolk.*

■ NORFOLK   *map page 65, B-2/3*

Most urbane of the Hampton Roads cities, Norfolk owes its cosmopolitan air to two things—a huge and profitable naval and NATO presence and the Chrysler Museum of Art. A sophisticated institution by any standards, the Chrysler sets a certain tone, and it extends its refined arms out to administer other historic sites in the city as well.

■ NORFOLK NAVAL STATION   *map page 65, B-2*

Norfolk Naval Station, the largest naval base in the world, is the place to go to see some Navy. More than 100 ships call this their home port, and at any given time the base's 15 piers resemble a bristling battlescape of subs, tenders, destroyers, cruisers, oilers, landing ships, and even an aircraft carrier (five are home-ported here). Stretching for 15 miles along the Elizabeth River and Willoughby Bay, off Hampton Boulevard or I-64, this huge complex of naval facilities employs more than 100,000 military personnel and civilians.

Men Coming Home from Work at the Shipyards, 1936, *by Paul Carter.*

Besides its run-of-the-mill brass, the base also claims two four-star admirals: the Commander-in-Chief, Atlantic, who is also in command of NATO's Atlantic operations, and the Commander-in-Chief, Atlantic fleet. These two men are responsible for the defense of the eastern half of the country, as well as a considerable chunk of the Western Hemisphere. Both they and other high-ranking elite live in a line of houses left over from the 1907 Jamestown Exposition held on this site. The exposition drew attention to the naval potential of the area, but no real construction began until 1917, late in World War I. By Armistice Day the following year, 34,000 enlisted men were stationed here.

The Navy presence in Norfolk has grown steadily ever since. Recently opened to the public, the base offers guided tours by bus and boat. The tours begin at Waterside, downtown on the Elizabeth River, or at the base's tour office off Hampton Boulevard. *757-444-7955.*

Downtown Norfolk from the air.

■ **DOWNTOWN NORFOLK** *map page 65, B-3*

Downtown today is something of a crazy quilt. A gleaming new shopping center has sprouted beside ancient St. Paul's Church; new high-rises loom above historic neighborhoods and a few old storefronts, and the waterfront, as always, the waterfront thrives. Try to spot some of the more than 20 original sculptures—historical and whimsical and just plain beautiful—scattered throughout downtown, some of them prominent, some hidden away.

Cannonball Trail

In about two hours you can follow an inviting promenade through downtown Norfolk past an array of places of historic and architectural interest. Granite inlays and medallions are set in the sidewalk to guide you, and narrative plaques tell you the history. The trail also goes along the Elizabeth River, where workboats and naval vessels glide by, and to a reception center, where you can refresh yourself and pick up information of interest. Below are some highlights.

Town Point Park is a 7-acre greensward and outdoor concert site. Connected by bridges to the southeast corner of the park is the affecting **Armed Forces Memorial,** where you can sit on a bench and contemplate the 20 or so letters from servicepeople who died in America's battles from the Revolution to the Gulf War. They've been cast in bronze and lie on the ground as if scattered by the wind.

Northwest of Town Point Park is the gunmetal gray **Nauticus, the National Maritime Center,** a fascinating high-tech "museum with a nautical slant." Built on a pier over the Elizabeth River, it contains exhibits about tides and weather and all the human uses of the seas. The Hampton Roads Naval Museum, on Nauticus's second floor, explains in paintings, artifacts, models, weapons, and documents the role the port has played in world maritime affairs. Docked alongside the pier is the *Wisconsin,* a battleship that can be boarded and is enormously popular with visitors. *1 Waterside Drive; 757-664-1000.*

Inland from this "new Norfolk" but within walking distance of it on the Cannonball Trail are several sites from the city's long past, among them **St. Paul's Church.** The graves under the magnolia trees in the churchyard date from the 17th and 18th centuries. The brick church itself, built in 1739, is the only building that survived British Lord Dunmore's destruction of the city on New Year's Day 1776. But St. Paul's did take a hit: A rusting British cannonball remains lodged high up in its south wall. *St. Paul's Boulevard and City Hall Avenue; 757-627-4353.*

The **Moses Myers House,** a dignified old Georgian/Federal brick house with exceptional furnishings, holds a unique place among Virginia's historic houses; it gives you a detailed picture of the life of a Jewish family in Federal Norfolk.

A bootstraps entrepreneur, Moses Myers came to Norfolk from his hometown of New York City in 1787 when he was in his mid-30s. The Revolution had forced him into bankruptcy, but Myers believed Norfolk would provide good business opportunities and he migrated south with his bride, Eliza. They established themselves as the first Jewish family in Norfolk. Within five years Myers's merchandising business was doing so well that he was able to erect the first stage of this impressive brick house. But the gods of fortune proved fickle, and a bank failure in the aftermath of the War of 1812 again destroyed Myers financially. He lost everything but his house and its furnishings.

For five generations, until 1931, the house stayed in the Myers family. Now owned by the city and administered by the Chrysler Museum of Art, it is furnished

Waterside Marketplace, on Norfolk's downtown waterfront.

mostly with Myers family pieces, from the exceptional mahogany case clock that Moses and Eliza brought with them from New York to portraits by such masters as Gilbert Stuart and Thomas Sully. Their home is now a shrine to fortitude and good taste. *331 Bank Street; 757-441-1526.*

The **Douglas MacArthur Memorial** is a shrine of a different cast. Begun through a grassroots effort of local admirers of Gen. Douglas MacArthur (1880–1964), the memorial opened in 1964 in Norfolk's old neoclassical city hall, built in 1850. MacArthur's remains are enshrined in the domed rotunda, and inscriptions of his words adorn the walls. The general's widow, a Norfolk native, is also buried here. Exhibits in the building trace MacArthur's meteoric rise to the rank of five-star general and his critical role in the Pacific theater during World War II. *Bank Street and City Hall Avenue; 757-441-2965.*

The **Willoughby-Baylor House,** owned by the city and administered by the Chrysler Museum of Art, is open for tours and slated to become a museum with changing exhibits on Norfolk's history. In 1794, William Willoughby, a prosperous building contractor, bought a lot on Freemason Street, part of his ancestor Capt. Thomas Willoughby's 1636 land grant. Some of that grant had become the "town of Norfolk" in 1682, and about a block away Moses Myers had just built his large brick house. Although smaller, Willoughby's house contains furniture and portraits of the period and has a charming 18th-century garden. *601 East Freemason Street; 757-441-1526.*

A hundred years after William Willoughby bought his lot, Boston architect W. D. Wentworth built a Richardsonian Romanesque house for the prominent Norfolk banker James Wilson Hunter. Now the **Hunter House Victorian Museum,** it has always been in the family and retains the original furnishings, creating a fascinating Victorian household today. *240 West Freemason Street; 757-623-9814.*

Chrysler Museum of Art *map page 65, B-3*

The Chrysler Museum's serene Italianate marble sits amid the decorous eclectic mansions of the neighborhood around the Hague, a small inlet of the Elizabeth River. Possessing one of the finest art collections in the country, the museum is a moving force in Norfolk's culture. It stages theater, dance, music, and poetry events, administers two historic houses, and has an outstanding art reference library.

There are exceptional exhibits of antique and art glass; Greco-Roman, Egyptian, and pre-Columbian antiquities; and art nouveau and art deco works. The wide-

The Chrysler Museum of Art in Norfolk.

ranging collection of paintings includes works by Americans Charles Willson Peale, Asher Durand, Winslow Homer, Edward Hopper, Jackson Pollock, and Richard Diebenkorn. European painting from the 14th to the 20th century is represented by such masters as Filippino Lippi, Gauguin, Rubens, Renoir, Velasquez, and Matisse.

The museum traces its origins to two schoolteachers, Irene Leache and Anna Cogswell Wood, who arrived in Norfolk after the Civil War. Their love of art inspired local citizens and eventually led to the founding in 1939 of the Norfolk Museum of Arts and Sciences, which underwent a transformation after Walter P. Chrysler Jr. donated a major portion of his art collection to the city in 1971.

The son of the founder of the Chrysler Corporation, Walter seems to have been born a collector—he bought his first serious piece, a Renoir nude, at the tender age of 14 (the dorm master at his boarding school destroyed it as "prurient"). In 1958 he established a museum in an old church in Provincetown, Massachusetts, but he soon outgrew this space. Hearing of his plight, Norfolk offered his collections a home at the Norfolk Museum of Arts and Sciences, which he accepted. He and his wife, a Norfolk native, moved to an old brownstone mansion within sight of the museum. Visitors to the house recall the soft glow of its Tiffany lamps, now on display in the museum. *245 West Olney Road; 757-664-6200.*

■ NORFOLK CORNUCOPIA

As you explore northward from downtown, you should drive through the old neighborhoods of Ghent. It's worth stopping at **Doumar's,** a 1950s-style drive-in, for its barbecue, ice cream, and history. The Doumars' illustrious relative Abe, a Lebanese immigrant, invented the ice-cream cone. The inspiration came when Abe was selling trinkets at the 1904 St. Louis World's Fair. Standing near a waffle vendor, Doumar suggested that he roll a waffle into a cone, fill it with ice cream, and call it a cornucopia. Hence, the ubiquitous treat Americans enjoy today.

After the fair, Abe invented his own four-iron waffle machine, and a year later he was hawking his cornucopias at the Raleigh State Fair, where President Theodore Roosevelt enjoyed a Doumar's confection. Eventually, Abe and his kinsmen settled in Norfolk, selling ice cream from stands along the beach, and by the 1930s, they had opened the drive-in that still operates today. Now, as then, the Doumars promise you any flavor you want—as long as it is vanilla, chocolate, strawberry, or butter pecan. *1919 Monticello Avenue; 757-627-4163.*

From Doumar's, head west on 21st Street, turn north on Hampton Boulevard, pass Old Dominion University, and cross the Lafayette River to an area, off North Shore Road, of picturesque creeks and backwaters with comfortable houses and tall trees. After lingering a bit there, take Little Creek Road east (you can pick it up by heading north on Colonial Avenue from North Shore) until you see signs for the Norfolk Botanical Garden, a riot of color and bloom.

The **Norfolk Botanical Garden** covers 155 acres in the lush vegetation of coastal Virginia. Edging lakes and lily ponds are forests of lacy conifers; rose, holly, and camellia gardens; a butterfly garden with 34 species; herb and fragrance gardens; rhododendron thickets; and banks of azaleas. About 12 miles of walking paths thread through this sylvan quietude; you can tour the grounds on foot, aboard the gardens' open-air trackless trains, or on canal boats that ply the lake.

The garden began as a WPA project in 1938, when local African-American women were hired to clear the area and plant 4,000 azaleas. Gradually, more azaleas were added, as well as camellias and rhododendrons. In the 1950s, the garden gained renown as the site of the International Azalea Festival, which still is held every year in April. With the young azalea queen and her court as hosts, the festival honors the North Atlantic Treaty Organization. Even in the forest, this city's military heritage is not forgotten. *6700 Azalea Garden Road; 757-441-5830.*

Wildflowers in the Norfolk Botanical Garden.

■ PORTSMOUTH *map page 65, A/B-3*

In 2002 Portsmouth celebrated its 250th birthday, and for all that time, it has been known as a shipbuilding town. Its Gosport Shipyard, established in 1767, went on to become the Norfolk Naval Shipyard in 1945, now the oldest and largest shipyard in the country. Workers here built the ironclad CSS *Virginia* (also known as the *Merrimac*), as well as the first U.S. battleship, the USS *Texas* (1892), and aircraft carrier, the USS *Langley* (1922).

The **Lightship Museum,** the retired Lightship *Portsmouth* freshly painted safety-red, is a fine specimen of the maritime past. The ship's spit-and-polish interior gives a good sense of what life was like for crews living aboard these floating beacons. This one saw service from 1915 to 1963 off Virginia, Delaware, and Massachusetts, and, among its other compelling features, it displays the old Fresnel lens from the Smith Point Lighthouse. *End of London Street; 757-393-8741.*

The first lightship ever built in this country was constructed in nearby Hampton in 1819. Within a year of that commission, four more lightships had been built and placed off dangerous shoals in the bay. The age of lightships peaked in the early 20th century, then rapidly declined as they were replaced by buoys and lighthouses or simply deemed unnecessary.

Close by at the **Portsmouth Naval Shipyard Museum,** model ships ride the motionless seas of display cases and wartime and maritime memorabilia are exhibited. A large audio-diorama of Portsmouth in 1776 brings the colonial town to life and tells about the city's history from then until now. *2 High Street, at Water Street; 757-393-8591.*

■ OLDE TOWNE PORTSMOUTH

You can get a full-scale taste of the 18th century by strolling through charming Olde Towne Portsmouth, just west of the waterfront north of High Street. With its trees, alleyways, and well-tended Georgian, Federal, and Victorian houses, Olde Towne, the original 65-acre tract laid out by Col. William Crawford in 1752, is a pleasure to explore. A free brochure, "Olde Towne Walking Tour," available around town, details the different houses, almost all of which are still private residences, open to visitors only on Candlelight Tours in December. In summer you can take a Trolley Tour or, at dusk, an Olde Towne Lantern Tour, led by costumed guides.

The Navy looms large along the Elizabeth River.

The Virginia (Merrimac) *and the* Monitor *in battle. This print published by L. Prang & Co., Boston, 1886, was one of a popular set known as Prang's War Pictures.*

Only the **Hill House** (circa 1820), the headquarters of the Portsmouth Historical Association, functions as a museum. A dignified white brick Federal house with an English basement, it holds furnishings collected by all the generations of the Thompson and Hill families who lived here until 1961. *221 North Street; 757-393-5111.*

Another way to visit an Olde Towne historic dwelling is to spend a night at the **Patriot Inn Bed & Breakfast,** which faces the Elizabeth River. Built in 1794 two doors from Hill House, it has four comfortable rooms (a couple with a fireplace) furnished suitably for the period, but with every modern convenience. *201 North Street; 757-391-0157.*

The **Ball-Nivison House** is a good example of an architectural trompe l'oeil known as a "tax dodger's" house. Its gambrel roof and dormer windows were designed to partially disguise its second floor and thereby persuade 18th-century British tax collectors to assess it as a one-story structure. The Marquis de Lafayette was feted here during his 1824 hero's tour of America. Andrew Jackson dropped by on an 1833 inspection of the town's naval facilities. *417 Middle Street.*

■ Downtown Portsmouth

Downtown Portsmouth melds into the edges of Olde Towne. Some buildings from the 1950s and 1960s along High Street have been put to innovative uses, as have some older landmarks.

The **Commodore Theatre,** a movie house built in 1945, has been returned to its original art deco splendor—but with a twist. Its lower level now serves as a theater-restaurant where audiences can enjoy a light meal and watch first-run movies at the same time. *421 High Street; 757-393-6962.*

When the streets of old Portsmouth were first laid out, the intersection at High and Court Streets marked the center of town, where on the four corners a church, a courthouse, a market, and a jail were erected. There today, sure enough, stands the Classical Revival red brick courthouse of 1846, and in the middle of Court Street rises a later addition, the Confederate monument. The **Courthouse Galleries** (entrance on Court Street; 757-393-8543), a museum in the courthouse, exhibits the multimedia works of regional and international artists. Lectures, classes, and performances also take place here.

Portsmouth has several historic churches, but **Trinity Church** was in at the start, built at the crossroads in 1762 as Portsmouth Parish of the Church of England. Modified several times, and named Trinity in 1830, the present building, with a few Tiffany windows, has an airy feel. *550 Court Street; 757-393-0431.*

■ Elsewhere in Town

Farther down the waterfront stands the **Ntelos Pavilion,** an open-air cultural-arts amphitheater, with 3,500 seats covered by tentlike sails and 3,000 lawn spots. *Harbor Center, 901 Crawford Street; 757-391-3260.*

Across from Olde Town, next to the Holiday Inn, is a large marina. The **Deck Restaurant,** upstairs from the marina's shop, has an attractive observation bar facing south toward Portsmouth and a more formal, glassed-in dining room with a view of the glorious harbor and the Norfolk skyline that defies description. And the food is wonderful too. You'll want to sit outside in summer on one of the many deck levels or at the Tiki Bar, and don't forget to bring your bathing suit for a dip in the floating swimming pool. *10 Crawford Parkway; 757-398-1221.*

It would be a shame to be this close to so much maritime bustle without joining in. **Elizabeth River ferries** leave regularly from the High Street Landing, go to North Landing, then across to Norfolk's Waterside and back. And, amid tugs and towering warships, the ***Carrie B.,*** a replica of a Mississippi paddlewheeler, plies the fascinating harbor on narrated tours to the naval base and the site of the *Monitor* and *Merrimac's* encounter. From April to mid-October she leaves from Waterside in Norfolk and stops at the North Landing ferry dock, at the Visitor Information Center. *6 Crawford Parkway; 757-393-4735.*

■ **GREAT DISMAL SWAMP**   *map pages 48–49, D-6*

The Great Dismal Swamp hardly deserves its gloomy name. Dismal it is not, though great it is, and for that reason it's now preserved as a National Wildlife Refuge. Straddling the Virginia–North Carolina border, these wondrous 107,000 acres of wetlands support a variety of migratory birds, as well as deer, fox, raccoons, otters, bobcats, bears, and many, many mosquitoes. The peaty soil also supports dense evergreen shrub bogs and forests and eerie cypress swamps, with the trees' knees poking out of the water. Tannin in tree bark and the peat bog underlying the marsh give the swamp waters their remarkable tea-brown color.

At the heart of the marsh lies **Lake Drummond,** a 3,100-acre natural lake whose water drains out of it into man-made canals. Canoeists and other boaters explore the lake and its tributaries and commercial boat tours provide day trips through the swamp; hikers and bicyclists can travel along a dirt road and an elaborate boardwalk raised above the wetlands.

The swamp and Lake Drummond got their start more than 4,000 years ago, created, the local Native Americans believed, by a "fire bird." Scientific evidence suggests that a peat fire did cause the lake's depression, and there is even speculation that a meteor may have landed in the vicinity.

The first whites thought to have seen the lake came on a hunting expedition in 1665. One of the party was North Carolina's governor, William Drummond, after whom the lake was named. Few followed after them, and those who did had little nice to say about the great marshland. Virginia's Col. William Byrd called it a "horrible desart" and advised that "Never was Rum, that cordial of Life, found more necessary than in this Dirty Place."

But George Washington, consummate explorer, surveyor, and developer, found it "a glorious paradise" and visited it repeatedly in the mid-1700s. An inveterate canal builder, Washington wanted to build a 5-mile-long waterway through the marsh to allow commerce between North Carolina's Albemarle Sound and Virginia's Chesapeake Bay. His plan was deferred by the Revolution, but in 1805,

TIMBER CUTTERS GOING INTO THE SWAMP.

This illustration of African-American timber cutters on a barge heading into the Great Dismal Swamp appeared in Harper's Weekly *in 1873.*

after his death, the Dismal Swamp Canal opened. Now more accessible, the swamp began to capture the public imagination. Henry Wadsworth Longfellow included it in his poetry, and in 1856 Harriet Beecher Stowe wrote *Dred: A Tale of the Great Dismal Swamp,* describing the exploits of runaway slave Nat Turner. And more than a century later William Styron brought it to widespread attention with his Pulitzer Prize–winning novel, *The Confessions of Nat Turner.*

Commerce did come to the Dismal, and throughout the 19th and 20th centuries, its rich forests were heavily logged. By the 1970s, it began to be viewed as more than simply timberland, and in 1973, Union Camp, the swamp's major owner, deeded its holdings to the Nature Conservancy, which conveyed the land to the U.S. Department of the Interior for a wildlife refuge.

Boat access is available from Feeder Ditch off Dismal Swamp Canal, on Route 17 south of Portsmouth. Hikers and bikers should proceed south from Suffolk on U.S. 13, and then take Route 32 to Washington Ditch. The city of Suffolk sponsors occasional guided tours of the swamp, and in the early fall there's a white-tail deer hunt. *Refuge Headquarters, 3100 Desert Road, Suffolk; 757-986-3705.*

■ HAMPTON   *map page 65, A/B-1*

For all its slow, Southern style, Hampton has been the scene of some truly pioneering ventures. The site of one of the first colonial villages, it rightfully claims to be the "oldest continuous English-speaking settlement in America" (although it has been burned twice—by the British in the War of 1812 and the Union in the Civil War). It's also the home of Hampton University, one of the country's first African-American institutions of higher learning. And it was at Hampton's NASA facilities that the Mercury astronauts trained for their orbits of the Earth.

In recent years the city has followed the trend of turning its downtown waterfront into a tourist attraction, but it has done so without forsaking its seafaring soul. The wharves where seafood trawlers dock and the processing plants where they offload their catch are still clustered along the Hampton River, just beyond which stretches a new brick-paved plaza. Adding its own nostalgic tone to the plaza, the restored **1920 Hampton carousel** from the city's Buckroe Beach amusement park, now gone, revolves in a flash of prancing, painted horses.

The **Virginia Air & Space Center** looms above the scene. An architectural tour de force completed in 1992, the glass, brick, and aluminum building has a winged roof, symbolic of the city's long association with flight. Ten historic aircraft are suspended from the center's high glass vaults, but its pièce de résistance is the Apollo 12 command capsule whose lunar passengers made "one giant leap for mankind." Also here is an IMAX theater and an interactive space gallery that gives visitors a hands-on experience of aeronautics and space travel. *600 Settlers Landing Road (I-64, Exit 267); 757-727-0900.*

In stark contrast to the high-tech center, small **St. John's Church** stands just a few blocks away. Built in 1728, it is the only part of the old colonial town that survives, though it too has been burned and repaired twice. Shaped like a cross, the brick chapel is surrounded by a walled graveyard with many 18th-century stones. The Victorianized interior includes a stained-glass window depicting Pocahontas. The church's most prized possession is its Communion silver, the oldest in America, made in England in 1618 and in continuous use ever since. *100 West Queens Way.*

The new **Hampton History Museum** opened downtown in 2003, covering the Kecoughtan Indians, Capt. John Smith's arrival, the pirate Blackbeard's downfall, and how Hampton got to be called Crabtown. *120 Old Hampton Lane; 757-727-1610 or 757-727-6436.*

In 1935, the **Aberdeen Gardens** neighborhood, 110 acres bounded by West Mercury Boulevard, West Queen Street, Briarfield Road, and the Newport News city line, was developed by and for African-Americans as part of Franklin D. Roosevelt's New Deal. In 2002 it won the Neighborhood of the Year award from Neighborhoods USA. The **Aberdeen Gardens Museum** (55–57 Mary Peake Boulevard; 800-800-2202), which preserves the neighborhood's heritage and honors the original residents, was dedicated in September 2002 and should be open on a limited basis by late 2003.

The **Harborlink passenger ferry** crosses Hampton Roads to Norfolk year-round, docking at Nauticus in Norfolk and at the Hampton Visitors Center near the Virginia Air & Space Center. *762 Settlers Landing Road; 757-722-9400.*

■ HAMPTON UNIVERSITY *map page 65, A-1*

Hampton University lies on the far bank of the Hampton River, its sloping, shaded grounds overlooking the sailboats and workboats that thread their way up and down. Standing on its campus, you can appreciate the feel of a civilized idea brought to elegant fruition and imagine the dreams that went into the founding of this African-American university, whose roots go back to the Civil War.

As the Union-held Fort Monroe attracted escaped slaves to the area during the war, the New York–based American Missionary Association dispatched personnel to Hampton to help the growing black population. One of its first projects was to open schools, and with the war's end, it pursued its educational efforts, establishing schools to train black teachers throughout the South. Hampton became the site of the Hampton Normal and Agricultural Institute, where classes began in 1868.

For years the school was guided by the visionary Gen. Samuel Chapman Armstrong, a staunch abolitionist who fought in the Civil War and became the head of Hampton's Freedman's Bureau at the end of the war. Armstrong believed that in addition to training teachers, the new black institutions should teach skills such as agriculture and mechanics, and he incorporated these into a highly successful curriculum. He also had a talent for raising money and managed to attract significant Northern benefactors. One of his innovative strokes was founding the Hampton Singers, a traveling student troupe whose performances garnered the school both fame and funds.

In 1878, the school extended its scope and began educating Native American students taken captive during the Indian Wars of the 1870s. To help with this task,

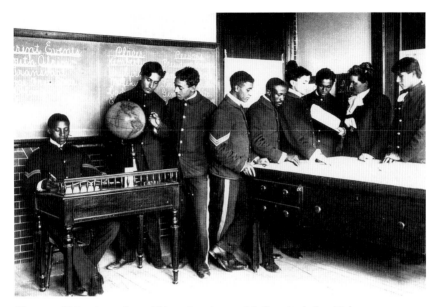

Hampton University students, African-American and Indian, in the late 19th century.

Armstrong called on Booker T. Washington, a former student. The institution's **Hampton University Museum,** started in 1868 and reputedly the oldest black museum in the country, has a fine collection of African and Native American artifacts, works of the early students, and paintings by other African-American artists. *Huntington Building; 757-727-5308.*

Two of the 19th century's most renowned architects, J. Cleveland Cady and Richard Morris Hunt, created buildings for the university. The clock tower of Cady's red brick **Memorial Chapel** (1886) has long been a waterfront landmark—the Italianate structure's pine pews were hewn by university students themselves as part of their education. Hunt designed the nearby rambling yet symmetrical **Virginia Hall.** Less showy but more moving is the **Emancipation Oak,** under which Abraham Lincoln's Emancipation Proclamation was read aloud, reputedly its first recitation in the South. *Off I-64, Exit 267; 757-727-5000.*

Another landmark associated with Hampton University is the **Little England Chapel.** The white clapboard church, built in 1879, is the only existing example of the black missionary churches that proliferated in Virginia after the Civil War.

Students on the Hampton University campus today.

This one began informally when a Connecticut printer employed by the Hampton Normal and Agricultural Institute invited a few neighborhood children into his home one Sunday to sing hymns. The following week, 17 children appeared on his doorstep, and in less than a year, 75 people were gathering on Sundays. At that point, the school got involved, sending teachers rowing across the river to help provide Sunday instruction. Very soon, the simple chapel that stands today was built. Services were held here until 1989. *4100 Kecoughtan Road, at Ivy Home Road, about 1 mile south of Settlers Landing Road West.*

Not far from the Little England Chapel is a reminder of an arcane bit of Hampton history, this one infinitely less spiritual. In the mid-17th century, word began to spread that the newly established sea lanes of the Chesapeake were swimming in valuable cargo. The news lured Caribbean pirates who holed up in the endless creeks and marshes of the Eastern Shore and attacked ships passing through the Virginia capes.

Merchant and tobacco ships were forced to travel in convoys to protect themselves from the brigands, the most notorious of whom was Edward Teach—or, as the world remembers him—Blackbeard. Cultivating his reputation for ferocity, he

Black Life Time Line

1619 First Africans arrive on a Dutch man-o'-war, to be sold as indentured servants.

1624 Birth of William, first black person born in Virginia.

1650 Black population of Virginia numbers 300.

1651 Anthony Johnson, bound servant, secures freedom. Imports five servants and acquires 250 acres on the Eastern Shore, making him the first black landowner in Virginia.

1653 Johnson petitions court for lifetime rights to his runaway servant, a black man who had committed no crime. First known judicial sanction in the English colonies of lifetime servitude where crime was not involved.

1667 Virginia House of Burgesses passes law to the effect that conversion of blacks to Christianity does not gain them their freedom from servitude.

1698 The English Parliament gives private traders approval to participate in the slave trade. Virginia's black population enters a phase of rapid and sustained growth.

1705 Virginia Black Code marks a major step in transformation of black indentured servants into slaves; declares black and Indian slaves to be real estate.

1730 Black population in Virginia numbers 30,000.

1776 Thomas Jefferson includes an indictment of slavery in his draft of the Declaration of Independence, but the clause is struck to appease representatives of Georgia and South Carolina.

1778 Importation of slaves barred by Virginia legislation.

1782 Manumission of slaves legalized. Provision that master must continue to support freed slaves deters emancipation.

ca. 1799 Dred Scott is born a slave in Virginia; later moves with owners to Missouri, where in 1846 he sues to obtain his freedom on grounds that he lives in free territory. Loses suit in 1857, but is emancipated that year by his owner.

1830 Black population numbers 517,100, of which 90 percent are slaves.

1830s American Colonization Society transports free blacks to Liberia; 3,000 of the state's 50,000 free blacks go.

1831 Nat Turner and small band of followers in Southampton County massacre his master's family and about 50 other whites in the vicinity; Turner is caught and hanged.

1850 Southerners demand a Fugitive Slave Act to guarantee return of slaves escaping to the North; the act is first invoked in the case of a fugitive from Norfolk named Shadrach, arrested in Boston. A sympathetic crowd of black Bostonians helps him escape his pursuers.

1860 Union troops invade Alexandria and release slave-jail inmates, turning the building into a prison for Confederate soldiers.

1861 General Butler's Union forces move into Fort Monroe near Hampton; thousands of black refugees flock to the fort to gain freedom.

Composite of scenes of Nat Turner's rebellion, 1831.

1863 President Lincoln issues Emancipation Proclamation, freeing Confederate slaves and allowing for recruitment of black soldiers; nearly 180,000 respond to the call.

1864 Battle of the Crater; black division charges on Confederate line. More than 1,000 blacks killed, wounded, or captured; charge fails.

1865 Confederates evacuate and set fire to Richmond. Black soldiers march in and, without orders to do so, stop at Lumpkin's slave jail to pay tribute to the inmates cheering through the bars. Thirteenth Amendment ratified in December, prohibiting slavery.

1868 Fourteenth Amendment ratified, declaring all persons born or naturalized in the United States to be citizens.

1870 Fifteenth Amendment ratified, banning voting discrimination based on race, color, or previous condition of servitude.

1880s Statutes enacted (the Jim Crow laws) throughout the South legalizing segregation of blacks and whites in schools and public facilities.

1901 State constitutional convention adopts a poll tax and "comprehension" requirement for prospective voters that has the effect of severely limiting the black vote.

1954 U.S. Supreme Court orders desegregation of schools.

1964 The Federal Civil Rights Act is enacted, repealing the South's Jim Crow laws and barring racial discrimination in voting and use of public facilities.

1965 Federal Voting Rights Act is passed; leads to a dramatic increase in black registered voters in the South and in the number of blacks holding elective office.

1990 L. Douglas Wilder becomes Virginia's—and the nation's—first elected black governor.

1998 British science journal *Nature* reports results of DNA testing on descendants of Thomas Jefferson and of his slave Sally Hemings, indicating he may have fathered one of her children.

2003 Virginia's General Assembly passes a resolution expressing "profound regret" over the closing of Prince Edward County public schools from 1959 to 1964 to avoid desegregation.

went into battle, an eyewitness said, with "lighted matches stuck under his hat, which appearing on each side of his face, his eyes naturally looking fierce and wild, made him altogether such a figure that imagination cannot form an idea of a Fury from Hell to look more frightful."

When British ships finally forced Blackbeard out of the bay, he sailed south to harass North Carolina shipping. At the behest of the population there, Virginia's Governor Spotswood dispatched two sloops to run the pirate down. During a pitched battle, the buccaneer, with 25 wounds in him, finally succumbed. His infamous head was then summarily detached from his body and hung from the bowsprit of one of the royal ships. When the victorious entourage returned to Hampton, the bloody trophy was placed on a point on the Hampton River now known as Blackbeard Point. The site today is a placid residential neighborhood—a far cry from "a Fury from Hell."

■ **FORT MONROE** *map page 65, B-1*

Fort Monroe is heavy with history, and legions of luminaries haunt its moated environs. In the tip of Old Point Comfort, the hexagonal stone casemate fort—still part of a functioning Army post—was begun in 1819, to better protect the coastline after the British sacked Hampton and sailed up the Chesapeake to capture Washington, D.C., during the War of 1812. Encircled by a moat 1.25 miles in circumference, enclosing 63 acres, and so impregnable it was called the Gibraltar of the Chesapeake, it remains the largest stone fort in the United States. *End of Mercury Boulevard (U.S. 258).*

A young lieutenant of engineers, **Robert E. Lee,** was posted here early in his career and oversaw the completion of the fort's outworks and approaches during the early 1830s. Three decades later he may have regretted his own handiwork, because Fort Monroe became one of the Union's most critical strongholds in the South during the Civil War. Although ensconced in Virginia territory, the fort was secured by the North at the outbreak of war. Thus, the North held the entrance to Hampton Roads, cutting off Virginia's major ports, all of which lay upriver.

In 1861, three Hampton slaves escaped their owner and sought protection here. The fort's commander, Gen. Benjamin Butler, a lawyer by training, gave them shelter. When his Southern counterpart, Maj. John Cary, demanded their return,

(following pages) An aerial view of Fort Monroe.

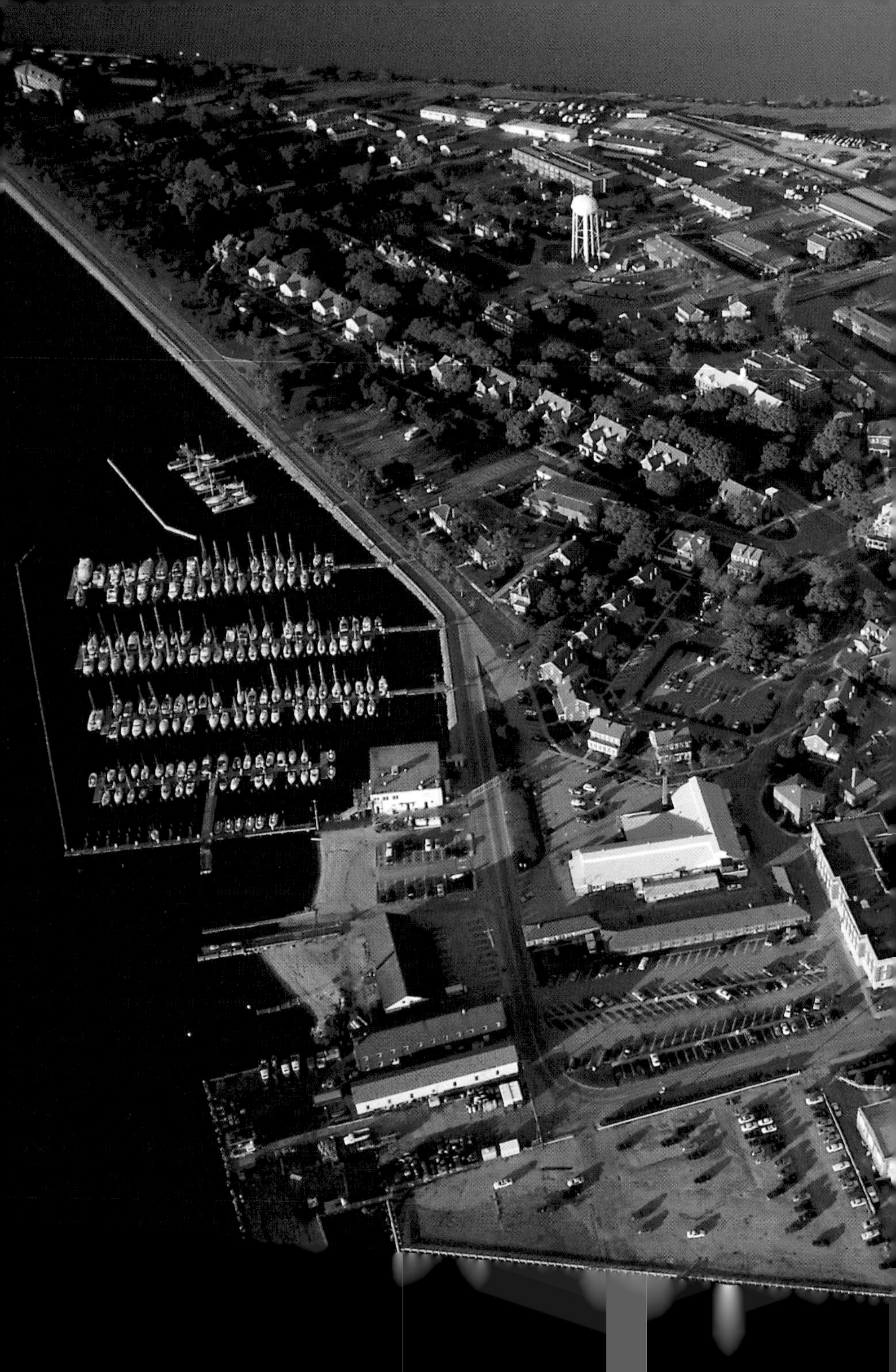

citing the Fugitive Slave Act, the clever Butler replied that the act did not apply to "a foreign country, which Virginia claimed to be." Butler's argument was soon adopted by Union commanders throughout the country and eventually by the War Department. It also caused something of a crisis at Fort Monroe, as runaway slaves inundated the "freedom fort." Nevertheless, the Union managed to shelter and clothe many and give them work. Refugees who couldn't be accommodated spread into the surrounding areas, building shantytowns.

At the end of the war, Harriet Tubman, the heroine of the Underground Railroad, came to the Colored Hospital at Fort Monroe to serve as a nurse and matron. Another child of the South also found himself here after the war: Confederate President Jefferson Davis. He came as a captive, having been apprehended in Georgia and falsely accused of plotting Abraham Lincoln's assassination. He spent almost a year imprisoned in one of the fort's casemates before he was released on a $100,000 bail bond, posted by such unlikely people as the Northern journalist Horace Greeley and Commodore Cornelius Vanderbilt.

You can view Davis's spartan cell in the sod-roofed **Casemate Museum** (757-788-3391), part of the original walled battlement, on a walking tour of Fort Monroe. Exhibits on the fort's history, including uniforms, weapons, models, and drawings, make up the remainder of the display. Across the street is the white, veranda-wrapped house where Robert E. Lee once lived. An even more impressive antebellum house, **Quarters Number One,** where both Lincoln and the Marquis de Lafayette once slept, is also at Fort Monroe, as is the memorable **Old Point Comfort Lighthouse,** built in 1802.

■ NEWPORT NEWS   *map page 65, A-1*

This city suffers from the same malady that Gertrude Stein ascribed to Oakland, California: There is simply "no there there." What used to be a thriving downtown in the mid-20th century has been down at the heels and, except for the immense Newport News Shipbuilding yard, virtually deserted for years. But despite its drawbacks, Newport News has some fine attractions, though they are spread out.

One of the few bright spots downtown is the **Newsome House Museum and Cultural Center,** a restored Queen Anne house built in 1896. The permanent exhibit documents the life and times of Thomas Newsome, a prominent African-American lawyer and community leader, and changing art exhibits are also mounted. *2803 Oak Avenue; 757-247-2360.*

The town got its name from Christopher Newport, an intrepid 17th-century mariner who brought many colonists across the Atlantic from Britain. Legend has it that when Newport tired of those endless sea voyages, he settled on the James River in the area that is now Newport News and opened a small store. People would come here to hear the news. Hence the name, which natives pronounce "NEWp't News."

If Christopher Newport gave the town its name, it was railroad baron Collis P. Huntington who put it on the map. Huntington had visited the area as a teenager hawking watches and hardware up and down the East Coast. Hampton Roads apparently made a lasting impression on him, because he returned decades later with enterprise on his mind. He was looking for a terminus for an eastern railroad so that he could link his Pacific lines to Atlantic shipping channels. In the early 1880s, he opened the Chesapeake and Ohio Railroad through the Virginia Peninsula. A few years later, he established the Newport News Shipbuilding and Dry Dock Company, to this day the mainstay of the city's economy.

Huntington was a character, but as colorful as he was, he was outdone by his second wife, a Richmond beauty named Arabella. Though called Belle, she was not the classic southern lady. Born of working-class parents in post–Civil War Richmond, she carried on a quiet affair with Huntington for almost 20 years, and when his first wife died they finally married. When he died 17 years later, she married his nephew Henry, slipped easily into the role of dowager, and became one of the world's most renowned art collectors—she and Henry established California's Huntington Library and Art Gallery. A British acquaintance said of her, "Mrs. Huntington allows herself manners which even the Empress of Germany cannot afford."

In Newport News the Huntington legacy lives on. Collis's shipyard, though it long ago passed from Huntington hands, has grown into the largest privately owned shipbuilding concern in the country. In the last half-century, it has produced the gargantuan *Nimitz*-class aircraft carriers, guided missile cruisers, and submarines, as well as the elegant luxury liner, the SS *United States*. Its dry docks, berths, and piers claim 2 miles of James River waterfront, and though no tours are given, you can get a glimpse of all this hardware from the James River Bridge and along the city's Huntington Avenue.

The **Mariners' Museum** is another Huntington gift. Collis's son, Archer Huntington, founded it in the early 1930s, spurred on by the shipyard's colorful president Homer Ferguson. Both men recognized the need for a nautical museum "devoted to the culture of the sea." The museum has flourished ever since. Its low-slung postmodern building overlooks the banks of tree-lined Lake Maury, and its interior houses one of the finest "mariner" collections in the country. The comprehensive maritime research library and archive contains, among other treasures, Capt. John Smith's map of the Chesapeake Bay.

The impact of the entrance gallery—a Chesapeake Bay exhibit—is enhanced by the romantic gleam of the lens from the old Cape Charles Lighthouse. The gallery also covers the dying culture of the region's watermen, the development of pleasure boats, and the inspiration for those frequently bare-breasted figureheads on old ships.

A dramatically darkened gallery exhibits the exquisite ship models produced by woodcarver August Crabtree. Other exhibits explore the age of exploration and the age of steam. A new small craft center adjacent to the main museum will house a collection of workboats and pleasure craft from around the world, including a Taiwanese canoe and Brazilian balsa-log rafts. But the most excitement nowadays is generated by the USS *Monitor* Center, where you can see bits and pieces of the Union ironclad before and after archaeological conservation and learn about the colossal effort of raising the vessel's anchor and turret. (Department of trivia: the *Monitor* had the first ever below-the-waterline flush toilet.) *100 Museum Drive (I-64, Exit 258A); 757-596-2222.*

More a wildlife complex than a museum, the **Virginia Living Museum** houses an impressive array of native animals. Its indoor exhibits include aquariums filled with bay and river critters, as well as woodpeckers, owls, and flying squirrels. A two-story, glass-enclosed aviary affords you a close-up look at songbirds, and a planetarium takes you to the stars. Outside, a boardwalk trail, cantilevered above a serene lake, leads past cages with larger animals, including raccoons, beavers, foxes, and bobcats. Many of these animals were injured in the wild and brought to the museum for humane reasons. *524 J. Clyde Morris Boulevard; 757-595-1900.*

The **Virginia War Museum** takes an enlightened look at America's wars, from the Revolution to the present. The museum and its 50,000 artifacts reveal the human impact of war—from its hardships and tragedies to its propaganda. There are galleries exploring the role of women and African-Americans in the military, but perhaps the most interesting collection is the propaganda posters. A number of Axis- and Allied-nation posters on display say something critical about how populations have been whipped into a frenzy in order to "destroy the enemy."

The Virginia Air & Space Center in Hampton.

The museum grounds bristle with an array of weaponry—pre–World War I howitzers, tanks, antitanks, and more. *Huntington Park, 9285 Warwick Boulevard (I-64, Exits 258A or 263A); 757-247-8523.*

At the northwestern tip of Newport News, only 3 miles from the Yorktown Victory Center, stands **Endview Plantation** (1769), which played a part in the Revolution, the War of 1812, and the Civil War. Outdoor living-history programs and reenactments of battles take place here—from the Revolutionary War and World War I as well as Civil War. The white clapboard house has been furnished to reflect both Union and Confederate occupation, with one room done as a hospital. *362 Yorktown Road (I-64, Exit 247); 757-887-1862.*

COLONIAL TIDEWATER

Although the spirit of 17th- and 18th-century Virginia speaks most loudly in the Colonial Triangle of Jamestown, Williamsburg, and Yorktown, colonial churches and plantations may be found throughout the Tidewater, as Virginians call their state's coastal plain. On the Peninsula (the land between the James and York Rivers), the Middle Peninsula (between the York and the Rappahannock), and the Northern Neck (between the Rappahannock and the Potomac), Virginia history is preserved from settlement through independence. This is where the great plantations used to be, the land of which gentry-loving Virginians used to say, "Gentlemen and oysters never leave the Tidewater!" though they never said it within hearing distance of their cousins from Albemarle County or Middleburg.

A great deal of this historic landscape is populated by people who live and work in the historic houses and are careful to preserve the colonial character of their abodes. In Colonial Williamsburg, for example, where the luckiest employees live in the historic district, this carefulness is mandated. Cars are parked out of view, and electric wires and all other signs of modernity are buried or tucked amid discreet greenery. If one wants to live here, one has to live intimately with the past.

■ HISTORIC JAMESTOWN *map pages 48–49, C-4*

Driving the Colonial Parkway to visit the three points of the Colonial Triangle, your first stop might be Jamestown, at the parkway's western end. Virginia's first colony began on a small peninsula called, oddly, Jamestown Island, which still looks as it must have when those three small ships landed in the New World in 1607. Herons strut through its tidal marshes, and tall pines wave stiffly in the breeze off the river, their resinous scent mingling with the fresh smell of the James.

A figure-eight road loops through the forests on this almost-deserted 1,500-acre spit of land, and imagination must serve to resurrect life here in the early 17th century. Now the only human activity on the island focuses around the **visitors center** and the excavated site of Virginia's first capital, under the joint auspices of the Association for the Preservation of Virginia Antiquities and the National Park Service—along with Yorktown, Jamestown is part of the Colonial National

Replicas of the three ships that brought the first European settlers to Virginia are anchored at Jamestown.

Jamestown Glasshouse.

Historical Park. In the visitors center, exhibits illustrate the history of the settlement. The excellent film that plays here doesn't try to romanticize the hardships of Jamestown's early decades.

Behind the visitors center, the narrow streets of modest old Jamestown are clearly visible, lined by the excavated foundations of the small houses that rose in an otherwise vast wilderness. One historic structure still standing is the ruined 17th-century church tower, attached to the reconstructed Jamestown Memorial Church. A statue of Pocahontas, erected decades ago, attests not so much to the Powhatan princess as to how far historical accuracy and interpretation have come since the statue was cast: she is shown dressed in the garb of a Plains Indian rather than that of a member of an Eastern Woodlands tribe. A heroic statue of Smith looks out across the river as well. For more than two centuries the original fort at Jamestown was presumed to have been washed away by the river. But in 1996 archaeologists unearthed traces of the palisades, two buildings, thousands of artifacts including armor and swords, and the skeleton of a young man. *Western end of the Colonial Parkway (from Williamsburg take Jamestown Road/Route 31S); visitors center, 757-229-1773.*

Leaving Jamestown Island now, and just before the bridge, you'll find something a bit more corporeal—the **Jamestown Glasshouse.** Of the many products those early colonists tried to wrest from Virginia to make their settlement pay, glass made from river sand proved one of the most viable. In the reconstructed glasshouse, near the ruins of the original 17th-century furnaces, skilled workers in knee breeches and muslin shirts stoke the beehive kilns and blow glass the old way, twisting their blowpipes into the molten mass, then blowing and turning the fiery globs into shapely green vessels and vases. These latter-day artisans spend several years in apprenticeship, as did their colonial predecessors. *757-229-2437.*

■ JAMESTOWN SETTLEMENT   *map pages 48–49, C-4*

Nearby, also on the Colonial Parkway, is the Jamestown Settlement, a living-history center that brings the old settlement resoundingly to life. Exhibits at the fine museum here survey the conditions in 17th-century England and Europe that forced the Elizabethans to look beyond their cramped motherland. Other displays illustrate Powhatan culture and describe the endurance of the early colonists. Outside, in a re-created Powhatan village, leather-clad interpreters cook native foods, tend fires, and explain how the Powhatan hunter-gatherers and farmers lived off the abundance of Virginia's forests and rich river shores. The Powhatans' simple but sufficient life contrasts strikingly with the re-created fort of the settlers. The stockaded fort seems tenuous and ill-conceived, its small,

Capt. John Smith, 1580–1631.

VIRGINIA'S NATURAL INHABITANTS

For their apparel they are sometimes covered with the skins of wild beasts, which in winter are dressed with the hair but in summer without. The better sort use large mantles of deerskins, not much differing in fashion from the Irish mantles—some embroidered with white beads, some with copper, others painted after their manner. But the common sort have scarce to cover their nakedness but with grass, the leaves of trees, or such like. We have seen some use of mantles made of turkey feathers, so prettily wrought and woven with threads that nothing could be discerned but the feathers. But the women are always covered about their middle with a skin, and very shamefast to be seen bare.

They adorn themselves most with copper beads and paintings. Their women, some have their legs, hands, breasts, and face cunningly embroidered with diverse works, as beasts, serpents, artificially wrought into their flesh with black spots. In each ear commonly they have three great holes, whereat they hang chains, bracelets, or copper. Some of their men wear in those holes a small green and yellow colored snake near half a yard in length, which, crawling and lapping herself about his neck, oftentimes familiarly would kiss his lips. Others wear a dead rat tied by the tail. Some on their heads wear the wing of a bird or some large feather with a rattle. Those rattles are somewhat like the shape of a rapier but less, which they take from the tail of a snake. Many have the whole skin of a hawk or some strange fowl stuffed with wings abroad, others a broad piece of copper, and some the hand of their enemy dried. Their heads and shoulders are painted red with the root puccoon [bloodroot] brayed to powder, mixed with oil; this they hold in summer to preserve them from the heat, and in winter from the cold. Many other forms of paintings they use, but he is the most gallant that is the most monstrous to behold.

—Capt. John Smith, *General History of Virginia,* 1624

A Virginia Algonquin, probably a Powhatan, sketched by Wenceslaus Hollar in 1645.

thatch-roofed, wattle-and-daub buildings dark and musty. It's easy to imagine why so many died from disease and starvation in a place like this. *757-253-4838*.

Docked at the shoreline are replicas of those three original ships—the *Susan Constant* (the largest at 110 feet), *Godspeed,* and *Discovery.* Visitors are welcome aboard, and "colonials" in knee breeches relate what it was like to cross the Atlantic in the dark, breathless hold of a tiny vessel, sharing quarters with too many other humans, not to mention livestock.

■ WILLIAMSBURG   *map pages 48–49, C-4*

When the Jamestown statehouse burned in 1698, colonial officials decided, after 91 disease-ridden years, to move the capital off the miasmic island. Middle Plantation, on higher ground 5 miles northeast, was chosen as the new site. A small village, it had recently become home to the College of William and Mary. Within a year, the new capital had been laid out and named for England's king, William III. Royal governor Francis Nicholson probably played the greatest role in turning the small settlement into a well-proportioned town.

Dominated by a central Market Square, its main thoroughfare was the mile-long Duke of Gloucester Street, buttressed at its west end by the College of William and Mary and at its east end by the impressive brick Capitol, which was completed in 1705. The new village quickly established itself as the administrative and cultural focus of the Virginia colony. As the century progressed, artisans' shops lined its streets, and dignified clapboard homes clustered around Market Square and the majestic Governor's Palace.

But as dissension grew in the colonies, Williamsburg became polarized. This, after all, was the seat of British royal government in Virginia—and a hotbed of popularly elected revolutionaries such as George Washington, Thomas Jefferson, Patrick Henry, and Richard Henry Lee. They had sat in the Capitol as burgesses, at first decorously tending the king's business. But decorum gave way to seditious oratory in the Capitol halls, including Patrick Henry's famous speech: "Caesar . . . had his Brutus, Charles the First his Cromwell, and George the Third may profit by their example. If this be treason, make the most of it." By 1774, the royal governor had been forced to dissolve the rebellious body, but the burgesses simply adjourned to nearby Raleigh Tavern, where they continued the business of government and revolution. Through the turmoil of the following years,

Williamsburg remained the home of the colony's elected government and the meeting place for many of the patriots who would eventually press the American colonies toward independence.

As the Revolution dragged on through the 1770s, Williamsburg seemed less and less defensible. In 1780, Jefferson, now governor, moved the capital 50 miles northwest, to more central Richmond. By 1781, war was upon Williamsburg; colonial and French commanders set up headquarters in residences and launched the decisive siege of Yorktown.

After the war, the old colonial capital, like Jamestown before it, lost its preeminence. Unlike Jamestown, however, it had the College of William and Mary and the county seat to keep it from lapsing into a backwater. Over the course of the 19th century, it survived as a quiet farming hamlet and college town, one with a rich architectural heritage. Many of its colonial buildings remained, though dilapidated or Victorianized with porches and frills. Some served as small stores, others as homes. Still, the layout and sense of the 18th-century village prevailed into the early 20th century, and visionaries who could imagine Williamsburg's past glory dreamed of a more promising future.

One of those visionaries was the Reverend W. A. R. Goodwin, rector of the town's Bruton Parish Church. Goodwin managed to convey his dreams to John D. Rockefeller Jr. and found in the philanthropist a receptive audience. For 30 years, Rockefeller poured money and enthusiasm into returning the little country town to its 18th-century grandeur. He and his family even maintained a residence at graceful old Bassett Hall.

Today, Williamsburg is surely the most elaborately restored and reconstructed colonial site in America. Nine miles northeast of Jamestown along the Colonial Parkway, the historic area—**Colonial Williamsburg**—now covers about 300 acres and comprises almost 90 restored colonial buildings, as well as a number of reconstructions built on original foundations. All this, along with Carter's Grove Plantation, 8 miles away on the James River, is maintained by the nonprofit Colonial Williamsburg Foundation.

More than a historic site, Williamsburg is sublimely genteel. Men in knee breeches and white stockings, and wide-skirted, mobcapped, and well-mannered, dames add a human dimension to the shops, taverns, inns, and historic sites.

(following pages) An 18th-century shoemaker's shop at Colonial Williamsburg.

(above and right) Keeping up to date is not part of the job description for the intepreters of the past at Colonial Williamsburg.

"People of the past" are stationed throughout the town, offering up colorful impersonations of colonial residents. Just wandering the historic area, even without paying to enter the buildings, will give you a taste of the past. Faithfully restored clapboard houses, surrounded by 18th-century gardens, are home to lucky Colonial Williamsburg employees, and no noisome traffic is allowed to detract from the swish of long dresses along Duke of Gloucester Street.

No traffic, that is, save that of the crowds. About a million visitors tour Colonial Williamsburg each year, anxious to take in the ambience and a little history along the way. Tricorn hats off to Williamsburg! It manages to teach history in an eminently palatable way, although it has cleaned up the 18th century. Its streets are hardly a muddy morass scented by animals and sewage; disease is no longer a threat. The former Virginia capital may be a bit too perfect to re-create colonial life authentically, but it does combine the best of two worlds—the quaintness of the past and the sanitized, air-conditioned comforts of the present.

■ Touring the Town

The best way to see Williamsburg is the old-fashioned way: on foot. Start at the **visitors center,** outside the historic area, where you can park and choose from several tour packages. Your ticket also allows you to use the bus that shuttles from the visitors center through the historic area. While you're here, take in the 35-minute docudrama, *Williamsburg: The Story of a Patriot,* about a fictitious planter faced with the decisions that all colonists had to make in the years before the Revolution: Should he support the perpetrators of the Boston Tea Party? Side with Britain? Declare independence? Once armed with that historical grounding, you're ready to attack the town itself. *I-64, Exit 238; 757-220-7645 or 800-447-8679.*

At the east end of **Duke of Gloucester Street,** the **Capitol** makes a good starting point. The brick building, with its uniquely rounded sides, is a reconstruction of the 1705 capitol, which burned in 1747. (It was replaced in 1753, but that building too was destroyed by fire, in 1832.) The distinctive H-shape of this reconstruction symbolizes the bicameral nature of Virginia government in the 18th century. The royal governor and his 12-man council of gentlemen, appointed for life by the king, were ensconced in the opulent quarters on the west side of the building. Here, they held court, presiding as justices over civil and criminal cases and serving as the upper house of the legislature. Publicly elected burgesses served in the lower house. Their space, on the east side of the building, is decidedly less extravagant, with no whiff of royal trappings. That difference in decor sums up the contrast between America's spirit of informality and practicality and the entrenched, autocratic conventions prevailing in England in that era.

As in the days of old, the neighborhood surrounding the Capitol is replete with taverns. To the east, on Waller Street, is **Christiana Campbell's Tavern,** a favorite of George Washington's and still popular with seafood lovers. West of the Capitol, on the first block of Duke of Gloucester Street, politicians and poohbahs had their choice of four taverns. **Shields Tavern** and the **King's Arms** once again serve colonial fare; **Wetherburn's** and the famous **Raleigh Tavern** operate solely as historic sites. The social and political center of the old capital, the Raleigh Tavern witnessed many a historic moment, from the meetings of patriotic burgesses to an 1824 ball in honor of the Marquis de Lafayette. Farther along, **Chowning's Tavern** also offers dining. (*Colonial Williamsburg's reservations number is 757-229-2141.*)

A sampling of colonial-era tradespeople also have their shops on Duke of Gloucester Street—the peruke (wig) maker, milliner, book binder, scrivener, apothecary, harness maker, and more. Some of these establishments sell their wares and a few allow free entry, but most require a general Colonial Williamsburg admission ticket.

On its westernmost block, Duke of Gloucester Street opens into **Market Square.** In colonial days, the greensward bustled with farmers who came to town to sell produce. The small brick **Courthouse** that served as the seat of government of James City County in the 18th and 19th centuries still stands in the square, as does the old **guardhouse** and the octagonal **powder magazine,** which played a prominent role in the buildup to the Revolution. In April 1775, Governor Dunmore ordered British troops to move in by night and stealthily remove the gunpowder from the magazine. When his deed was discovered, Virginians were outraged and mustered troops to move against the British. The governor backed down and paid for the purloined powder.

Once the most prestigious address in town, Market Square is faced by several fine colonial houses, including the sprawling clapboard home of the distinguished Randolph family. Built in 1715 and expanded several times, the **Randolph House** still contains much of its original interior paneling. One member of the family,

Peyton Randolph, presided over the First and Second Continental Congresses in Philadelphia.

Market Square's western side gives onto **Palace Green,** at the far end of which rises the **Governor's Palace,** an elaborate reconstruction of the original, which was completed in 1722. Perhaps the most impressive piece of architecture in British colonial America, the original palace housed seven royal governors, as well as Patrick Henry and Thomas Jefferson, the Commonwealth's first two governors, but it was turned into a hospital for troops injured in the siege of Yorktown after the capital was moved to Richmond. On the night of December 22, 1781, the building burned to the ground in three hours. The richly paneled entry hall of the current palace contains a remarkable display of musketry and armaments arranged in swirling, decorative patterns on the walls. There's an elegant supper room, and a ballroom and private quarters for the governors and their families. Behind the palace are extensive formal and informal gardens.

Two notable buildings face the Palace Green. One is the brick manor **house of George Wythe**—jurist, law professor, mentor to both Thomas Jefferson and John Marshall, a signer of the Declaration of Independence and generally acknowledged sage of Williamsburg. The other is **Bruton Parish Church,** whose walled cemetery contains graves dating from the late 17th century. The current brick cruciform church wasn't built until 1715, but it has been used continuously since then as a house of worship. Its interior is elegantly simple, with high enclosed box pews, clear glass windows, and a cantilevered pulpit.

In the block beyond the church, Duke of Gloucester Street suddenly rejoins the 20th century. Boutiques and eateries cluster here at the easternmost point of the **College of William and Mary,** but when you enter the walled grounds of the Wren Yard, the college's ancient campus, you quickly reenter the past.

Chartered in 1693 by its namesakes, King William and Queen Mary, this college boasts the oldest structure in continuous academic use in the United States. The stately brick **Wren Building**—named after the English architect Sir Christopher Wren, who reputedly designed it—has been restored several times and now reflects the style of the early 1700s. The well-proportioned interior contains bare 1700s-colonial classrooms, a chapel, and a Great Hall for dining. The piazza along the rear overlooks a sunken garden and a portion of the serene college campus. Flanking the building's front are the brick **President's House** (1732) and the **Brafferton** (1723). Built as a school for Native Americans, the

Brafferton was made possible by funds from the estate of eminent 17th-century English scientist Robert Boyle. Notable early William and Mary alumni include four U.S. presidents: George Washington, Thomas Jefferson, James Madison, and John Tyler. *West end of Duke of Gloucester Street, between Jamestown and Richmond Roads.*

Francis Street, Colonial Williamsburg's second thoroughfare, parallels Duke of Gloucester Street on the south and is appealing and quieter, which is suitable for the **Williamsburg Inn,** set back on its own lawn.

A couple of blocks west you come to the site of a rather unusual museum concept. On the eve of the Revolution a **Public Hospital** for the mentally ill opened in Williamsburg, and a reconstruction of that hospital now traces the history of mental health treatment from 1773 through the late 19th century. It also serves as a clever historically correct entrance to the entirely modern museum structure behind it, the **DeWitt Wallace Decorative Arts Museum,** designed by the noted architect Kevin Roche. The low-slung, partially underground building encompasses 26,000 square feet of exhibit space and displays one of the world's finest collections of 17th- through early 19th-century British and American decorative

Canoeing on Lake Matoaka, on the William and Mary campus.

arts. Among its masterworks are Charles Willson Peale's portrait of George Washington as commander of the American forces during the Revolution; mid-17th- and 18th-century furniture, ceramics, silver, and pewter; and some extraordinary historic prints. *Francis Street; 757-220-2946.*

Providing the counterpoint to the DeWitt Wallace is the nearby **Abby Aldrich Rockefeller Folk Art Museum.** The wife of John D. Rockefeller Jr., Abby Rockefeller was one of the nation's foremost collectors of American folk art, and her weathervanes, naive portraits, and wood carvings form the core of the offerings. The exquisite galleries also display textiles, ceramics, and a number of *Peacable Kingdom* paintings—American classics by self-taught early 19th-century artist Edward Hicks, a Quaker minister who painted this theme throughout his lifetime. Also here is the renowned portrait *Baby in Red Chair. South England Street; 757-220-7698.*

■ MODERN WILLIAMSBURG *map pages 48–49, C-4*

Banking on the notion that modern travelers might want to leaven their colonialism with some 21st-century diversions, several enterprising concerns have set up not far from the historic area. One of these is **Busch Gardens Williamsburg,** a theme amusement park that tumbles across 360 precisely landscaped acres 3 miles east of town. Adding to the megamagic is nearby **Water Country USA,** a water theme park with 40 acres of water slides, wave pools, and meandering streams. *800-343-7946 for both.*

On the other side of the historic area, along the old Richmond Road, factory outlets between Williamsburg and Lightfoot attract shoppers. The granddaddy of all is the **Williamsburg Pottery Factory.** More like a flea market than an outlet mall, this mind-boggling complex of more than 30 warehouses is filled to overflowing with glassware, furnishings, foods, plants, and other items. Don't be misled by the name: This is no factory; this is a merchandising marathon. *757-564-3326.*

For a more serene interlude, drive west of town to the **Williamsburg Winery,** the state's largest producer. Its wines range from simple ones for casual consumption, like the Governor's White, to more complex reds like the Gabriel Archer. In addition to a tasting room, there is a restaurant. *Off Route 199 east of Jamestown Road; 757-229-0999.*

In the fast lane at Williamsburg: Busch Gardens.

Lee Hall   *map pages 48–49, C-4*

A few miles east of Williamsburg lies **Lee Hall,** a village named for the foursquare brick Italianate mansion built there in 1858 by Richard Decauter Lee. The home played a part in the Peninsula Campaign in 1862, when it was headquarters for Confederate generals Magruder and Johnston. From earthworks on the lawn, a spy balloon was sent aloft to glean intelligence about Gen. George McClellan's whereabouts and strength. *163 Yorktown Road, Lee Hall (part of Newport News); take Exit 247 from I-64 or take Route 60 east; 757-888-3371.*

And while you're in the neighborhood, you might stop for a meal or stay overnight at the **Boxwood Inn,** a Victorian mansion that's served as the Warwick County Hall of Records, a general store, post office, and military housing but is now a bed-and-breakfast whose owner has studied French cooking. *10 Elmhurst Street, Lee Hall; 757-888-8854.*

■ **YORKTOWN** *map pages 48–49, D-4*

Of the three parts of the Colonial Triangle, Yorktown, 14 miles from Williamsburg at the eastern end of the Colonial Parkway, in some ways seems the most compelling. Now, as in the past, it drowses on high banks above the York River, while traffic arcs across the nearby Coleman Memorial Bridge and ships come and go from the Naval Weapons Station upriver. People still swim and picnic along its sandy strip of beach or visit **Cornwallis' Cave,** which is just a hole in the red-clay bank. Legend has it that British troops took cover in the cave while Revolutionary forces pummeled their position during the Siege of Yorktown. It is that 1781 siege, of course, that makes Yorktown more than just another lazy little river hamlet. How did history come to choose it as the culminating spot of the Revolution?

By the time the Revolution reached Yorktown, Washington's men—ill-clothed, sick, underfed, underpaid, and undervalued by the Continental Congress—were

Storming a Redoubt at Yorktown *(1840), by Eugene Lami, hangs in the Old Senate Chamber of the Capitol in Richmond. The painting shows Revolutionary War soldiers overrunning British breastworks, leading to the surrender of Cornwallis.*

on the verge of deserting. Victory had rarely visited the Colonials, and the British seemed to have the men and resources to fight forever. The one bright spot for Washington lay in the new French commitment to the cause. Since the Franco-American Treaty of 1778 the French had been sending money and supplies to the Americans, but they did not send troops until 1780. Fortified by this fresh infusion from a powerful ally, the success of the Revolution again seemed possible.

Late summer of 1781 found Washington's forces in New York, preparing for a campaign to drive the British out of New York City. To the south, Britain's daunting Lord Cornwallis had swept through Virginia, and then, under orders from his superiors in New York, had fallen back to the sea, situating his troops on the banks of the York River. Here, strategically near the mouth of the Chesapeake Bay, he prepared a naval depot and waited for reinforcements by water.

The French commander, the Comte de Rochambeau, sensed something precarious in Cornwallis's position, and when on August 14 Washington learned that France's Adm. Joseph Paul de Grasse and his fleet were en route to the Chesapeake, he decided to move south and attack. In one of the great moments of military stealth, Washington pulled his men out of New York, leaving behind a token force, and covered the 500 miles to Virginia in four weeks. Perhaps believing that what was coming would spell ultimate victory or defeat, Washington made a detour and, after six long years of war, stopped at Mount Vernon to see his family.

Meanwhile, the British Rear Adm. Thomas Graves and his 19 warships had set sail from New York to reinforce Cornwallis at Yorktown. Rounding the Virginia capes on September 5, the fleet was taken by surprise by 24 ships under Admiral de Grasse's command. The Battle of the Capes sent the British limping back to New York and left Cornwallis in Yorktown unfortified, unsuspecting, and vulnerable, with his back to the sea, where the French battle fleet had him blockaded.

By mid-September the combined allied force of 17,600 men had reached Virginia and positioned themselves at Williamsburg, where they prepared to lay siege to Cornwallis's 8,300 men. On October 9 the bombardment began. In classic 18th-century tradition, both sides dug fortifications, as the Revolutionary forces continually bombarded the British. Cornwallis realized he faced defeat and on October 17 requested a parley. The opposing parties met in the nearby Moore House and worked out the formal terms of surrender. On October 19 troops of

Yorktown National Battlefield in spring.

both sides gathered on what is now called Surrender Field to witness a ceremony that would ultimately lead to freedom for the 13 colonies.

■ **VISITING YORKTOWN**

Pick up a map of the site at the **Yorktown Visitor Center,** just east of town. Exhibits here include Washington's field tent and a 15-minute film explaining the decisive events that happened here. A lookout area on the roof provides a good overview of the earthworks that still make serpentine scars across the old battlefield, and 1.5 miles away, on a beautiful site overlooking the river, stands the little clapboard **Moore House.** *Route 238 off Colonial Parkway, east of town; 757-898-3400.*

Just another grassy meadow today, **Surrender Field** rests quietly now, though at twilight white-tailed deer drift across it like Revolutionary ghosts. *Route 238, 1.5 miles south of the visitors center; 757-898-3400.*

About a mile north on Route 238, casualties of another war lie in the brick-walled **Yorktown National Cemetery:** Civil War soldiers killed during George McClellan's infamous Peninsula Campaign and the Second Siege of Yorktown. The Union commander spent a month here in a face-off with Confederate Gen. John B. Magruder's far weaker forces, until Gen. Joseph Johnston's reinforcement arrived. "No one but McClellan," Johnston said, "could have hesitated to attack." But hesitate he did, laying siege instead, and giving the Confederates time to slip away without terrible losses.

Although it's an easy walk from the visitors center to the historic area (and all around the town), you can take a free trolley. At the first stop rises the **Victory Monument** (1884), a pedestal topped by a classical rendition of Victory, arms outstretched in hope, on the bluffs above the river. Along **Main Street** and the cross streets off it stands a scattering of nice old colonial buildings large and small, most built in the first half of the 1700s, when Yorktown was a prosperous tobacco port. By the time the war struck, the soil of surrounding plantations had been depleted and the port had lost its product.

The grandest structure still standing from that period is the brick **Nelson House,** the Georgian home of Thomas Nelson Jr., ardent patriot, signer of the Declaration of Independence, and, briefly, governor of Virginia. Built around 1730 by Nelson's grandfather "Scotch Tom," the house, now restored, re-creates a piece of life in Yorktown before the war. In 1774 Nelson led the local tea party, tossing tea overboard from a British vessel. During the war, when the British were

Diary of a Plantation Owner

William Byrd II, a member of Virginia's ruling class and the builder of the mansion at Westover Plantation, was born in 1674 and died in 1744, by which time he had become president of the Virginia Council of State. Much of his life, intimate and public, is known to us because Byrd, who was a voracious reader and also a writer, began, in 1709, to keep secret diaries. Besides his day-to-day routine, the diaries reveal a man with a pro-forma religiosity and a randy sexuality. (By the time he wrote the entries below, he had sown his wild oats.) The diaries, written in an obscure form of shorthand, did not come to light until 1939. Only three, covering 1709–1712, 1717–1721, and 1739–1741, survive.

January 21

I rose about 6, read Hebrew and Greek. I prayed and had hominy. The weather was cold and clear, the wind southwest. The Doctor and Mr. Anderson went away. I read records and Latin till dinner when I ate sparerib. It snowed again a little till the evening, then danced because could not walk. At night talked with my people. Mrs. Byrd had the headache pretty much. I prayed.

January 26

I rose about 6, read Hebrew and Greek. I prayed and had sage tea. I danced. The weather was cold and clear, the wind northwest. My son was hurt in the eye with a snowball; God preserve him. I read records and Latin till dinner when I ate pork griskin. After dinner my man Peter ran here from above. I played billiards and danced. I had letters from England, and prayed.

January 27

I rose about 6, read Hebrew and Greek. I prayed and had tea. I danced. The weather was cold and cloudy, the wind west. I sent Peter up again with Bob. I put myself in order and sent Mr. Procter over the river. The boat came from the Falls, where all were well, thank God. Mr. B-r-n came and Mr. Ravenscroft and Mr. Wendey to dinner and I ate sparerib. After dinner we talked and had coffee. The company went away. In the evening I talked with my people and discoursed my family till 8, then retired and prayed.

—William Byrd II, *Secret Diary,* 1740

assumed to be headquartered here, it was Nelson, as commander of the Virginia militia, who ordered the house shelled. That was not Nelson's only selfless act; he borrowed heavily against his fortune to support the war effort. *757-898-2410 or 757-898-3400.*

Across Read Street from the Nelson House stands the **Custom House,** the oldest such building in the country. It dates from about 1721, during Yorktown's bustling days of commerce.

Small and lovely **Grace Church** (1697) stands nearby on Church Street, its marl walls having endured both the Revolutionary and Civil Wars. In its walled cemetery are the graves of Thomas Nelson Jr. and Nicholas Martiau, the first American ancestor of George Washington. *757-898-3261.*

The Yorktown waterfront offers two other attractions. In the shadow of the Coleman Bridge, the **Watermen's Museum** (309 Water Street; 757-887-2641) evokes the centuries-old and now troubled culture of the Bay's oystermen, crabbers, and fishermen. **Nick's Seafood Pavilion** (324 Water Street; 757-887-5269), down the street, cooks to perfection fresh catches from the bay in a setting of Grecian and Italian statuary.

Northwest of the historic area, at Route 238 and the Colonial Parkway, the Jamestown-Yorktown Foundation maintains its **Yorktown Victory Center,** a museum and living-history site where costumed interpreters work a 1780s-style farm site and a Revolutionary-period military encampment. The center's film, *A Time of Revolution,* supplies a particularly good explanation of the area's history. *757-253-4838.*

■ PLANTATIONS AND HISTORIC BUILDINGS
map pages 48–49, B/C-3/4

Along the middle stretch of the James River, from roughly Williamsburg to Richmond, lies a virtual gold mine of colonial and Georgian mansions. Virginia planters built these palaces in the heyday of the plantation, and the houses epitomize that genteel life. Most are privately owned and some have remained in the same family since they were built. Though they dot both sides of the river, the greatest concentration can be found in **Charles City County** near or along Route 5, the renowned Plantation Route. Several historic houses along this scenic wooded lane are now B&Bs. Others are open for guided tours, but some open their doors only during Historic Garden Week. Those mentioned below deserve special attention for their historic or architectural merit.

Eight miles east of Williamsburg, atop an 80-foot bluff, **Carter's Grove** was built in 1750 by Carter Burwell, a grandson of Virginia's rich and powerful Robert "King" Carter. By the early 20th century the plantation was deteriorating, but in 1928 it was bought by the Archibald McCraes, who, with their Richmond architect and deep pockets, raised the roof and restored the house.

Carter's Grove is now owned by the Colonial Williamsburg Foundation. An orientation slide show provides an overview of the almost 400 years of history at this stately mansion, and at the archaeological dig that is uncovering the 17th-century Wolstenholme Towne settlement, you can take a walking tour enlivened by audiotapes. *Route 60E; 757-220-7645.*

Sherwood Forest lays claim to being the only house owned by two U.S. presidents, William Henry Harrison (who owned it but never lived here) and his running mate John Tyler, who bought it from a Harrison relative. Tyler did live at Sherwood Forest, and at the behest of his young second wife, he added Greek Revival touches to this already elegant Georgian clapboard house. Tyler's descendants still live here. *14501 John Tyler Memorial Highway (Route 5), 18 miles west of Williamsburg; 804-829-5377.*

One of the oldest (1726) large brick houses in Virginia, the Georgian mansion at **Berkeley Plantation** is memorable even more for its history and its boxwood gardens than its beauty. It is reputedly the site of the first official Thanksgiving, in 1619. Benjamin Harrison, a signer of the Declaration of Independence, built it, and his son, the future president William Henry Harrison, was born here. *12602 Harrison Landing Road, off Route 5, 18 miles west of Williamsburg; 804-829-6018.*

The elegantly proportioned Georgian manor house that is **Westover** was built circa 1730 by William Byrd II, the man credited with founding Richmond. Though the house is open only during Historic Garden Week, the grounds alone, with their fine gates, are well worth a visit. The striking facade of the house with its famous Westover doorway faces the James across a lawn punctuated by a line of centuries-old poplars. It's said that the McCraes, who bought Carter's Grove, really wanted Westover, which wasn't for sale, and that the renovation they did was intended to make Carter's Grove more closely resemble Westover. *7000 Westover Road; 804-829-2882.*

(following pages) Berkeley Plantation.

Shirley, Virginia's oldest plantation, was established just six years after the founding of Jamestown. The house, birthplace of Robert E. Lee's mother, has been in the Hill-Carter family since it was built in 1723. A remarkable walnut staircase seems to rise unsupported for three stories through its center, and the three rooms on the first floor (the only ones open to the public) are furnished with museum-quality paintings and antiques. The outbuildings give a fascinating insight into plantation life. Revolutionary War reenactments are held on the grounds. *501 Shirley Plantation Road, off Route 5, 35 miles northwest of Williamsburg; 804-795-2385.*

If you take the little **ferry** across the river from Jamestown to Surry County, you'll come to **Smith's Fort Plantation,** the site of the fort John Smith built in 1609 to protect the Jamestown settlement. A few years later, Powhatan gave the land to Pocahontas when she married John Rolfe, and their son Thomas built a house on it. Today a small 18th-century dormered brick house stands here, beautifully restored and furnished. *Route 31; 757-294-3872.*

Bacon's Castle, a short distance southeast, is the only remaining example of High Jacobean architecture in America. Built in 1665 by Arthur Allen, a planter,

Shirley Plantation

the brick manor was occupied by Nathaniel Bacon's forces during Bacon's Rebellion in 1676, though Bacon never lived here. The house, with high triple chimneys and curved gables, is furnished in the fashion of the 17th and 18th centuries, and there's a large, well-preserved colonial-era garden. *Route 10 in Surry County; 757-357-5976.*

■ RIVER COUNTRY

Virginia's Middle Peninsula, between the Rappahannock and the York Rivers, and the Northern Neck, that long arm of land between the Potomac and the Rappahannock, are both rich in colonial sites and history and are still flavorfully rural, stretching away in corn and soybean fields bordered by oak and evergreen forests. Meandering creeks burrow inland along the big rivers. Sailboats glide in and out of the marinas that dot peninsulas where they jut into the bay, and little seafood houses, specializing in crabs, fish, oysters, and clams, nestle on inlets.

■ THE MIDDLE PENINSULA *map pages 48–49, C/D-1/3*

From Yorktown, take the Coleman Bridge (Route 17) across the York River to the low-key Middle Peninsula, and you come first to **Gloucester Point.** This strategic tip of land was first fortified in 1667, and during the Revolution Lord Cornwallis established a base here, believing the narrow part of the York River ideal for naval defense. Cornwallis also counted on Gloucester as an escape hatch, and two days before the surrender, was prevented only by a vicious storm from evacuating his men in boats from Yorktown by night.

In the Civil War too, these narrows were seen as vital to the defense of the Upper York River and Richmond, so Lee established fortifications at the Point. They defended Yorktown during McClellan's siege of April 1862, staving off for a while the Union advance. But early in May the Confederates withdrew and Federal troops occupied Gloucester Point and later the town of **Gloucester,** 13 miles north, usually called **Gloucester Courthouse.**

Gloucester Courthouse Circle (Main Street; 804-693-0014), in the center of town, comprises a cluster of charming brick buildings from 1766 enclosed by a low circular brick wall. Among them are the restored **Clayton Clerk's Office,** now a visitors center, and the old courthouse building, which contains a wonderful assortment of large bronze plaques that bear close perusal—they're dedicated to Pocahontas, 23 members of the "illustrious Page family" from 1659 to 1902,

Dr. Walter Reed, and Nathaniel Bacon, among others. Along with nearby **Lawyers Row,** the **Botetourt Building** across the street, and a 1770 brick tavern, now the **History Museum** (6539 Main Street; 804-693-1234), these buildings are worth spending a morning to visit. The museum is crammed with bits and pieces of local archaeology, artifacts from an old country store and post office, relics of the Revolutionary and Civil Wars, and a fascinating exhibit on John Clayton (1694–1773), the botanist who between 1739 and 1743 published his famous *Flora Virginica,* an illustrated guide to the state's plants.

Gloucester County, reputed to have been the main residence of Powhatan and Pocahontas, celebrated its 350th anniversary in 2001. It has two beautiful brick churches: the large, cruciform **Abingdon Church** (1755) and **Ware Church** (circa 1690–1713), an imposing brick rectangle with 3-foot-thick walls. There's also **Rosewell,** the gorgeous ruin of the Page family's huge mansion (1725–-1738), which has an excellent visitors center. Not far away, on the Severn River bayward of Gloucester Point, stands **Warner Hall** (4750 Warner Hall Road; 804-695-9565), a large white mansion built circa 1895 on the foundations of an earlier building—Warner Hall Plantation was established in 1642 by Augustine Warner, George Washington's great-great-grandfather. Once Nathaniel Bacon's headquarters, the house is now a comfortable B&B. To reach it, take Route 17 south from Gloucester Courthouse about 6 miles, and then go left on Featherbed Lane to Warner Hall Road.

You can drive through **Mathews County** (Virginia's second smallest) in a minute, but it has 200 miles of shoreline and not a single stoplight. Once a steamship and shipbuilding area, it's now a place for kayaking, birding, and fooling around on the water. Its **New Point Comfort Lighthouse** began service in 1805. Essex County's **Tappahannock,** once a deepwater trading post and port, offers seafood, antiques, and early architecture.

■ THE NORTHERN NECK *map pages 48–49, C/D-1/2*
Cross the Rappahannock from the Middle Peninsula to the Northern Neck, and you can hardly tell the difference. In some ways, this land is as unspoiled and unpretentious as it was centuries ago. If you cross from Greys Point on Route 3, you'll pass by the **Tides Inn** (480 King Carter Drive, 804-438-5000)—not really old, only about six decades, and not pretentious, but a favored resort of the sailing rich. It does possess an antique diesel yacht that's on the National Register of Historic Places, the 127-foot *Miss Ann.*

Continue north on Route 3, and before long you'll be directed to a real architectural treasure. The little cruciform **Christ Church** with its pagoda-like roof, called the finest colonial church in North America, was completed in 1735, when George Washington was three years old, and it has remained virtually unchanged since then. A National Historic Landmark, it was built by Robert "King" Carter and contains a rare triple-decker pulpit of native walnut, its original limestone paving slabs, and elegant high-backed box pews. Bricks for the 3-foot-thick walls were fired in a kiln near the churchyard. *Route 646 near Kilmarnock; 804-438-6855.*

It would be nice to live in **Reedville;** it's a lovely little finger of land, with water to the left of you, water to the right of you, and a slew of pretty Victorian houses. It seems as if every house on Main Street has a dock in its own backyard. There's the restored and furnished **Walker House** (1875) and the **Fishermen's Museum,** where you can learn about fishing for menhaden (Main Street; 804-453-6529). At **Tangier Island & Chesapeake Cruises** (468 Buzzard's Point Road; 804-453-2628) you can take a boat to Tangier Island across the bay for a visit and lunch.

The Northern Neck was the birthplace of four of Virginia's most illustrious sons—George Washington, James Monroe, James Madison, and Robert E. Lee. All but Madison are from Westmoreland County, and Washington and Lee were born within 10 miles of each other. Besides geography, destiny and even marriage linked the lives of the two men, whose kin mingled and meshed in byzantine Southern fashion.

New Point Comfort Lighthouse.

Stratford Hall   *map pages 10–11*

Take Route 3 north to Route 214, looking for signs to Stratford Hall, which is as imposing as the people who lived here, one of Virginia's most illustrious families: the Lees. The unusual Georgian great house, an H-shaped brick mansion with broad exterior staircases and dominant chimney clusters, is most famous as the birthplace of the South's enduring hero, Robert E. Lee. The Lees who preceded him were also a striking lot, and their story is worth telling.

A Shropshire gentleman named Richard Lee arrived in Jamestown in the 1630s and established the family on American soil. His descendants would distinguish themselves as colonial officials, military heroes, and mothers of presidents. (Zachary Taylor's mother was of the Lee line.) With what would prove to be a family talent for land acquisition, Richard Lee got off to a fine start, leaving his heirs several plantations, including one on the Northern Neck. It was Richard's grandson Thomas who built Stratford Hall.

Thomas was raised on the Northern Neck on the family's Machodoc Plantation. For years he apparently had had his eye on a nearby piece of land called the Clifts, and in 1716 he bought it from the Pope family—the same people who once owned the farm on which George Washington was born. Early in the 1730s his new house was complete, and he and his wife and numerous children moved in. A well-respected colonial official and a member of His Majesty's Council of Twelve (the upper house of the Virginia Legislature), Lee went on to serve briefly as chief executive of Virginia during the royal governor's absence.

Thomas's sons continued in their distinguished father's footsteps. As conditions with Britain grew strained, however, several of the sons became vocal proponents of more freedom for the colonies. When the Continental Congress met in Philadelphia, Richard Henry Lee introduced the resolution that "these United Colonies are, and of right ought to be, free and independent States absolved from all allegiance to the British Crown." Several months later, Richard Henry and Francis Lightfoot Lee affixed their names to the Declaration of Independence, the only brothers to do so.

After a generation Stratford Hall passed to Thomas Lee's granddaughter, the "divine Mathilda." This is where the Lee story becomes more complicated. At the end of the Revolution, Mathilda married her second cousin, the dashing Revolutionary War hero Lighthorse Harry Lee, who earned his romantic sobriquet from his lightning-quick raids on the British. A compatriot of George Washington, he remained a hero after the war and delivered Washington's eulogy, with its famous words: "First in war, first in peace, and first in the hearts of his countrymen."

Lighthorse Harry Lee had a talent for politics, but not for managing his private affairs. Under his guidance, or lack of it, Stratford Hall gradually fell into financial ruin. After only eight years of marriage, Mathilda died, leaving Lee with three children. Several years later, while serving as governor of Virginia, Lighthorse Harry took a second wife, Anne Hill Carter, a descendant of Virginia land mogul Robert "King" Carter. In January 1807 the couple's fifth child, Robert Edward, was born, but by the time he was learning to walk, his father had been sent to a nearby debtors prison. When Lighthorse Harry regained his freedom, he took his family to Alexandria, where family members were willing to lend assistance. And so

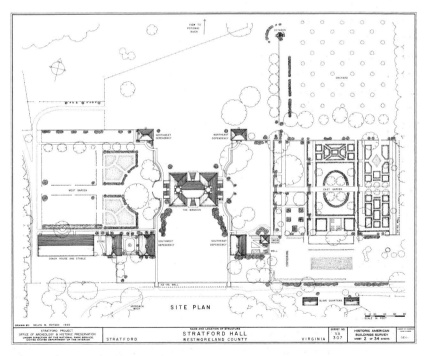

The great house, outbuildings, gardens, and grounds of Stratford Hall sit high above the Potomac River.

Robert E. Lee left Stratford Hall behind before he had reached the age of 4. Although Robert had been born here, the great estate really belonged neither to his father nor his mother, and so it passed to his half-brother, Mathilda's son Henry Lee. Sadly, this Henry too seemed star-crossed, and in the early 1800s he sold the house out of the family.

Decades later a disconsolate Robert E. Lee wrote his wife this letter from the battlefield. It was Christmas Day, 1863, and their house in Arlington, Virginia, was in the hands of the Union:

> In the absence of a home, I wish I could purchase Stratford. That is the only other place I could go to, now accessible to us, that would inspire me with feelings of pleasure and love.... It is a poor place, but we could make enough cornbread and bacon for our support, and the girls could weave us clothes.

Happily, Stratford is no longer a poor place but a huge, thriving "towne in itself." In the 1930s Mrs. Charles Lanier, inspired by a poem about Lee written by her father-in-law Sydney Lanier, founded the Robert E. Lee Memorial Association. Through grass-roots efforts, the association raised the funds to restore the property. The large rooms on the main floor are filled with 18th- and 19th-century antiques, including the crib, daintily draped with mosquito netting, that once held the infant Robert E. Lee. The Great Hall, with its tray ceiling, full paneling, and generous proportions, is one of America's most elegant rooms.

Outside the house lie a boxwood garden and a vegetable garden, kitchen and office dependencies, a smokehouse, a coach house and stables, slave quarters, and a stone gristmill. The 1,800 acres of green and wooded grounds overlooking the Potomac are a working farm supporting 800 head of cattle. *Route 214; 804-493-8038 or 804-493-8371.*

George Washington Birthplace National Monument *map pages 10–11*

Continue a few miles northwest on Route 3, and turn right onto Route 204; you'll know you've arrived when the fields abruptly end at a replica of the Washington Monument. Beyond the white granite obelisk, picturesque Popes Creek meanders past red cedars that edge Washington's birthplace. Destroyed by fire on Christmas Day 1779 while Washington was away at war, the old house was never rebuilt. Its outline is marked on the ground by a gray line of oyster shell, and behind it stands the brick memorial house, built in the 1930s, a story and a half, spacious but not grand. Not intended as a replica but as typical of what an upper-class 18th-century tobacco planter would have built, it is furnished in the style this same planter would have enjoyed.

Washington's roots in Virginia went back five generations, and in this area, three. His paternal grandmother, Mildred Warner, who married into the Washington family, was the great-granddaughter of Nicholas Martiau, a French Huguenot and naturalized Englishman who arrived at Jamestown in 1620. On the Washington side, his great-grandfather, John, had come from England to Virginia in 1657. A year later he married Anne Pope, whose father, Nathaniel, owned much of the Popes Creek area. By the time George was born, his father, Augustine, was comfortably ensconced at Popes Creek Plantation with his second wife, Mary Ball. Washington was the couple's first child. When George was three and a half, the family moved farther up the Potomac, to Augustine's Little Hunting Creek farm, the property the world now knows as Mount Vernon. Augustine soon relocated his family again, this time at Ferry Farm on the Rappahannock below Fredericksburg.

Augustine died when George was 11, leaving behind his young family by Mary Ball and two older sons by his first wife. One of these, Augustine Jr., inherited the Popes Creek land, and the other, Lawrence, became the squire of Little Hunting Creek. Young George spent time with both brothers, and so as an adolescent he became reacquainted with the languid charms of Popes Creek.

Today, the property again functions as a working colonial-type farm. Horses and cows graze behind split-rail fences, costumed cooks work in the tidy kitchen dependency beside the memorial house, and vegetables ripen on the vine. If the season is right, you might pick a fig from a row of trees that date to Washington's time. A long, lovely country lane leads past Dancing Marsh and Dogwood Swamp back to the brick-walled family cemetery. The remains of more than a score of Washingtons reside here. *1732 Popes Creek Road, off Route 204; 804-224-1732.*

P I E D M O N T

Rolling across the center of Virginia, the Piedmont sweeps through farm fields and pastureland and some of the most sought-after horse country in the nation. Punctuating all this ruralness are several of the Old Dominion's most winsome cities—places full of themselves and their histories. Things here are done with old-school Virginia grace and refinement. To some that style may seem passé, but it's a dying art form well worth appreciating.

■ RICHMOND   *map page 132, D-5, downtown page 134*

All roads lead to Richmond, or at least most of the state's major highways do. This is fitting, because to some Southerners this city is "the navel of the universe" and to others, mostly outlying students, "the holy city." Richmond is many things to many people: the industrial hub of Virginia; a cultural mecca rich in museums and historic sites; the place where Patrick Henry proclaimed "Give me liberty or give me death"; the capital of the Confederacy; and the current capital and headquarters of state officialdom, which is working hard…and slowly…to rid itself of some antebellum (not to say antediluvian) attitudes. Richmond has been home to Justice John Marshall, Edgar Allan Poe, tap dancer Bill "Bojangles" Robinson, and the tennis star Arthur Ashe. A linchpin of the New South and host to Fortune 500 companies, it is the Tobacco Capital of the World and the unrepentant heartland of the old Virginia aristocracy. A new city, an old city, a mild city, a harsh city. An enduring city. An endearing city.

It must have been a Richmonder who wrote the anonymous but ubiquitous dictum, seen on ashtrays, paper napkins, and tea towels: "To be a Virginian, either by birth, marriage, adoption, or even on one's mother's side, is an introduction to any state in the Union, a passport to any foreign country, and a benediction from the Almighty God."

Richmond's high-rises thrust suddenly into view, startling to the senses, really, in a state with so few pockets of towering urbanism. Devoted mostly to state government, banking, and financial interests, the high-rises cluster just above the downtown edge of the James River, and they leave a somewhat misleading first

The grounds surrounding a grand old Richmond mansion, Maymont, are now a public park.

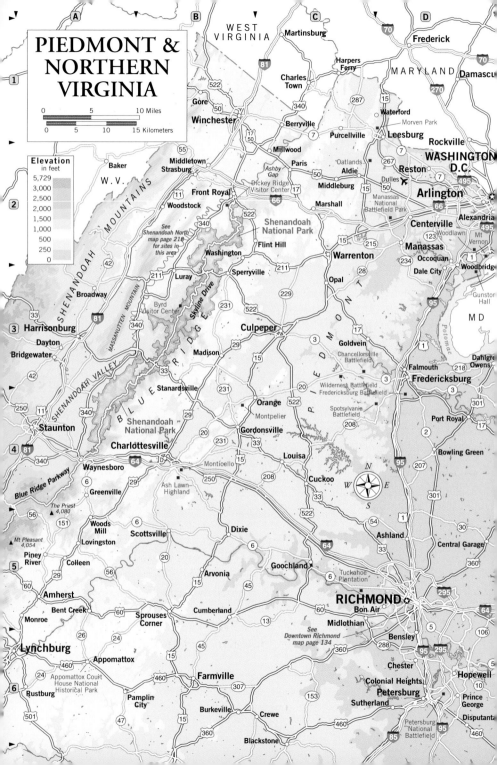

impression. Richmond, ultimately, is more horizontal than vertical. Its avenues spread out across seven hills through neighborhoods like Church Hill, the Fan, and the Boulevard, where restored Victorian row houses overlook shady streets, and lead into inner-city neighborhoods like Jackson Ward, a place with an illustrious history that's emerging at high speed from a period of desolation.

■ **ABOUT DOWNTOWN**   *map page 134*

In many ways, Richmond is the heart of Virginia, literally and figuratively. Built on the fall line of the James, the city marks the transitional point between the hilly Piedmont region to the west and Tidewater to the east.

At the onset of the Civil War, Richmond was the South's shining city of industry. This legacy continues, only today the large manufacturing companies, including Alcoa, in the city's fashionable West End, and Philip Morris, with its sprawling state-of-the-art complex on Richmond's southern outskirts, have been joined by companies at the forefront of high finance and high technology.

Richmond's downtown once ranked as the most fashionable place to shop in the South, but stores on Broad Street now stand boarded up, and despite the city's efforts, most of downtown's business has gone to suburban malls. Interestingly, some of the older shopping districts are enjoying a renaissance: Carytown, in the near West End, which earlier in the last century was a vibrant area of shops, movie theaters, restaurants and entertainment, is experiencing a new vitality today, and a plan is afoot to revitalize the Broad Street area.

Buildings that once housed the mighty **Tredegar Iron Works** rise by the riverfront. In its day, Tredegar, the chief industrial center in the South, produced half of all the armaments used by the Confederates. This was a progressive employer that watched out for its workers, who were immigrants, free blacks, and slaves, either owned by the company or rented from other owners. Tredegar provided a hospital and housing, and in the mid-1800s, when white artisans demanded that blacks be removed from certain skilled jobs, the whites went and the blacks stayed.

The Tredegar Iron Works is now the site of the **Richmond National Battlefield Park Civil War Visitor Center,** which traces the long torturous history of the war here and the fall of Richmond. The staff will tell you about the battles that took place near the city and help you plan a tour of the battlefields. *470 Tredegar Street; 804-771-2145.*

After nearby Petersburg fell in April 1865, Robert E. Lee sent word to Jefferson Davis that the North would be moving on the Confederate capital. Davis fled, and the South set fire to tobacco warehouses along the riverfront to keep their contents out of Northern hands. The fire spread, Richmond burned, and much of the white population bolted in fear. Much of the black population secretly rejoiced that they would be free at last. By April 4, Abraham Lincoln had entered the city, triumphant. Hand in hand with his young son Tad, he walked quietly through the streets. Recognizing him, many newly liberated slaves followed after them, some of them calling Lincoln "messiah" and bowing before him. But the Great Emancipator would have none of that. "You are free," he told them. "Free as air." Ten days later, Robert E. Lee rode into the city astride his horse Traveller to face defeat. He was going home to his wife and their temporary home at 707 East Franklin Street. The townhouse is still there, surrounded by—and a part of—modern Richmond.

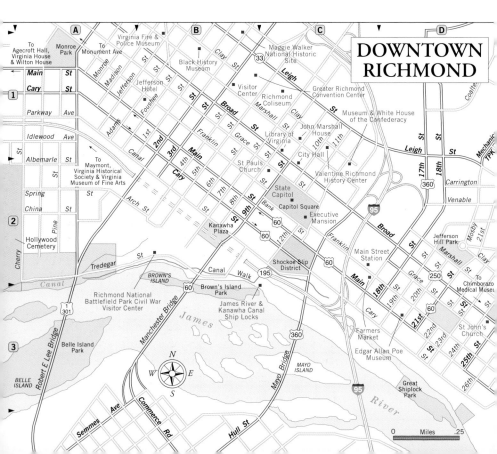

DOWNTOWN RICHMOND

Wickham House and its famous staircase.

The Valentine Museum, beloved in Richmond for decades, has expanded its mission as the **Valentine Richmond History Center,** aiming to "locate Richmond in the mainstream of American history." The complex now includes the **Wickham House,** an 1812 showcase of Federal architecture and furnishings; the museum galleries, in several adjoining townhouses; and the Edward V. Valentine Sculpture Studio. The center also offers tours of the city.

The house was built by John Wickham, a New York lawyer who moved to Richmond and became a prominent citizen (he defended Aaron Burr in his treason trial before Justice John Marshall). Notable for its exquisite murals and curving staircase, it speaks of urbanity and fine living—for Wickham if not necessarily for his slaves or his wife. She rarely went out, as she was confined by 17 pregnancies.

In the late 1800s, Mann Valentine, a Richmond merchant, bought the house from the Wickham family, and in his will he established the museum, with his brother, Edward Virginius Valentine, as president. Edward, a popular sculptor who did the beautiful recumbent statue of Robert E. Lee at Washington and Lee University in Lexington, was a social animal, and prominent people flocked to his studio (which in 1937 was moved to the museum garden from its location several blocks away). *1015 East Clay Street; 804-649-0711.*

After the subdued elegance of the Wickham House, the stuccoed, porticoed, neoclassical **White House of the Confederacy,** a block away, is a study in contrasts. Here, Jefferson Davis had his brief reign as president of the Southern states. The interior, done as it was then, is truly something to see. Its brocaded, chandeliered, red-velvet bordello-esque decor is aptly characterized by some of the tour docents as "gosh-awful Victorian." The decor notwithstanding, they do a good job of tracing the Davis family's poignant and tragic history. The **Museum of the Confederacy,** in the same complex, has paintings, war memorabilia, and accurate exhibits about the history of the Civil War. *1201 East Clay Street; 804-649-1861.*

A few blocks away is the large Federal brick **John Marshall House** (1790), home of the precedent-setting Great Chief Justice. In 1801 Marshall became the country's fourth chief justice of the Supreme Court, taking the post somewhat reluctantly, as he believed the judiciary to be the weakest of the three branches of government. During his 34-year tenure (the longest of any chief justice), Marshall decisively changed that state of affairs, making the court an equal partner in a tripartite governmental system. Over the objections of his political nemesis, Thomas Jefferson (who also happened to be his cousin), he interpreted the Constitution in a way that firmly established the federal government's authority over individual states.

Marshall was not by nature an intellectual. Robust and athletic, he liked sports, and a set of quoits still lies in the family parlor where he used to play. Even while serving as chief justice, Marshall lived here with his beloved wife, Polly, and their brood of children. *818 East Marshall Street; 804-648-7998.*

Lee's frock coat in the Museum of the Confederacy.

State Capitol Building.

In those days, the Supreme Court had no home of its own, and its members often convened nearby in the Virginia capitol. In fact, it was at the **State Capitol Building,** not in the Circuit Court, that Marshall heard the famous treason case against Aaron Burr.

The suave Burr cut quite a figure when he came into court as a prisoner in 1807. Even though he stood accused of plotting the overthrow of the federal government in territories west and south of Virginia, society welcomed him. While awaiting trial, he was housed in a three-room prison suite, and his admiring public dispatched servants daily with notes and gifts of fruit. Legal sensibilities were apparently different in those days, as Burr attended a dinner party at the home of one of his attorneys, none other than John Wickham. Other guests included some of those who would sit on his jury—and the chief justice himself.

During the trial, Marshall seemed to favor Burr's cause, and ultimately the dashing "traitor" was acquitted of the charges against him. A cynic might conclude that in Richmond, lack of charm was a far greater offense than treason. And Burr was a charming man.

The Hall of the House of Delegates, where Burr was tried, still occupies the north end of the gracefully pillared State Capitol, which was designed by Thomas Jefferson, that consummate lover of the classical. After studying various Greek and Roman temples and thoroughly steeping himself in the classical architectural orders, he modeled the building after the Erectheum in Athens and the Maison Carrée, a temple built by the conquering Romans in Nîmes, France. The original building (exclusive of the wings, which were added later) has been in use since 1788, making it the second-oldest working capitol in the United States, after the one in Annapolis, Maryland. It is filled with images of Virginia's favorite sons, including a statue of George Washington done from life by French sculptor Jean-Antoine Houdon. Washington, looking somber and dignified, occupies the place of honor under the dome, and in the niches around him are busts of the seven other Virginia presidents, as well as one of the Revolutionary War hero the Marquis de Lafayette. As the guides explain it, Lafayette is merely a place holder, there only until the country elects its ninth Virginia-born president. Guided tours of the capitol are free and worth the time. *Ninth and Grace Streets; 804-698-1788.*

(above) An old view of Richmond—pictured here around 1850. (opposite) Dining out in a revitalized Schockoe Bottom.

EDGAR ALLAN POE

Tortured and brilliant as an adult, Edgar Allan Poe spent an apparently contented childhood in Richmond as the foster son of the Allan family. (His mother, an acclaimed young actress, died when he was two, and his father before that.) When Poe got to the University of Virginia, his relations with his foster father began to sour, and money became a problem, one that would haunt him the rest of his life. To continue his education, he enrolled at West Point, but the military milieu was crippling to his creativity, and so he deliberately got himself dismissed. After the academy, he spent some time with his aunt, Maria Clemm in Baltimore, and there he fell in love with his young—very young—cousin, Virginia Clemm.

Edgar Allan Poe (1809–1849), who spent a happy childhood in Richmond.

By then he had published three volumes of poetry, but his financial situation was deplorable. In 1835, he took a job in Richmond as critic for the newly established *Southern Literary Messenger.* In his 18 months on the magazine, its circulation went from 500 to 3,500. It was during this time that the 27-year-old Poe married the 13-year-old Virginia. As much as he apparently loved his wife, the marriage did not settle Poe's situation. His bouts with depression and alcoholism led to his dismissal from the magazine, and he and his wife left Richmond for the North.

Though Poe's literary reputation flourished, his personal life did not. In 1842, his young wife suffered a ruptured blood vessel in her brain and lingered as an invalid for five years. In 1849, the writer made his final visit to Richmond and was warmly received. He wrote to his mother-in-law, "I have been invited out a great deal—but seldom go, on account of not having a dress coat." A few months later, he sailed for Baltimore, with plans to return to Richmond. He never did. He was found semiconscious and ill in Baltimore and died soon thereafter.

The old Shockoe Slip and Shockoe Bottom tobacco warehouses on Cary Street down along the river are the focus of Richmond's riverside revitalization. The cavernous red brick buildings have been trendified into a variety of upscale shops, restaurants, lively taverns and music clubs. And for the city's newest attraction, **Canal Walk,** the long neglected canals have been transformed into an area of waterfront walkways that will soon be flanked by shops, restaurants, and apartments and that can be traversed either by canal boat or on foot. There will be monuments, markers, and exhibits (some of them interactive), explaining life in Richmond over five centuries. They'll tell about historic areas—such as early Shockoe, where in the late 17th century tobacco, furs, rum, and Africans were traded—and events, such as Henry "Box" Brown's daring escape from slavery, when he shipped himself in a crate to Philadelphia and freedom.

The **17th Street Farmers Market,** in Shockoe Bottom, with a pedigree dating back 300 years, claims to be the oldest of its kind in the country. Its stalls are full of fresh produce from the surrounding countryside, and its vendors are full of the city's soft-spoken bonhomie.

The **Edgar Allan Poe Museum,** in a complex of buildings surrounding a courtyard, holds Poe memorabilia, his writings, even parts of the Richmond buildings in which he lived or worked. The complex includes a separate piece of history—the **Old Stone House,** built in the late 1730s and the oldest structure in the city. *1914 East Main Street; 804-648-5523.*

■ AFRICAN-AMERICAN RICHMOND

Race relations have a complex past in this city. Long a hub of black culture, the city today is about 55 percent African-American. In the antebellum era, house slaves apparently lived well here—if any human who is considered property can be said to live well. In any case, there was a strong social network among blacks, and even a kind of "downstairs" aristocracy that mirrored the city's white aristocracy. Some blacks were able to purchase their freedom and set up shop as artisans or small businessmen. But for most blacks, slavery was the only life they knew, and they waited with high hopes for the North to win the Civil War.

After the war, they had freedom, but suffered the shame of the Jim Crow laws that plagued the South. In spite of that, Richmond became a mecca of black enterprise and culture. The music scene flourished, black businesses did well, and a black middle class filled the well-kept row houses of Jackson Ward.

One woman who understood how to negotiate her standing in this ambiguous color-coded world was Maggie Walker. She was the daughter of a former slave who was an assistant cook in the Church Hill mansion of Elizabeth Van Lew, a passionate abolitionist and Union spy. Despite her rather humble beginnings, Walker let neither social conditions nor her own physical handicap (she was a paraplegic during the last years of her life) impede progress. Early in the 20th century, she took a small fraternal society and turned it into a lucrative business concern that owned a newspaper (of which she was editor) and a bank (of which she was president—the first female bank president in the United States). An early champion of civil rights and African-American pride, she remained actively committed to improving educational opportunities, economic development, and racial cohesiveness in her community until her death in 1934.

The **Maggie L. Walker National Historic Site** (110½ East Leigh Street; 804-771-2017), a substantial brick Italian Revival house of 25 rooms, stands amid the restoration of Jackson Ward, once "the Harlem of the South," a thriving black community of prospering business, famous for the nightlife in its jazz and ragtime clubs along "the Deuce," or Second Street. Today the whole of Jackson Ward is a National Historic Landmark—the largest in the country associated with black history and culture. Many of its row houses have been renovated and small businesses have been started—and you'd have to stand in line to buy one of the best 19th-century houses, dripping with cast-iron lace.

In an 1832 mansion a couple of blocks away from Maggie Walker's, the **Black History Museum** (00 Clay Street; 804-780-9093) exhibits artifacts and documents illustrating the history of African-Americans since the early 17th century. While in the area, walk a block south and west to the **Virginia Fire and Police Museum** (200 Marshall Street; 804-644-1849), an 1849 firehouse, to see fire and police uniforms and helmets, antique firefighting equipment, and early fire engines.

Now, if you're ready for lunch, head back to the Deuce, to **Croaker's Spot** (Second and Leigh Streets; 804-421-0560), where two young entrepreneurs have opened what seems to be the most popular place in town. The line for takeout trails out on the sidewalk, and the wait for the tables or the high-backed booths in the bar can be long, but persevere: the soul food is first-rate.

Maggie Walker (1867–1934), in a studio portrait taken in New York circa 1900.

■ LEAVING DOWNTOWN

Heading west on Franklin Street, you'll soon spot the towers and turrets of the **Jefferson Hotel,** a resurrected stalwart of the Gilded Age that opened in 1895 with the wedding reception of Charles Dana Gibson and the beautiful Irene Langhorne, the original Gibson Girl. Beneath its capacious skylit rotunda, an ornate mezzanine is ringed by rich faux-marble columns, and broad marble staircases reminiscent of Scarlett's Tara sweep upward. A statue of Thomas Jefferson by Edward V. Valentine stands beneath its own Tiffany skylight in the lobby. *Franklin and Adams Streets; 804-788-8000.*

Continue west on Franklin, which soon becomes wide and sedate **Monument Avenue,** whose circles sweep around the heroic monuments that give the street its name. Almost all are Civil War heroes astride their steeds—Lee, Jackson, Jeb Stuart, Jefferson Davis (not on horseback, but gesticulating), and finally, Matthew Fontaine Maury, best known for his groundbreaking charts of Atlantic currents. At the western end of the row stands Monument's most recent addition, a statue immortalizing tennis pro Arthur Ashe, a native son. Small side streets, rich in Victorian architecture, lead southwest off the avenue to the Fan district, a triangular residential section whose avenues fan out from an apex near Monroe Park. This eastern part of the Fan, peppered with bookstores, cafés, and shops and swarming with students, serves by default as campus for the uncentralized Virginia Commonwealth University.

Monument Avenue eventually intersects yet another glorious thoroughfare— The Boulevard. This is where the city keeps much of its culture. The acclaimed **Virginia Museum of Fine Arts,** founded in 1936 and endowed by such philanthropic giants as the Mellons, houses a collection that spans 5,000 years. Highlights include Egyptian, Roman, and Greek works; wonderful art nouveau and art deco decorative arts; modern and contemporary works; art from India, Nepal, and Tibet; Impressionist and Postimpressionist paintings; and outstanding Fabergé eggs. The museum sponsors an active program of performing arts in its auditorium. *2800 Grove Avenue at The Boulevard; 804-340-1400.*

The **Virginia Historical Society,** near the Virginia Museum of Fine Arts, is yet another example of a changing Richmond. The Cheek Gallery displays "Arming the Confederacy," a huge collection of Confederate-made weapons, and is lined

A classical Thomas Jefferson in Carrara marble stands amid the beaux arts splendor of his namesake hotel.

Detail of a painting in the Virginia Museum of Fine Arts.

with towering murals (the *Four Seasons of the Confederacy*) depicting Southern heroism and struggles in the Civil War. The rest of the building is devoted to imaginative, interactive exhibits that portray the story of Virginia, from prehistory to the present. There's also a good history and genealogical research library. *428 North Boulevard; 804-358-4901.*

Fantastical **Maymont** occupies a sweeping 100 acres in southwestern Richmond. On a knoll above the James River, this turn-of-the-century estate glimmers with cascading Italian fountain gardens and Japanese gardens and has an arboretum, a children's farm, native wildlife exhibits, a carriage collection, and a nature center. The austere, turreted stone house (1893) is remarkably intimate, with all the personal possessions of its original owners, Richmond attorney and businessman James Dooley and his wife, Sallie May. Her feminine French furnishings vie with the dark Germanic pieces in his rooms. Mrs. Dooley's boudoir is not to be missed. Her bed, designed as a swan, was created for their country estate,

BELLES OF THE DEBUTANTE BALLS

In both antebellum and Reconstruction Virginia, the dearest dream of any girl was to be a southern belle—a beauty with all the social graces, from a worthy family. Perhaps the most famous were the five daughters of Chiswell (Chillie) Langhorne, a Virginia gentleman from Danville who had been ruined by the Civil War, but subsequently made a fortune on the railroads. The family lived in Richmond before relocating to the Blue Ridge Mountains, and the five Langhorne sisters—Lizzie, Irene, Nancy, Phyllis, Nora—became quintessential southern belles, a persona that, according to James Fox, the grandson of Phyllis, made such young ladies as much objects of admiration as the fair maidens of chivalrous romance. These belles of the debutante balls had their pick of suitors—Irene (born 1873) achieved a celebrity equivalent to that of a supermodel today. Her younger sister Nancy (born 1879) married Waldorf Astor, the richest man in the world at the time, lived in London, and became the first woman to take a seat in the British Parliament.

The adulation of the Belles had a direct relation to Virginia's sense of defeat, the sense of injustice that could hardly be addressed in conversation. They had an electrifying effect on Richmond society....

...Irene had never been groomed for her part. She had simply emerged from Mr. Langhorne's circus—no makeup, no attendant hairdresser.... She had been noticed by the New York papers while she was still a schoolgirl, to the annoyance of her father, who threatened to go to New York to shoot the editor. "She is tall and fair," wrote the *New York Times* in the offending passage, "and dances like a dream. Her carriage is queenly and her complexion perfect." . . .

Lizzie disapproved of Irene's success, thinking it the height of vulgarity to be in the newspapers at all. And the crepe-veiled widows of Richmond were beginning to look down on Mr. Langhorne for having broken ranks by collaborating with the Yankee occupation and getting rich. The social system of Richmond deliberately excluded money.... Nancy Lancaster recalled how "People in Virginia looked very down on the Astors and the Vanderbilts. They were supposed to be fur traders and Mr. Vanderbilt was meant to have ferried a boat.... There was that terrific feeling that there was nothing better than a Virginian. You felt that was the passport."

—James Fox, *Five Sisters: The Langhornes of Virginia,* 2000

Swannanoa (still standing in the Blue Ridge Mountains). Her dressing table is a sterling silver Tiffany confection with posts and legs made of narwhal tusks. *2201 Shields Lake Drive; 804-358-7166.*

Not far from Maymont, you can find yourself in the whispering glades of **Hollywood Cemetery,** whose serene hillsides are the final resting place of a host of famous Virginians, including Presidents James Monroe and John Tyler, Confederate president Jefferson Davis, nine governors of Virginia, and 24 Confederate generals. *412 South Cherry Street; 804-648-8501.*

■ WEST OF THE BOULEVARD   *map page 134*

West of The Boulevard on Cary Street is Windsor Farms, a rich old suburb containing two remarkable historic houses that are a lesson in what money can do—especially pre-Depression money. They're part of English, not American history; both are Tudor in style and both were brought here from England in pieces and reassembled in the mid-1920s. **Agecroft Hall** (4305 Sulgrave Avenue; 804-353-4241), a half-timber manor built in Lancashire in the late 15th century, has 23 acres of beautifully landscaped grounds and gardens. **Virginia House** (4301 Sulgrave Avenue; 804-353-4251), a 12th-century Warwickshire stone priory, has a west wing (1926) that is a replica of Sulgrave Manor, George Washington's ancestral home in Northamptonshire, England.

To reenter American history, continue west on Cary, turn south to the banks of the James, and there is **Wilton House,** a serene Georgian brick plantation house built by William Randolph III in 1750. It was moved here in 1933 from another riverfront site 25 miles east in Henrico County to save it from industrial encroachment. Open for tours, it has a beautiful parlor, floor-to-ceiling paneling, and period furnishings. *215 South Wilton Road; 804-282-5936.*

About 7 miles up the James River from Richmond lies **Tuckahoe Plantation,** the boyhood home of Thomas Jefferson. The H-shaped frame house and its outbuildings (1733–1740) are considered classic 18th-century plantation architecture. Jefferson went to school in one of them. The gardens are open daily, but you must call in advance to tour the house. *12601 River Road; 804-784-5736.*

President James Monroe's tomb at Hollywood Cemetery in Richmond.

■ EAST OF DOWNTOWN   *map page 134*

Edgar Allan Poe's young actress mother rests at **St. John's Church,** a few blocks from Poe's museum (see page 141), as do Henry Clay and George Wythe, a signer of the Declaration of Independence who tutored Thomas Jefferson at the College of William and Mary. The large white clapboard building (begun in 1742) was built on land donated by William Byrd II in 1737, and it has its original altar and dark wood box pews, with cream plaster walls. It is probably best known as the site of Patrick Henry's famous "Give me liberty or give me death" speech. *2401 East Broad Street; 804-648-5015 or 804-649-7938.*

Church Hill, the area around St. John's, is Richmond's oldest intact neighborhood, and it is full of wonderful architecture. The church is the only colonial building; most of the houses are early-19th-century, and during Reconstruction, Victorian ones blossomed north of Broad Street.

On a nearby high hill facing south lies the site of **Chimborazo,** the sprawling Confederate hospital complex of barracks and tents where 76,000 sick and wounded were cared for during the Civil War. The hill is now a city park, surrounding a building that houses the National Park Service headquarters for all of Richmond's National Battlefield Parks and the **Chimborazo Medical Museum,** which documents the state of medicine and medical knowledge on the eve of the war in 1860. *3215 East Broad Street; 804-226-1981.*

■ FREDERICKSBURG   *map page 132, D-3*

This little city has rested beside the falls of the Rappahannock River, near its confluence with the Rapidan, for about 250 years. Like Richmond, on the fall line of the James 58 miles to the south, Fredericksburg was built here not by mere whim. The fall line, the point of transition between the rocky Appalachian uplands to the west and the coastal plain to the east, is the site of waterfalls and the upper limit of a river's navigability, the logical place to locate water-powered industry and a natural center of transportation and commerce.

Small Colonial and Federal brick buildings, leftovers from the prosperous days of the 18th and 19th centuries, make Fredericksburg's eminently walkable waterfront historic district a charming place. You can get an all-day parking pass at the **Visitor Center** (706 Caroline Street; 540-373-1776), or a ticket for the trolley tour. The buildings here, filled with antique and craft shops, sophisticated little restaurants, and galleries, bear witness to the resilience of this town, because, as every Virginian

TERRIFIC CHARGE OF THE FEDERAL TROOPS (SUMNER'S DIVISION) UPON THE CONFEDERATE FORTIFICATIONS LOCATED ON THE TERRACE BEHIND FREDERICKSBURG, VA. DECEMBER 13TH, 1862.

Federal troops attack fortifications on the terrace behind Fredericksburg, December 13, 1862.

knows, Fredericksburg was ravaged during one of the worst battles of the Civil War. Though it took close to 100 years to rebuild itself, the town has achieved that now, and any visitor is guaranteed to be charmed. You can even stay overnight right in Old Town, at the **Richard Johnston Inn** (711 Caroline Street; 540-899-7606), an 18th-century brick double row house with a wonderful shaded courtyard. A comfortable B&B named for its early builder, it's famed for its lavish breakfasts.

You can't walk more than a few feet along Fredericksburg's streets before encountering the name Washington. George himself spent a good bit of his youth at Ferry Farm, a few miles downriver, but it was his siblings who left an indelible mark on the town. His brother Charles built an understated frame house on Caroline Street in about 1760 and lived in it for about 20 years.

In the early 19th century, the house became the **Rising Sun Tavern,** and the restored building celebrates that incarnation.

Nowadays, when you walk up onto the tavern's low-slung veranda, mob-capped serving "wenches" greet you and take you on a memorable tour of the darkly inviting rooms. The descriptions of tavern life highlight the robust side of early America—like the diners' passing their dirty wooden plates along to the next arrival. Why bother washing them, after all, when everyone took pot luck—whatever was in the pot hung over the hearth. Baths were offered only in July and August, because, except during the hottest months, who needed them? *1304 Caroline Street; 540-371-1494.*

Things are more genteel a few blocks away at the **Mary Washington House.** George purchased this clapboard cottage in 1772 for his 64-year-old mother, "to make her more comfortable and free from care...." He enlarged the house at least once, raising the roof and adding two rooms, and his mother planted the boxwood gardens. Mary lived here for 17 years, just a quick walk away from her daughter and son-in-law, Betty and Fielding Lewis. *1200 Charles Street; 540-373-1569.*

George, a safe distance away at Mount Vernon, might have thought this a fine setup. But one wonders whether his brother-in-law, Fielding Lewis, would have concurred. Influential and respected, Lewis came from Tidewater gentry, settling in Fredericksburg in 1746. Commerce in the burgeoning river town quickly made him wealthy; he acquired much of a 1,300-acre plantation on the edge of town in 1752, and in the early 1770s began building a Georgian manor house, the town's finest.

Today the estate, now known as **Kenmore** after the ancestral Scottish home of owners who succeeded the Lewises, is reduced to 4 acres of lawn, gardens, and shade trees. The house itself is undergoing restoration, its high-ceilinged rooms to remain empty until 2005. Tours begin in a modern gallery, where much of the furniture is displayed, and there are fascinating video exhibits detailing the restoration. When you enter the house, you can focus on Kenmore's most memorable feature: its ornate plasterwork, particularly on the ceilings. The craftsman first responsible for this artistry also did work at Mount Vernon, but history, like the Washington family, remembers him simply as the "Stucco Man." In the late 19th century, the decorations were made more elaborate by an owner who was himself a craftsman of talent. His embellishments are not always distinguishable from the originals, but in the drawing room it is clear that he added floral swags to clothe some of Stucco Man's naked putti. *1201 Washington Avenue; 540-373-3381.*

For decades the low-slung dormered brick cottage that is now the **James Monroe Museum** was believed to have been Monroe's law office, but preservationists from the museum's owner, Mary Washington College, also in Fredericksburg, have dated the building to the 19th century, decades after Monroe's stint in Fredericksburg. No matter, because the museum is filled with an impressive amount of Monroe memorabilia, including the Louis XVI desk on which he signed the inaugural address that would form the basis of his famous Monroe Doctrine. Lawrence Hoes, Monroe's great-great-grandson and the man who helped found the museum, grew up with the desk in his family home. Since boys will be boys, he managed as a young child to topple it. When the desk was taken to a local cabinet-maker for repair, a secret compartment was discovered, something fairly common in such old pieces. Only this one was still filled with more than 200 pieces of Monroe's personal correspondence, some from the greatest thinkers of the day. *908 Charles Street; 540-654-2110.*

Two blocks away, at the corner of William and Princess Anne Streets, a handsome brick Federal building (1816), once the town hall and a market house, is now the **Fredericksburg Area Museum,** which houses a collection of art and artifacts that survived (like the building) the Civil War. Holdings range from Indian artifacts, Revolutionary relics, and Civil War weapons to furniture, silver, and documents. *907 Princess Anne Street; 540-371-3037.*

Time spreads out from the river in Fredericksburg, climbing away from the Colonial/Federal downtown and into the morass of the Civil War. The war visited Fredericksburg and the surrounding countryside—Chancellorsville, Spotsylvania, Wilderness—three times: in December 1862 and in the spring of 1863 and 1864. The four battlefields together, all within 17 miles of town, make up the multi-site **Fredericksburg and Spotsylvania National Military Park,** where the war, all told, took 100,000 lives.

At the infamous Marye's Heights (pronounced Marie's), the now green hills terrace gently up to a national cemetery memorializing the 1862 Fredericksburg carnage. The Union boys fell in heaps that cold winter, when they charged across open ground toward this hillside and the Southerners entrenched on the "sunken road."

The battle of Spotsylvania ended essentially in a draw, but it did allow the Confederate forces to fare better in later battles near Richmond and in the Shenandoah Valley. In the Wilderness, the Confederates marked a tactical victory, losing half as many men as Grant's army.

Plan your tour of any part of the park at the **Fredericksburg Battlefield Visitor Center** (1013 Lafayette Boulevard; 540-373-6122), where there are audiovisual presentations and exhibits, maps, and brochures, not to mention interpretive assistance from park historians.

Also part of the park but across the Rappahannock is **Chatham Manor** (120 Chatham Lane; 540-371-0802), a beautiful Georgian plantation house built by

VIRGINIA WINE

The wine-making tradition has deeper roots in the Old Dominion than anywhere else in the East. Those first Jamestown diehards produced wine from native grapes within two years of their arrival. In 1619, the first House of Burgesses passed Act Twelve, which required that all settlers "tend their own vineyard." Problem was, their product wasn't very drinkable. They kept trying, though, even importing French *vignerons* (winegrowers) to oversee vineyards planted in European stocks. But even the redoubtable French failed to make a successful Virginia wine.

Thomas Jefferson, a wine aesthete, tried his hand at Monticello, but alas, Virginia winters were too harsh for the delicate European viniferas. Then, in the 1830s, an American hybrid, the Norton Virginia grape, gave the state an award-winning claret. Sought after on the Continent and in America, it received the gold medal in Paris in 1892.

Still, it took almost a century and a half and the pressures of late-20th-century living to firmly establish a flock of Virginia winegrowers. In the 1970s, as wine fever spread across the country, a number of amateur Virginia vintners began experimenting, more or less in their own backyards. Many of them started their vineyards simply as a labor of love, but as the fever heightened, retired professionals or those weary of the workplace began to look to wine growing as an alternative lifestyle. They found that vinifera varietals and French hybrids did well in the sun and soil of the Commonwealth.

Today, there are more than 80 wineries scattered across the state, which trails only California, Oregon, Washington, and New York in total production. A few big-time operators, such as Williamsburg Winery and Prince Michel Vineyards, are among them, but most are small family-run farms that nonetheless produce some respectable commercial wines. The greatest concentration is in the Charlottesville-Culpeper and Middleburg–Front Royal areas. Big or small, Virginia's wine makers are a welcoming lot, happy to show visitors around their wineries and offer them a taste of their chardonnay, Riesling, vidal, or cabernet sauvignon. Roadside markers, with a grape cluster logo, lead the way to vineyards. At gourmet and grocery stores and at state-run ABC (Alcoholic Beverage Control) stores, shelves are well stocked with Old Dominion vintages.

William Fitzhugh in the late 1760s that was visited by both George Washington and Abraham Lincoln. The house served as Union headquarters during the battle of Fredericksburg but is best known for its service thereafter as the Union hospital where Clara Barton and Walt Whitman tended the wounded.

If you drive west out of Fredericksburg, past the sprawl of strip malls that line Route 3, you'll suddenly return to the woods and pastureland that mark the historic **Chancellorsville Battlefield** (visitors center, 9001 Plank Road; 540-786-2880). Here Lee and Stonewall Jackson squared off against Northern general Joseph Hooker on May 2, 1863, and Lee scored probably his most brilliant success. The battle cost him dearly, though, because as every Civil War buff knows, this is where the mythic Stonewall stood his last. After a victorious day, Jackson was wounded by Southern men who mistook him for the enemy when he rode out on an evening reconnoiter.

After his left arm was amputated at a field hospital at Wilderness Tavern, Jackson was taken to a small frame plantation office—now the **Stonewall Jackson Shrine**—in the rural community of Guinea Station, a railroad crossing to the southeast. For almost a week, he lay here fighting his own wounds—and the North. In his delirium, he called out battle instructions to his fellow officers. He also had cogent moments, when he knew that his wife was by his side. Pneumonia gradually gained on him, and on May 10, a Sunday, the devout Jackson calmly remarked, "I have always desired to die on Sunday." He lapsed briefly back into delirium, shouting final battle orders for Gen. A. P. Hill. Then he grew serene again. "Let us cross over the river," he said at the last, "and rest under the shade of the trees." *15 miles south of Fredericksburg; 804-633-6076 or 540-371-0802.*

■ THOMAS JEFFERSON COUNTRY   *map page 132, B-4*

Albemarle County dips and rises in the lavish greenness of classic Virginia horse country, virtually in the center of the state, along the eastern flank of the Blue Ridge Mountains (take I-64 northwest from Richmond). Leggy Thoroughbreds graze its neatly fenced pastures, and the very rich and sometimes even the famous live at the end of tree-lined entrance lanes in houses that have stood as long as two centuries.

The word *tony* best describes the ambience of much of the county, and this ambience extends somewhat to the city of Charlottesville, which the county surrounds. Some of the high tone comes from the fact that this is Jefferson country, and early on he gave the county a sophisticated taste for the good life. Old-line

VIRGINIA ARCHITECTURE: AN AMATEUR'S CRITIQUE

The private buildings are very rarely constructed of stone or brick, much the greatest portion being of scantling and boards, plastered with lime. It is impossible to devise things more ugly, uncomfortable, and happily more perishable. There are two or three plans, on one of which, according to its size, most of the houses in the State are built. The poorest people build huts of logs, laid horizontally in pens, stopping the interstices with mud. These are warmer in winter, and cooler in summer, than the more expensive construction of scantling and plank.... The only public buildings worthy of mention are the capitol, the palace, the college, and the hospital for lunatics, all of them in Williamsburg, heretofore the seat of our government. The capitol is a light and airy structure with a portico in front of two orders, the lower of which, being Doric, is tolerably just in its proportions and ornaments, save only that the intercolonations are too large. The upper is Ionic, much too small for that on which it is mounted, its ornaments not proper to the order, nor proportioned within themselves.... Yet, on the whole, it is the most pleasing piece of architecture we have. The palace is not handsome without, but it is spacious and commodious within, is prettily situated, and with the grounds annexed to it, is capable of being made an elegant seat. The college and hospital are rude, misshapen piles, which, but that they have roofs, would be taken for brick-kilns. There are no other public buildings but churches and courthouses, in which no attempts are made at elegance.

—Thomas Jefferson, *Notes on Virginia,* 1784

Virginia gentry live here on estates with long pedigrees, but they have been joined in recent decades by industrial barons and celebrities who like the low-key character and intense beauty of the area.

Discretion is a cultural byword here, and celebrity stalking is frowned upon. Novelist William Faulkner, who spent two years in the 1950s as writer-in-residence at the University of Virginia, explained his version of it this way: "I like Virginia, and I like Virginians. Because Virginians are all snobs, and I like snobs. A snob has to spend so much time being a snob that he has little left to meddle with you, and so it is very pleasant here."

Not all the county reeks of money and manners. There are pockets, particularly on the west side, of simple, rural Virginia, where musty, plank-floored general stores stand at crossroads and farmers keep modest herds of cattle or tend apple orchards.

Down along the James, outside the little town of Scottsville (Route 6 and Route 20), one of the few remaining hand-poled cable ferries in America, the old **Hatton Ferry,** still crosses the river. If you don't feel comfortable having the ferryman struggle to pole you across, you can rent an oversize inner tube at the adjacent **James River Runners,** but mind the snakes the outfitters keep in cages on their porch. With a tube under you, you can float downriver with your backside for ballast and the wooded shoreline of the James conjuring an image of an earlier, simpler time.

Naturally, since this is Virginia, love of the past is never far way in Albemarle. In fact, it springs tellingly to life every Thanksgiving, when the equestrian crowd don their bright pink coats (Pink was a London equestrian tailor), collect their horses and hounds, and gather for the annual blessing of the hounds outside the stone walls of Grace Episcopal Church, in a wooded glen on the southern side of the county, 10 miles east of Charlottesville at Keswick. The old stone church is a noble structure any time of year, and its graveyard is replete with Jefferson's kinsmen and the early leaders of Albemarle. On Thanksgiving Day, the sight of those horses, steam rising from their flanks into the autumn air, seems to epitomize Albemarle's centuries-old devotion to living well.

■ MONICELLO   *map page 132, B-4*

The county got its taste for the good life from Thomas Jefferson, so it is fitting that his remarkable "Little Mountain," Monticello, on Route 53 southeast of Charlottesville, remains its most prominent feature. A lifework and a passion, this domed, columned manor house has become a living emblem of Jefferson—and a well-minted symbol for the nation, appearing as it does on the nickel. Jefferson devoted 40 years to Monticello, rethinking it, redesigning it, laying out and experimenting with its gardens. "Architecture," he said, "is my delight. And putting up and pulling down one of my favorite amusements."

Though he was born in Albemarle when it was the frontier, Jefferson was no backwoodsman. He clearly had the soul of a philosopher, and his interests ranged the globe, though he had a strong preference for things Roman or French. His gifts and how he employed them have made him the hero of many, including John F. Kennedy, who, addressing a group of Nobel Prize winners at a White House dinner, said that they were "the most extraordinary collection of talent, of human

(following pages) "Where has nature spread so rich a mantle under the eye?" asked Thomas Jefferson writing about the setting of his "own dear Monticello."

The parlor at Monticello contains much of Jefferson's painting collection.

knowledge, that has ever gathered together at the White House—with the possible exception of when Thomas Jefferson dined alone." Yet as a man Jefferson was eminently informal. While serving as the third president, he sometimes answered the door to the White House himself—and in slippered feet.

All of Jefferson's sophistication and experience went into his home. Building on Roman, French, and Palladian models, he called Monticello his "essay in architecture." A visiting French nobleman was so impressed with the manor (and apparently so unimpressed with other American edifices) that he declared Jefferson to be "the first American who has consulted the fine arts to know how he should shelter himself from the weather." As classic as the house is, it is nonetheless full of the quirky character of Mad Tom, as his political enemies called him. An inveterate tinkerer, Jefferson placed his gadgets throughout the house—like a seven-day clock, operated by weights that descended to the basement, and a "polygraph" device for making a copy of a document as one wrote it.

He also exhibited his inventiveness in the garden. "No occupation," he once wrote, "is so delightful to me as the culture of the earth, and no culture comparable to that of the garden." He kept up a lively correspondence with horticulturists and friends concerning his experiments with vegetables, flowers, even wine grapes. Today, Monticello's grounds have become famous. Flowers of Jefferson's day line the "roundabout" on the West Lawn, and vegetables grow in a terraced plot below the house; an orchard and vineyards lie farther down the slope.

Because a great deal of everything used in the house had to be made on the plantation, south of the house, extending for 1,000 feet, were dwellings, a blacksmiths' shop, an ironworking shop, a joinery, a dairy, and a carpenters' shop. Excavations along "Mulberry Row" have located the buildings, turned up thousands of artifacts, and thrown light on the life of Monticello's field, skilled, and house slaves. A well-documented self-guided tour and a guided tour tell this story, and as part of an ongoing project called Getting Word, all possible descendants of former Monticello slaves are being interviewed for an oral history.

The supposition that Sally Hemings, a slave at Monticello, may have become Jefferson's mistress in the years following the death of his wife, Martha, clings to the Jeffersonian story. It is possible but still under dispute that Hemings, three-quarters white, was Martha's half sister. Recent DNA testing has indicated that at least one of several black families claiming the Jefferson lineage is related to the Jefferson family line, although not necessarily to Jefferson himself. Members of that branch have been invited to attend Jefferson family reunions at Monticello.

Had Jefferson followed his private instincts, he might never have left his mountaintop to participate in the fray of politics. But his public instincts pushed him into the arena of nation-building and marked him forever as one of this country's Founding Fathers and its "Great Democrat." Ironically, he died on the half-century anniversary of the Declaration of Independence, as did his longtime friend and sometime enemy, John Adams. Jefferson is buried at Monticello on a quiet slope below the house. In predictable style, he penned his epitaph, remembering himself to the world for three accomplishments: his authorship both of the Declaration and of Virginia's statute of religious freedom, and the founding of the University of Virginia. *Route 53; 434-989-9822.*

(following pages) The slave quarters at Ash Lawn–Highland. The prosperity of James Monroe's plantation depended on slave labor, as did those of the previous three presidents from Virginia.

■ ASH LAWN–HIGHLAND   *map page 132, B-4*

James Monroe, the fifth president of the United States (1817–1825), was a busy man. He negotiated the Louisiana Purchase under Jefferson, was secretary of state and secretary of war at the same time, ambassador to England, Spain, and France, a U.S. senator, a congressman, and four times the governor of Virginia. His Monroe Doctrine (1823) changed forever U.S. relations with Europe, and for his skills of negotiation in difficult times, his presidency was called the "Era of Good Feeling."

In 1793, Monroe bought Highland, a piece of land 2.5 miles from Monticello, at Jefferson's suggestion. His mentor also chose a site on the property where the Monroes' small house would be built and sent his gardeners to establish the orchards. In 1799, the Monroes moved in, and their first guests were James and Dolley Madison. When you visit today, the first thing you see is a gorgeous white oak, three times taller than the house and with a wingspread twice as wide. The small, homey rooms, with period furnishings, give an immediacy to 18th-century life that's missing from many grander mansions. James must have been out of town the day the tiny Mrs. Monroe approved the construction of the hall archway that supports the chimney, because at his more than 6 feet, he had to duck his head to pass through. People come to Ash Lawn–Highland today (its name was changed from Highland to Ash Lawn after the Monroes died, but it now goes by both names) for the summer music festival, Historic Garden Week, and other annual events. *1000 James Monroe Parkway; 434-293-9539.*

As you come down the mountain from Monticello and Ash Lawn, stop in to see the historic **Michie Tavern** and its museum. You can lunch here on colonial fare, write your name with a quill pen, learn to dance the Virginia reel (a sort of square dance probably brought from England and possibly the first dance the colonists ever did in the New World) and generally steep yourself in the late 18th century. There's a printer's market that sells old and reproduction currency, newspapers, documents, pamphlets and books; a general store in an old gristmill; and a gift shop. *683 Thomas Jefferson Parkway; 434-977-1234.*

■ UNIVERSITY OF VIRGINIA

From Monticello, Jefferson could look through a spyglass down on the town of Charlottesville and the university he founded. These days, he would no doubt enjoy progressive-minded Charlottesville and its offerings—fine restaurants, brew pubs, upscale boutiques, and plenty of bookstores.

At play on the Lawn of Mr. Jefferson's University.

The University of Virginia remains Mr. Jefferson's University and the center-piece of the city. Though it was long the bastion of the Virginia gentleman, the school can hardly be classed as an entrenched gentlemen's institution anymore. For one thing, it has been coed for decades, and for another, with close to 20,000 students, it has become an eclectic modern university. The Greek tradition is alive and well in the Rugby Road fraternity mansions, but there are plenty of non-Greek pockets, and all told, the tenor on the "grounds" (never say "campus" here) is like that at many burgeoning state institutions elsewhere in the East. The forward-looking, eccentric Jefferson would probably feel more at home wandering the grounds today than he would have felt amid the hard-drinking, button-down, "gentleman's B" crowd (an A grade would show you were a grind) that populated his university earlier in the 20th century.

Happily, however, time has not much altered the famous "academical village" Jefferson designed. Now a designated World Heritage Site, the buildings have also been proclaimed an outstanding achievement of American architecture by the American Institute of Architects.

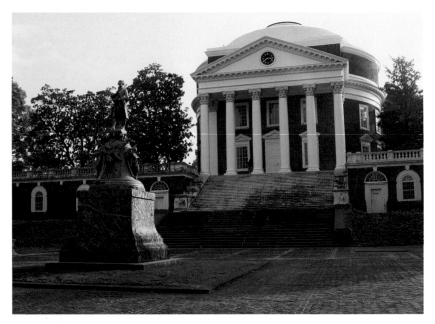

The Rotunda was the University of Virginia's original library building.

The "village" essentially comprises the university's Rotunda and, extending east, two long, low colonnaded buildings flanking a lawn and holding rows of spare yet charming student rooms punctuated by 10 two-story pavilions.

The **Rotunda** was originally meant to house a library and classrooms but had been outgrown by the mid-19th century and an annex was built. A fire in 1895 destroyed much of both, and the Rotunda reopened in 1898, its style changed markedly by the architect Stanford White. In the 1970s it was restored to Jefferson's design: on two levels, large oval chambers used for meetings and hour-glass-shaped hallways, and above, the exquisite dome room, encircled by pairs of columns and cleverly unobtrusive bookcases. The pavilions interrupting the colonnades of student rooms were intended by Jefferson to house professors, so that students would have easy access to their mentors.

Today, faculty clubs and such occupy the pavilion spaces, but the small student rooms remain in the hands of the school's top students. To have a room on the Lawn, as it is called, is a cherished honor.

■ CHARLOTTESVILLE   *map page 132, B-4*

Beyond the Lawn and U.Va.'s hallowed halls, the city of Charlottesville sweeps west toward the Blue Ridge and east toward a thriving downtown. Fine old neighborhoods still grace the city, and most of the inevitable strip-mall grotesquerie has been confined to the corridor along U.S. 29 N.

The university still dominates the town, and an intellectual and artistic renaissance, encouraged by the city, is making Charlottesville more and more enticing. Young people are flocking to buy and renovate small houses downtown, and the arts are flourishing. Small businesses, a theater company called Live Arts, an ice rink, museums, and shops center on East Main Street's **Historic Downtown** mall, which also has sophisticated restaurants, antiques shops, bookstores, and galleries. This brick pedestrian refuge, whose trees cast that necessary shade that Jefferson called "our elysium," is the heart of downtown, but there's plenty of activity at University Corner and on West Main too. Except on Sundays, a free trolley connects downtown with the university. Charlottesville also has a free outdoor concert series, Fridays After Five, a wonderful City Market, and, in October, the Virginia Film Festival. The **Kluge-Ruhe Aboriginal Art Collection** (400 Peter Jefferson Place; 434-244-0234), off Route 250 east of town, is one of the world's foremost private collections of Australian Aboriginal art, and its study center houses extensive research materials for scholars.

Also east of town, by 15 miles, is **Prospect Hill** (2887 Poindexter Road, Trevilians; 540-967-2574), a wonderful 1739 plantation house–turned–B&B (make that B&B&D, because delicious dinners are served). You can stay in the Victorianized main house, the slave quarters, or one of two other dependencies, where taking a dip in the anachronistic swimming pool seems delightfully sinful.

Northeast of Charlottesville, a pretty byway (Route 20) takes you to Orange, and on the way you can visit three special places. One, **Clifton: The Country Inn** (1296 Clifton Inn Drive; 434-971-1800), is a spectacular bed-and-breakfast in a house built in 1799 by Thomas Mann Randolph, a governor of Virginia, member of Congress, and Thomas Jefferson's son-in-law. A national landmark, it has a cascading swimming pool, a tennis court, a croquet ground, and an award-winning dining room. There are rooms in the main house, but the most interesting ones are in the carriage house, garden house, and other 18th-century outbuildings.

The next stop you should make is at **Barboursville Vineyards** (17655 Winery Road; 540-832-3824), whose setting includes the still picturesque and romantic

Barboursville Vineyards.

ruins of the Barbour mansion. Thomas Jefferson designed the brick house, with Palladian porticos and an octagonal parlor, as a grand residence for his friend James Barbour, who was a governor of Virginia (1812–1814), a U.S. senator, the secretary of war, and the ambassador to Great Britain. The Barbour family lived here until the house burned at Christmas in 1884, then in a Georgian dependency on the grounds until the 1940s. At the winery's restaurant, Palladio, you can have lunch or dinner, by the fireplace in winter or on the loggia in fine weather. And of course you can taste and take home the products—among them a noteworthy pinot grigio—of this respected winery.

Finally, you'll come to **Montpelier,** the home of James Madison. This enormous, white-columned house, the oldest section of which was built by Madison's father about 1760, was enlarged by Madison himself in 1797 to receive his new bride, Dolley Payne Todd, and her son. He needed more space again in 1810, while he was our fourth president, and there the historic part stops. Then came the duPonts, who more than doubled its size and established an equestrian tradition that persists today. A 15-minute documentary on Madison's life orients you, and a self-guided tour takes you past two Madison rooms with period and original furnishings and three duPont rooms. A guided behind-the-scenes tour takes you upstairs into some unrestored rooms with furniture from Madison's day. You can see the grounds and outbuildings with a guide or alone. Don't miss the graveyards and the 200-acre Landmark Forest of old-growth trees. The Montpelier Hunt Races are held here in November, and other fairs and celebrations take place throughout the year. *Route 20, 28 miles north of Charlottesville, 540-672-2728.*

■ **LYNCHBURG**   *map page 132, A-6*

About 66 miles southwest of Charlottesville on U.S. 29 South sits Lynchburg, on seven hills. It traces its lineage to 18th-century Quakers who settled here on the banks of the James. Though they stayed only a few decades before economic conditions and their abhorrence of slavery pushed them on, the aura of those gentle folk still pervades this city. And by the way, its name has *nothing* to do with lynching: it commemorates John Lynch, who in 1786 donated the city's original 45 acres. The Quakers must also have given the town its religious bent, because today Lynchburg calls itself the City of Churches. Up on Court House Hill, overlooking the river, steeples reach heavenward like an array of supplicating hands.

Lynchburg might also be called a city of learning, since in its neighborhood there are five college-level institutions: Randolph-Macon Woman's College, with its wonderful American painting collection at the **Maier Museum of Art** (1 Quinlan Street; 434-947-8136); Lynchburg College; Sweet Briar College; the Virginia University at Lynchburg; and Jerry Falwell's Liberty University, which attracts busloads of tourists hoping to catch a glimpse of the televangelist.

The college scene doesn't encroach much on the heart of the old downtown. The James runs right through here, and historically it has served as Lynchburg's lifeblood. These days, though, the riverfront languishes, run-down and uninteresting—except for a weekend in mid-June, when the James River Batteau Festival takes place. Then, the James comes alive with an armada of re-created batteaux—those open, low-slung boats that carted goods up and down the river in the 18th century—once again heading downriver on the eight-day journey to the capital.

Lynchburg calls five of its seven hills the five Historic Districts, and they are full of splendid architecture. Driving up and down the grid, you get spectacular views down to the river and across to outlying countryside, but the up-close looks at the wonderful examples of Federal, Second Empire, Queen Anne, Stick style, Italianate, Beaux Arts, Gothic, and Greek and Georgian Revival are hard to beat.

Federal Hill has the earliest houses—many from 1812 to the 1820s. Skinny **Daniel's Hill,** across Blackwater Creek, was developed during the 1850s, extending north from **Point of Honor** (112 Cabell Street; 434-847-1459), the 1815 mansion on the point overlooking the James River Basin. The mansion, once the home of the Cabell and Daniel families, is now a beautifully furnished house museum.

Court House Hill slopes up from the river, ornamented by Lynchburg's renowned **Monument Terrace,** a 139-step stone staircase set with soldierly statues. At its top rises the Old City Court House, a columned Greek Revival antique that now houses a local-history museum. More vintage architecture crowns **Diamond Hill,** a few blocks southeast, where resplendent Italianate, Georgian, and Victorian mansions from the city's tobacco heyday mix with fine little cottages. After some rough years during the mid-20th century, Diamond Hill is becoming grand once again.

If you head out 12th Street, to a decidedly less patrician neighborhood, you'll find the **Anne Spencer House and Garden,** where the poet, a respected member of the Harlem Renaissance of the 1920s, lived for much of the 20th century. Though the surrounding neighborhood is nothing special, Spencer's shingle home is a charming place with an illustrious past. Here she entertained James Weldon Johnson, Marian Anderson, Paul Robeson, Martin Luther King Jr., and many other luminaries. Congressman Adam Clayton Powell Jr. even honeymooned in the house. Though the house is open only by appointment, the walled garden behind it is accessible. Sitting out there in her studio cottage, Spencer took much of her inspiration from the intimate garden itself. "What is pain but happiness here," she wrote, "amid these green and wordless patterns...." *1313 Pierce Street; 434-845-1313.*

The **Old City Cemetery,** founded in 1806, is worth a visit, to inspect its variety of decorative ironwork, see and smell its beautiful collection of antique roses, and view the early buildings moved here for their preservation. More than 20,000 people are buried at the cemetery, including veterans of every major American war and more than 2,200 Confederate soldiers from 14 states. Three-quarters of the graves are those of Africans and Native Americans; more than one-third are infants and children under the age of four. In the **Cemetery Center,** a museum of 19th-century mourning customs, you can research cemetery records. Also on the grounds

A memorial to Confederate soldiers tops Lynchburg's Monument Terrace.

Point of Honor, built on a bluff, has wonderful views of Lynchburg.

are the **Pest House Medical Museum,** a one-room doctor's office showing the horrible conditions in times of epidemic during the Civil War; the **Station House Museum,** telling everything there is to know about this small railway depot from Amherst County; and the **Hearse House and Caretaker's Museum,** displaying an old hearse and an undertaker's wagon and tools. *401 Taylor Street; 434-847-1465.*

After all this, you can repair to the **Main Street Eatery** (907 Main Street; 434-847-2526), where an enterprising Swiss couple has turned a run-down men's clothing store bought at auction into a popular restaurant, and, despite the everyday name, serves anything but ordinary food. And if you want to stay a night in Lynchburg, call the **Federal Crest Inn** (1101 Federal Street; 434-845-6155), a spacious Colonial Revival house, now a B&B, with beautiful plantings. Some of its rooms have a fireplace.

■ **POPLAR FOREST** *map pages 264–265, F-4*

An earlier Virginian also took inspiration from the green countryside surrounding Lynchburg. In 1806 that inveterate builder, Thomas Jefferson, then in his second term as president, turned his eyes in this direction, perhaps wistfully contemplating a life of rural quietude after his long public years. He knew he would never have much true privacy at Monticello, and so he began planning a villa, hidden away on land in Bedford County a few miles southwest of Lynchburg.

Jefferson and his wife, Martha, had inherited the Poplar Forest land from her father, and they had stayed here in the overseer's house in 1781, when the British threatened to capture Jefferson at Monticello. Now it seemed the ideal place for a retreat. Besides, there was nothing that gave him greater pleasure than designing and building. The 63-year-old Jefferson knew exactly what he wanted, and he proclaimed that Poplar Forest would be the "best dwelling house in the state, except that of Monticello. Perhaps preferable to that, as more proportioned to the faculties of a private citizen." He brought along John Hemings, master carpenter at Monticello and Sally Hemings's younger half-brother, to make all the interior moldings on the place.

High on a knoll above dipping pastoral hills, the intimate octagonal villa is stunningly proportioned and seems almost an extension of Jefferson the private man. He entertained no one but family and neighbors here, so he planned the villa to his own quirky tastes. The columned, classical portico, characteristically Jeffersonian,

Jefferson's Poplar Forest.

opens onto a narrow front hall that leads back to a soaring two-story dining room, a 20-foot cube, overarched with one of those skylights of which he was so fond. According to his granddaughter, who often accompanied him here, the house was furnished "in the simplest manner, but had a very tasty air; there was nothing common or second-rate about any part of the establishment."

Unfortunately, in 1845 a fire damaged the house, and the Hutter family, who then owned it, took the opportunity to modernize. Those innovations stood in place for a century, giving Poplar Forest the look of just another brick farmhouse. The Watts family, who bought the house in the 1940s, tried to do some restoration, but it wasn't until more recent years that scholars began to plumb the depths of this Jeffersonian jewel.

Now owned by a nonprofit organization founded by concerned businesspeople and civic leaders of the area, Poplar Forest has become a cause célèbre among preservationists. The house has been gutted and is in the midst of restoration, and the public is being let in on the process. The masonry work, roof, exterior walls and windows are complete, and in this skeleton, before the interior walls go up, you can get a true sense of the thinking of Jefferson the architect. One room is to be left skeletal, so the bones beneath the skin will be evident.

Jefferson's characteristic outflung terraces, covering his "wing of offices" (kitchen, laundry, and storerooms), extend to the east, and the ground floor of the house contains an exhibit of artifacts. You can visit the remains of the slave quarters and learn about the families who lived there. Note the sunken lawn and the mounds, and the two outdoor privies that flank the mansion. Like the house, they are octagonal. *Route 661, Poplar Forest; 434-525-1806.*

■ PETERSBURG   *map page 132, D-6*

We now jump east from Lynchburg to Petersburg, so we can follow Robert E. Lee's retreat to Appomattox and the end of the Civil War. But first, Petersburg itself, a town that has had more than its share of hard luck. It's a small city and a historic one—older than Richmond, as locals will remind you, and equally aristocratic.

The city was named for Peter Jones, who owned a trading post on the Appomattox River. Remnants of the unmortared stone building date from the mid-17th century. Officially a town in 1748, incorporated in 1784, its agriculture, manufacturing, and transport made it by 1860 the third-largest city in Virginia. As a rail and shipping center supplying Richmond, Petersburg drew the attention of

Lincoln and Grant, whose aim became its destruction, and from June 1864 to April 1865, Petersburg suffered the longest siege in American military history, ending only when Lee was forced to evacuate on the road to Appomattox and surrender one week later.

Would you like to own a beautiful antique house? They are to be had on many streets in Old Towne Petersburg today. Drive down Grove Avenue, for example, to the **Historic Petersburg Foundation** (420 Grove Avenue; 804-732-2096), and look around you. The historic districts here have seen hard times for years, beginning with the great fire of 1815 (350 buildings were destroyed), continuing with the siege and bombardment of 1865, and, the last straw, the 1993 tornado that devastated Old Towne. It didn't help that Brown & Williamson Tobacco moved to Georgia in 1985, taking away hundreds of jobs; or that when Wal-Mart opened in nearby Colonial Heights, business followed and Walnut Mall closed down. But buildings of distinction still stand, and the potential is there.

On your tour, first stop at the **Petersburg Visitors Center** (425 Cockade Alley; 804-733-2400) in the pretty old McIlwaine House (1815) and get a walking-tour map. In Old Towne, the beautiful **Exchange Building** (15 West Bank Street; 804-733-2404) houses the **Siege Museum,** which examines the Civil War from a purely local perspective, focusing on the details of ordinary life in embattled Petersburg during the last year of the war. Actor Joseph Cotten (Petersburg-born) narrates a short film. Drive or walk by the 1817 brick **Trapezium House** (244 North Market Street), which is now privately owned, to see that there's not a right angle in the place. Its builder was said to have been influenced by a Caribbean servant's superstition that parallel lines and right angles harbor evil spirits. In the basement of **Centre Hill Mansion** (Centre Hill Court; 804-733-2401) you can see part of a tunnel that connected the house and the river. Built in 1823, the mansion was remodeled along Greek Revival lines in the 1840s, with ornate woodwork and plaster, and furnished accordingly.

General Grant believed that "the key to taking Richmond is Petersburg," and after his frontal attack on the capital failed at Cold Harbor in early June 1864, he began moving his forces south, across the James River, and set up headquarters at City Point, northeast of Petersburg, where the Appomattox joins the James. In mid-June, Grant attacked Petersburg, but Lee's army arrived from the north just in time, and after four days of unsuccessful combat, Grant dug in for a siege. He began to gradually cut the lines of supply one by one, slowly tightening the noose

around Petersburg before settling down for the winter. By February, it was only a matter of time, and when Sheridan smashed the Confederates under Gen. George Pickett at Five Forks, west of the city, the last line was in Union hands.

Drive to **Petersburg National Battlefield** (East Washington Street; 804-732-3531), where both Union and Confederate fortifications are preserved. At the City Point Unit you can also visit Grant's headquarters, to which Lincoln paid two visits, one in the last weeks of his life. Early in the siege, an extraordinary episode occurred: Union soldiers of the 48th Pennsylvania Infantry, many of them coal miners, decided to tunnel under the no-man's-land between the lines and explode four tons of gunpowder under the Confederate fort, blowing a gap in their defenses. If it succeeded, they could take Petersburg without a long siege and shorten the war. The tunnel worked; the explosion was all they'd hoped for, creating **The Crater,** 170 feet by 60 feet and 30 feet deep; but the Union troops, instead of going around it to attack, plunged directly in and couldn't get out. The Confederates retook the position, inflicting more than 4,000 Union casualties and assuring that the siege would go on.

Take Crater Road to **Old Blandford Church** (319 South Crater Road; 804-733-2396), built in 1735 in Bristol Parish, which was founded by Peter Jefferson, father of Thomas. The church was used as a hospital during the siege and was restored in 1901, when each Confederate state donated a Tiffany stained-glass window in honor of its dead. Some 30,000 Confederates are buried in the churchyard, and it's said that the first Memorial Day was observed here.

■ **APPOMATTOX COURT HOUSE**   *map page 132, A-6*

Appomattox Court House is the East's most compelling ghost town. Its cluster of brick and log buildings appears unexpectedly in the middle of pastureland, along the old dirt stage road that once ran between Richmond and Lynchburg. Plenty of living and breathing people come here every day, either out of curiosity or respect, but it is the dead, not the living, that populate this place.

To most Americans the name Appomattox symbolizes the end of a gruesome, fratricidal war, an end in which all the players acted with dignity and humanity. The events that culminated here had been years, even centuries, in the making. One could say that as far back as the 1600s, the North and the South had begun to

Petersburg National Battlefield.

develop separate cultures, separate expectations—that the Mason-Dixon line was a kind of political fault line waiting to quake and pull apart. Appomattox was the place where the knitting back together of the fault began.

In the spring of 1865, Lee's Army of Northern Virginia was a bedraggled, hungry mass of men who somehow had managed to endure 10 months under siege in Petersburg. By early April, Grant's movement southwest of the city had forced Lee to retreat, and Petersburg finally gave way. Without Petersburg as a buffer, Richmond could not hold, and soon the Confederate capital was a chaos of fleeing bodies, fire, rioting, and looting. Meanwhile, Lee, desperate for fresh supplies, marched his army west toward Amelia Court House, expecting to find rations waiting there. Through some bureaucratic mix-up, there were none. Out of food and out of will, the Confederates had to spend a precious day foraging for rations while Grant drew the noose ever tighter.

The Union army was quickly closing in on the South. Yet one of the North's army heroes, Joshua Chamberlin, recalled that "we could not help admiring the courage and pluck of these poor fellows, now so broken and hopeless." On April 6, at **Sailor's Creek,** the Union advance forces overtook the Confederate rear (capturing nearly 8,000 prisoners, including eight generals), and left the Confederates in such disarray that Lee, watching in disbelief, lamented, "My God, has the army been dissolved?"

Time raced against the war-ravaged Southern army as it staggered toward the railroad depot called Appomattox Station and the hope of new supplies. By nightfall of April 8, it was clear that that hope was futile. As Lee camped with his advisers in the forest outside **Appomattox Court House,** they could see the fires of the Union army twinkling a dozen miles in the distance around Appomattox Station. Late in the afternoon of April 7, Grant had sent a dispatch to Lee concerning the hopelessness of further resistance and broaching the subject of surrender; Lee had replied simply, stating that he was not of the same opinion concerning hopelessness, but asking Grant's terms.

When Grant's answer came, after dark on April 8, there was only one: That Lee's men would be "disqualified for taking up arms against the Government of the United States." Lee wrote back, clearly stating that he was not speaking of surrender, that the "restoration of peace" was his sole object. To know whether Grant's proposals could lead to that, he asked that the two generals meet the following day.

The village of Appomattox Court House, where the Civil War surrender took place.

During the night, the South made one more attempt to break out of the Northern stronghold, but that quickly proved a failure. When it was reported to Lee, he concluded that there was nothing left to do but to go and see General Grant, "and I would rather die a thousand deaths." He now spoke of surrender, and to a dissenting officer, he admitted that history would judge him harshly. "They will not understand how we were overwhelmed by numbers," he said. "But that is not the question, Colonel: The question is, is it right to surrender this army. If it is right, then I will take all the responsibility."

On the morning of Palm Sunday, he sent his aide, Col. Charles Marshall, into Appomattox Court House to make arrangements for the meeting. The village was shut up tight. The first resident he encountered was Wilmer McLean, who took him to a locked-up house that was in such disarray Marshall found it unsuitable for the surrender. McLean then offered his own home. Lee, accompanied by a fellow officer, rode forward to wait for Grant in the McLean parlor.

Grant, meanwhile, made his way to the village. General Sheridan (who had marched on the Shenandoah) and General Ord were anxiously awaiting him, to warn him that the whole surrender scheme was a ploy on the part of the Confederates so that they could slip away. Grant waved them off and rode on to meet Lee.

Muddy, disheveled, wearing a slouch hat, and with his soldier's shirt unbuttoned, Grant arrived in the McLean parlor and greeted Lee. The two men chose a common ground to oil their meeting; they discussed the Mexican War and army life. Then Lee brought the pleasantries up short, asking Grant to name the terms of surrender and then to write them out. Grant sat quietly at a small desk and wrote. The short paragraph he handed Lee required Confederate "arms, artillery, and public property to be parked, stacked and turned over." When that was done, the Southern men could go home.

Lee recognized how generous the terms were, but he raised one more issue: Could the men take their horses with them, to help them replant and replenish their land? Grant agreed. Before they parted, Grant also offered to send through rations to Lee's starving army.

Lee, astride the gray bulk of Traveller, rode through the ranks of men who had gathered to salute him. "Men," he said, "we have fought the war together, and I have done the best I could for you …. Goodbye."

Later, Grant recalled that he "felt like anything rather than rejoicing at the downfall of a foe who had fought so long and valiantly." When his troops tried to set off cannons to celebrate, Grant halted them, saying, "The Rebels are our countrymen again" and that the Union troops therefore should "abstain from all demonstrations in the field."

On April 12, the Confederate army marched forward to lay down its arms in a formal ceremony of surrender. Maine's Joshua Chamberlin, who presided over the event, remembered the Southern men as "thin, worn, and famished, but standing erect, and with eyes looking level into ours…. [W]as not such manhood to be welcomed back into a Union so tested and assured." Chamberlin ordered his army to salute the vanquished, and the Southerners returned the salute. As the last arms were stacked, the Union army once again saluted the South, this time with a spontaneous three cheers that rose from within the ranks.

Appomattox was the finest moment in the nation's long, arduous road to recovery and healing. It was no more than a moment. Almost immediately, Lincoln's assassination, factional politics, and greed intervened to make Reconstruction a nightmare. As to the small village itself, it lapsed back into rural quietude. In 1892, the brick courthouse burned down, and the county seat was moved to Appomattox Station, thereafter known simply as Appomattox. Still the commercial hub of the area, it is now cluttered with small malls and fast-food franchises. Which is good, because historic Appomattox has been saved from all that.

In 1935, Congress passed a bill turning the virtually deserted village into the **Appomattox Court House National Historical Park,** and since then the National Park Service has been busy restoring its original buildings. The old burned courthouse, now reconstructed, houses the Visitor Center, and although the park rambles over almost 1,800 acres, it focuses on the village. *Route 24, off U.S. 460, 80 miles west of Petersburg; 434-352-8987.*

The park also contains a reconstruction of the substantial though simple two-story brick **McLean House.** As soon as the surrender meeting ended, the house was virtually attacked, as souvenir-hunting Union soldiers descended on its parlor, carrying off, among other things, the two chairs the generals had sat in. Four years later the McLeans moved to Alexandria, and in 1893, the house was dismantled brick by brick by a speculator who hoped to reconstruct it in Washington, D.C. When funds for this project weren't found, the bricks were left in a heap in Appomattox, easy prey for relic-hunters. Thanks to careful drawings done at the time, though, the house and its historic parlor have been rebuilt as they were.

Also in the village, at the old **Clover Hill Tavern,** you can see the rooms where the Confederate paroles were hastily printed, and the Southern men were, at last, granted official leave to go home. About half a mile away stands the **Sweeney Cabin,** where a little-known artist named Joel Sweeney (born 1810) may have lived for a few years. As a child Joel listened to slaves making music on gourdlike instruments, and as a young man, with the skin of the family cat, he made the first American-born instrument—the five-string banjo. He played it widely and grew famous, as did his brother Sam—Queen Victoria gave Joel a money belt containing gold, and in 1862 Sam rode with Jeb Stuart and played for General Lee at Winchester. You can look at the house from outside, but it's not open to the public.

A few miles northwest of Appomattox stands **Spring Grove Farm** (Route 613; 434-993-3891), a wonderfully comfortable bed-and-breakfast in a restored 1842 plantation house. The property is 200 acres, and there's a feeling of spaciousness here—the rooms are large; there are private porches and decks, and wood-burning fireplaces.

NORTHERN VIRGINIA

It's not uncommon to hear old-line Virginians point a finger north and proclaim that they "should never have let those Yanks come across the Potomac into Virginia territory." They're not referring to troop movements so much as to urban encroachments. In truth, northern Virginia shares more, by way of attitude, politics, and lifestyle, with its neighbor Washington, D.C., than with the rest of the state. For one thing, it tends to be one of the few jurisdictions in the state that consistently votes Democratic in national elections. And of course, it also tends either to go boom or bust, depending on the spending mood of Congress. Money coming out of the nation's capital has always oiled the economy of northern Virginia, though in recent years the area has begun to attract nongovernmental businesses, and its cities and counties proclaim themselves more than mere bedroom communities. Maybe. But they remain satellites, well within the gravitational pull of their world-class neighbor across the river.

Still, northern Virginia does belong to the past—and the present—of the Old Dominion. All you have to do is cross from Washington into Old Town Alexandria and you can sense the pace slowing down and vowels drawling a shade more. As in the rest of the state, history, here in the form of historic battlefields and other landmarks, curls around the area as surely as the wide Potomac curves around its edges. In some ways, it's the best of Virginia: its roots are as rich and deep as any place in the state; it's got all the cultural offerings of an urban center; and it's become a robust and dynamic melting pot where Asian, African, and Middle Eastern immigrants add spice to the old-Virginia mix.

■ MANASSAS NATIONAL BATTLEFIELD PARK
map page 132, D-2

Old battlefields can feel remarkably peaceful, and somehow, the more lives lost on them, the quieter they seem. Manassas is almost hushed, as if embarrassed by the frivolous gaiety with which it began. After all, these smooth green hills and clustered forests, watered by a little creek called Bull Run, witnessed the first real battle

(left) Alexandria today.
(following pages) The Battle of Manassas, also called the Battle of Bull Run, where both sides suffered heavy losses.

of the Civil War. In fact, it was at this site that a naive populace became convinced that the war was real. So certain was Washington society that the battle here would provide them with simple, lighthearted entertainment that they packed picnics and drove out to watch it on a late July morning in 1861. They must have come to regret their choice of picnic spots, because when the smoke cleared, their men had suffered 2,700 casualties, to the South's 2,000.

How did the two armies come to face off for the first time on this piece of ground? As with most things in war, it had to do first with politics. Anxious for an early victory, Lincoln, in the summer of 1861, pressed Gen. Irvin McDowell to engage the Southerners and work toward Richmond. McDowell argued against it, knowing that his men, most "90-day volunteers," were woefully untrained and untested. "You are green," Lincoln admitted, "but they are green also; you are all green alike." And so McDowell marched forward with 35,000 men, heading first to the railroad junction of Manassas and its guard of 22,000 Southern troops. But Confederate spies in Washington had warned of the attack in time for a Southern contingent of 12,800 men under Joe Johnston to move stealthily up from nearby Winchester and reinforce the Confederates. On July 21, McDowell struck the Southern line at a weak spot near its rear. By noon, rebels were being driven south to Henry Hill. The North, already claiming victory, stopped to regroup at the base of the hill. When they resumed their charge up the hill a couple of hours later, the South was ready for them. Johnston's first brigade, under Thomas J. Jackson, had formed a defensive line out of sight of the North. Seeing their solid ranks, Confederate general Barnard Bee of South Carolina yelled, "There stands Jackson like a stone wall. Rally behind the Virginians!"

By late afternoon the Union was in retreat, awarding the Confederacy a great victory, at least of morale. But the South too had suffered heavy losses and exhaustion, and consequently Johnston did not pursue the retreating enemy.

Perhaps if he had, the Second Battle of Manassas (Second Bull Run) would not have happened 13 months later. By then Stonewall Jackson had waged his brilliant Valley Campaign against the North in the Shenandoah, and he was the prize that the North most wanted to take. When he and his men raided the Manassas supply base, by then in the hands of the North, Union general John Pope gleefully ordered his army to "bag" Jackson. But Jackson outwitted them, as he usually did, by hiding, and by the time he came out to fight, he had been reinforced by Lee's army of 50,000. By nightfall on August 30, 1862, in an eerie déjà-vu, the Union troops were again in retreat toward Washington. No picnickers had come to this battle: By now everyone understood that the war was in deadly earnest.

Today, the park's visitors center has interpretive displays and a 45-minute movie explaining what happened here—and how it came to happen twice. *Route 234 off I-66, Exit 47B; 703-361-1339.*

■ LOUDOUN COUNTY

A pastoral realm of country estates, picturesque hamlets, and winding country lanes, Loudoun County occupies the northeastern tip of the state. Its rolling Blue Ridge foothills make it perfect hunt country, and the local population takes its equine amusements seriously. Here, they still anoint a master of the hunt and honor the "sport of queens" with a glamorous steeplechase season. Steeplechase and point-to-point races are open to the public, and you can bring a picnic lunch and spend a fine afternoon watching Thoroughbreds streak by and leap over fences. Or you can simply observe the way the horsey set socializes. Most of them set up tailgate parties with fine food and drink.

Loudoun actually has several distinct faces. Dulles Airport, the Danish architect Eero Saarinen's wonderwork, dominates the county's southeast corner and creates a kind of break in the dam, letting urban sprawl seep through. Bedroom communities are now being built on farmlands that have been cultivated for centuries. These fields roll on and on, right up to the edge of the Blue Ridge.

■ LEESBURG *map page 132, D-1*

The little town of Leesburg, Loudoun's county seat, is a mix of the trendy and the traditional. Quaint 18th-century stone houses dot the historic core of town, and King Street, the main drag, offers several nouveau colonial restaurants. The place maintains a neighborly, distinctly Southern charm, and there's a free parking garage right in the center of things. The **Loudoun Museum** (16 Loudoun Street; 703-777-7427) has a Civil War exhibit, and the turreted brick courthouse is guarded by an ever-vigilant copper Confederate soldier.

At the well-stocked **visitors center** (222 Catoctin Circle SE, 703-771-2617) you can find a walking map of downtown and information on the county's sumptuous bed-and-breakfasts. Some are old estate cottages, others are in historic homes, and almost all are uniquely charming. You can get a map to the scenic byways too. Loudoun's narrow lanes bob and weave across some of the loveliest hill

country in Virginia, past Thoroughbreds sunning themselves and sheep grazing in green pastures.

It's a county made for easygoing, unplanned driving trips, and its rural simplicity appeals to all sorts of worldly characters. Russell Baker, for example. That famous chronicler of growing up in America and now a host of television's *Masterpiece Theatre,* has a home here. And Gen. George Marshall retired to the peace of Leesburg after fighting in World War II and then creating what became known as the Marshall Plan to reconstruct Europe. His low-key but charming **Dodona Manor,** an early-19th-century house on a shady street, should have reopened for tours as you read this, after undergoing some restoration. *212 East Market Street; 703-777-1880.*

More splendid **Morven Park,** the estate of Virginia's popular reform governor Westmoreland Davis, lies north of Leesburg off Old Waterford Road. Its 1,200 acres of rolling hills and rich green grounds, now housing an equestrian center (not open to the public), a carriage collection, and a horse museum, are still dominated by the boldly columned manor house, which began as a farmhouse in the late 18th century, but has far outgrown its humble origins. The manor's rooms are filled with tapestries, oriental rugs, paintings and porcelains, and all sorts of high-style furnishings. It looks like a movie set, waiting for a couple in riding pinks and with British accents to enter the scene. *17263 Southern Planter Lane; 703-777-2414.*

■ **WATERFORD**   *map page 132, C/D-1*

The quiet little town of Waterford, north of Leesburg, is a lingering shadow from the past that has taken an interesting step to ensure the beauty of its future. A National Historic Landmark since 1970, it has bought up its "viewshed," so that in perpetuity what residents see as they gaze at the surrounding countryside will contain no nasty surprises.

An unbelievably quaint collection of 18th-century stone and clapboard cottages and white-chinked log houses, the town grew up around an old gristmill that Amos Janney, a Quaker who had migrated here from Pennsylvania, built about 1740. The town site was later gridded into lots, and Waterford became a strangely eclectic community. The Quaker reputation for tolerance attracted freed blacks and other Pennsylvanians with unorthodox religious views. These days Waterford

Steeplechase at Oatslands Plantation in Loudon County.

The Old Mill at Waterford.

still claims a rather unorthodox citizenry—those who want to preserve the grace and humanism of the 18th century from the cacophony and inhumanity of the 21st. Every year on the first weekend in October there's a huge fair—one of the largest juried craft shows on the East Coast—where costumed exhibitors and performers entertain and the townspeople open their wonderful little houses.

■ **MIDDLEBURG** *map page 132, C-2*

From Waterford, country lanes twist and bend southwest through the toniest part of Loudoun County and finally into the unofficial capital of Virginia hunt country: Middleburg. This small cluster of upscale shops with equestrian themes serves an impressive clientele. The late Paul Mellon, for example, had a training farm not far away, and the Mercedes seems to be the preferred vehicle on Middleburg streets. The town's fieldstone **Red Fox Inn** (2 East Washington Street; 540-687-6301) has housed and fed travelers since 1728, making it the second-oldest tavern in the nation. The **Aldie Mill,** a few miles east of town on U.S. 50, has also withstood the test of time. Built in the early 19th century, the two-wheel gristmill churns over the waters of Little River, grinding corn once again. Just off Washington Street (Route 50) stands the splendid new home of the **National Sporting Library** (102 The Plains Road; 540-687-6542), a research center for turf and field sports that has an extraordinary collection of 15,000 volumes and presents monthly lectures on its chosen sports.

If you'd like to taste life on a working horse farm, in a house built in 1775, surrounded by the faded elegance of an aristocratic past, spend a night—or a month—at **Welbourne,** a few miles west of Middleburg, where everything in sight is antique—some of it shabby, much of it exquisite, and none of it purpose-bought. The coonhounds will make you welcome, your hospitable host will make you a bourbon and branch, and you'll never forget the breakfast—the service *or* the food. *22314 Welbourne Road; 540-687-3201.*

■ OATLANDS *map page 132, C-2*

Six miles south of Leesburg on Route 15, a tree-lined country lane leads into **Oatlands,** a memorable example of an early Classic Revival Virginia country house. Now owned by the National Trust for Historic Preservation, the stuccoed yellow house was built in the Federal style in 1804 by George Carter, a great-grandson of Virginia's 18th-century land baron Robert "King" Carter. An enormous columned portico, elaborate plasterwork, and sweeping stairways, added in the 1820s, leave no doubt that this is a house in the grand style. It is the most visited house in Loudoun County.

There's a feeling of spaciousness to the estate as you stroll up to the house from the visitors center, which is in the 1903 carriage house, beneath tall trees and past the dairy (circa 1821) and the propagation greenhouse (1810). East of the house, across the lawn there's a 4.5-acre terraced, walled garden with gorgeous plantings and statuary, specimen trees, and romantic old brick dependencies, one of them a smokehouse-turned-studio. The ancient oak grove, though planted by George Carter, seems to have been there since the time of the Druids. Nowadays, Oatlands is the scene of sheepdog trials, the Loudoun Hunt point-to-point, the Middleburg dog show, and other events: the place is jumping eight months of the year. There's an ongoing archaeology program investigating slave life on the plantation, and in winter, lecture series, seminars and workshops, and plays are offered in the carriage house. *20850 Oatlands Plantation Lane; 703-777-3174.*

One other Loudoun note: **White's Ferry,** the only cable-guided ferry on the East Coast, plies the Potomac a few miles north of Leesburg, taking cars and passengers back and forth between the Virginia and Maryland shorelines. A ferry line has operated here since 1828.

■ THE GRAY GHOST

Loudoun County's favorite ghost is its gray one, Confederate major John Singleton Mosby. A legend in his own time, Mosby, along with his Partisan Rangers, patrolled Loudoun and its environs so well during the Civil War that the area became known as Mosby's Confederacy. Given Loudoun's proximity to the North, it was constantly crisscrossed by both armies and experienced terrible looting as a result. As one chronicler claimed, Loudoun "probably suffered more real hardships and deprivations than any other community of like size in the Southland." Though Mosby couldn't protect the population against this, he did manage to deal the North payment in kind. For several years, he and his small band of rangers harassed and humiliated Union forces passing through their territory.

Fleet of foot and virtually invisible, the Gray Ghost and his men were constantly on the move and frequently scattered to keep their whereabouts unknown. But they could "gather at my call," Mosby claimed, "like Children of the Mist."

After the war, they evaporated. Though the North feared that independent raiders like Mosby's band would insist on fighting even after the surrender, Mosby responded to their fears in his characteristically cavalier style. "We are soldiers," he said, "not highwaymen." Laying aside his trademark red-lined cape and ostrich-plumed hat, he returned to the practice of law—and went on to serve his country. He eventually was appointed U.S. Consul to Hong Kong and an assistant attorney for the Justice Department.

In 1995 the **Mosby Heritage Area** (540-687-6681) was formed to increase awareness of the history, culture, natural beauty, and landmarks of three centuries in northern Virginia. It covers parts of Loudoun, Clarke, Warren, Fauquier, and Prince William Counties, including the towns of Leesburg, Middleburg, Purcellville, Berryville, Front Royal, Warrenton, and Haymarket, as well as Manassas National Battlefield Park. The organization has produced driving tours on tape and CD, narrated by historian Robert O'Neill and introduced by Willard

Ginger, an Italian greyhound, outside the Red Fox Inn in Middleburg.

Maj. John Singleton Mosby, the "Gray Ghost" of Loudoun County.

Scott, that guide you to 10 sites associated with the Mosby Battalion from 1863 to 1865, covering 25 miles from Truro Church in Fairfax to Rector's Crossroads (modern-day Atoka).

■ MOUNT VERNON

map page 132, D-2

South along the Potomac from Washington and Alexandria lie the gates to one of America's favorite historic sites, George Washington's Mount Vernon. Close to a million people a year make a pilgrimage to this pleasant knoll above the river, not because the columned and cupolaed red-roof farmhouse ranks as an exceptional architectural landmark, but because it was the beloved home of the beloved father of our country.

After 250 years, Washington has become more monumental than mortal. Coming here to his home does seem to rehumanize him, transform him back into what he was at heart—a practical, hardworking planter who considered farming "the most delectable occupation."

Washington was not technically to this manor born. He spent a few young years here after his family had established the fledgling farm, but most of his childhood was spent on the smaller Ferry Farm, east of Fredericksburg. When George was 11, his father died. Exposed to little formal education, the boy could have grown up to be another unsophisticated colonial frontiersman had not his elder half-brother, Lawrence, intervened.

When their father died, Lawrence inherited Mount Vernon, and young George began to spend more and more time here. It was through Lawrence, who had married into the planter aristocracy, that George was introduced to Virginia society. Upon Lawrence's death, the 20-year-old George leased the farm from his sister-in-law, and he eventually inherited it in 1761. Returning victorious and with distinction from the French and Indian War, the young man soon conquered the heart of wealthy young Tidewater widow Martha Dandridge Custis, the mother of two young children. About their marriage, in 1759, historians have often disagreed. It seems certain that young George had suffered a serious infatuation for Sally Fairfax, the wife of his good friend George Fairfax. That love was obviously doomed, though romantic letters from Washington to Sally were uncovered after her death in England. Whatever his deeper longings, George apparently treated Martha with affectionate respect. Though the couple never had children of their own, Washington raised his stepchildren and his stepgrandchildren as though they were his. Contrary to his reputation as a womanizer, he seems to have been a dedicated family man. At the end of his life he sought escape in the role that seemed to please him above all others: squire of Mount Vernon.

Just as in Washington's time, a steady flood of visitors streams through Mount Vernon's rooms, admiring the ornate wall paneling and marble mantels and furnishings and walking out on the mansion's piazza overlooking the river. Probably the most moving place is the master bedchamber, where the great man died in 1799. After a miserable winter day overseeing outdoor work, Washington came down with a serious throat inflammation called quinsy. His doctors treated him with leeches and other remedies, but the 67-year-old hero did not recover. "I die hard," he whispered, "but I am not afraid to go."

George and Martha lie side by side in marble sarcophagi in the family burial ground above the river. Washington would likely be pleased with the shape his estate is in. The gardens are well tended, and the score of dependencies—including laundry room, smokehouse, greenhouse—are freshly painted and in good working

Life of George Washington: The Farmer, *by Junius Brutus Stearns (1810–1885).*

order. And on the bowling green fronting the house stand some of the tulip trees that Washington himself planted, in summer their foliage luxuriant and rustling in the river breeze. *Eight miles south of Alexandria along the Potomac on George Washington Memorial Parkway; 703-780-2000.*

After years of research and restoration, the water-powered **gristmill** 3 miles west of Mount Vernon is grinding grain again, with costumed millers to demonstrate its operation. Next to the mill you can watch archaeologists at work on the site of a 1797 whiskey distillery. *Route 235; 703-780-2000.*

■ WOODLAWN *map page 132, D-2*

Woodlawn is a compelling coda to Mount Vernon. This estate was a wedding gift from Washington to his stepgranddaughter, Eleanor Parke "Nelly" Custis, and his nephew Lawrence Lewis. Considered an exceptionally accomplished young woman, Nelly was raised at Mount Vernon and met her husband there.

Both Lawrence and Nelly appear to have had a fine aesthetic sense and a love of good living. Their Georgian brick house (1805) was designed by the prominent

Washington architect Dr. William Thornton, who was responsible for the U.S. Capitol, and Woodlawn is still decorated with many of the couple's own tasteful furnishings. Apparently, though, they lived their lives in the shadow of their great ancestor. They tried, perhaps too hard, to keep up Washington's high standards, but they lacked his business sense and were perpetually in debt.

The grounds, overlooking the Potomac, are renowned for their boxwood hedges and rose garden. The National Trust for Historic Preservation now owns the property, which also contains an unexpected architectural jewel nestled in the woods behind Woodlawn. The unpretentious yet remarkable **Pope-Leighey House** was architect Frank Lloyd Wright's response to the need for affordable but well-designed housing for the middle class. Designed in what he called his Usonian style, the simple L-shaped house shows how Wright blended functionalism and aesthetics. He built it in 1941 for a northern Virginia journalist named Loren Pope. But Pope's family of four found the house a bit too precious to live in and so sold it to the Leigheys. In 1964, they donated it to the National Trust, which had it moved here from its original site in nearby Falls Church. *Woodlawn and Pope-Leighey Visitors Center, 3 miles west of Route 235 North; 703-780-4000.*

■ GUNSTON HALL   *map page 132, D-2/3*

This dignified 18th-century brick manor house was the home of George Washington's friend and fellow patriot George Mason. A brilliant thinker and statesman, Mason tends now to be overlooked when Virginia's greats are listed. That's unfortunate, because he deserves to be admired as one of the "pens" of the Revolution. Anyone will recognize his language in the Virginia Declaration of Rights, written in May 1776: "That all men are by nature created free and independent and have certain inherent rights…the enjoyment of life and liberty…and pursuing and obtaining happiness." Two months later, similar sentiments found their way into the Declaration of Independence, written by Mason's younger friend and admirer, Thomas Jefferson.

Perhaps Mason's relative obscurity is a holdover from his lifetime. A private man who abhorred the fray of politics, Mason used his influence quietly through his writings and in behind-the-scenes conversations with friends. He refused to take a more active public role, in part because of his devotion to his nine children, who had been left motherless when his wife died fairly young.

HOME ALONE IN WARTIME

Alexandria, May 4, 1861.—I am too nervous, too wretched to-day to write in my diary, but that the employment will while away a few moments of this trying time. Our friends and neighbors have left us. Every thing is broken up. The Theological Seminary is closed; the High School dismissed. Scarcely any one is left of the many families which surrounded us. The homes all look desolate; and yet this beautiful country is looking more peaceful, more lovely than ever, as if to rebuke the tumult of passion and the fanaticism of man. We are left lonely indeed; our children are all gone—the girls to Clarke, where they may be safer, and farther from the exciting scenes which may too soon surround us; and the boys, the dear, dear boys, to the camp, to be drilled and prepared to meet any emergency. Can it be that our country is to be carried on and on to the horrors of civil war? . . .

I go from room to room, looking at first one thing and then another, so full of sad associations. The closed piano, the locked bookcase, the nicely-arranged tables, the formally-placed chairs, ottomans and sofas in the parlor! Oh for some one to put them out of order! and then the dinner-table, which has always been so well surrounded, so social, so cheerful, looked so cheerless to-day, as we seated ourselves one at the head, the other at the foot, with one friend,—but one,— at the side. I could scarcely restrain my tears, and but for the presence of that one friend, I believe I should have cried outright. After dinner, I did not mean to do it, but I could not help going into the girls' room . . . . Why did we think it necessary to send off all that was so dear to us from our own home? I threw open the shutters, and the answer came at once, so mournfully! I heard distinctly the drums beating in Washington. The evening was so still that I seemed to hear nothing else. As I looked at the Capitol in the distance, I could scarcely believe my senses. That Capitol of which I had always been so proud! Can it be possible that it is no longer our Capitol? And are our countrymen, under its very eaves, making mighty preparations to drain our hearts' blood? And must this Union, which I was taught to revere, be rent asunder?

—Judith Brockenbrough McGuire, Diary, 1861

So Mason let his authority radiate from his home, in which he must have taken great pride, because it remains quite a showplace. William Buckland, an indentured servant who arrived here in 1755, was responsible for much of the interior design and the supervision of the other craftsmen. The elaborate paneling is the work of William Bernard Sears, who arrived in the colonies from England in 1752 and apparently attempted to prove his talent by lining Mason's walls with exquisite woodwork. One wonders if Mason had a gardener with similar ambitions, because the grounds are impressive, particularly the double line of black heart cherry trees flanking the carriage driveway and the centuries-old boxwood allée. (Those English boxwoods, planted along a 12-foot-wide walkway, have grown so massive over the years that they're now only 3 feet apart.) *Mason Neck, Lorton, 15 miles south of Alexandria, off I-95, Exit 163; 703-550-9220.*

■ **OLD TOWN ALEXANDRIA** *map page 132, D-2*

Tree-lined, brick-paved, and charming, Old Town looks much as it did 200 years ago, when this was a rowdy little tobacco port on the middle Potomac. Now genteel, Old Town is a mix of carefully tended 18th- and 19th-century homes fanning out from a vibrant café-style commercial district with galleries, craft shops, and veritable bouquets of boutiques. Old Town also boasts some truly monumental ghosts—among them George (Washington) and Uncle Robert (E. Lee). Both heroes "slept here" and left their mark on the little town, which is reachable from Washington via the George Washington Parkway (which becomes Alexandria's Washington Street).

You have to admire Old Town's equanimity. The place has had its ups and downs over the course of two and a half centuries, but its basic character has remained remarkably solid. It traces its beginnings to a scattering of tobacco warehouses on the Potomac in the 1730s. This "last and best Virginia anchorage for ocean vessels before the Potomac Falls" served the planters whose tobacco farms dotted the countryside. The new spot on the northern frontier also attracted a number of Scottish merchants, whose stalwart traits can still be whiffed in the town's character.

In 1749 the Virginia General Assembly honored a petition jointly submitted by the planters and merchants to found a town on a 60-acre plot along the river. Since the land was owned by the Alexander family, the town, naturally enough, was to be

called Alexandria. In the best 18th-century style, the site was laid out in a precise grid, and, on what was probably a hot July day in 1749, a public auction was held to sell the half-acre lots. The savvy town planners wanted real people in Alexandria—people who had the desire to turn a gridded riverfront into a town, and so they prevented land speculators from buying up large parcels. The planners got what they wanted. Old Town grew up quickly, its waterfront lined with ship-yards and tobacco wharves and taverns, its streets fronted by modest brick and clapboard homes, as well as by imposing Georgian townhouses.

A quarter-century later the Revolution struck, and George Washington, who had a small townhouse in Alexandria and a plantation just downriver, became a national figure. The town managed to stay out of the direct line of fire. Only once did the British sail up the Potomac, fire a few shots at the seaport, and then leave.

The aftermath of war, however, and the making of America struck the town with full force. In 1789, Virginia generously ceded the town of Alexandria to the nation, to be part of the new diamond-shaped federal capital on the banks of the Potomac. With Washington not much more than farmland and marsh, Alexandria became a boomtown almost overnight, catering to the politicians and pundits who quickly congregated around the federal district. There was a problem for the bur-geoning seaport, though. Congress passed an amendment prohibiting the building of any government structures on the Virginia side of the Potomac. Historians believe that President Washington, ever mindful of his integrity, was behind the amendment: he owned land in Alexandria and didn't want to appear to be taking advantage of the situation.

Slowly, as Washington became a true city and other seaports captured more and more of Alexandria's trade, the town went bust. By 1846, it was ready to return to Virginia, and Congress graciously retroceded the struggling burg back to the state. And there, happily, it has remained ever since.

■ EXPLORING OLD TOWN ALEXANDRIA

Walking is the best way to see Old Town. You can poke around the commercial shops, then detour onto residential streets where the architecture is intriguingly varied. The Alexandria citizenry, by the way, take inordinate pride in their small but perfectly tended gardens and in the plaques that officially declare their resi-dences to be of historic merit. King Street is the city's main commercial row,

Old Town looks a lot like it did 200 years ago.

stretching west in a mile-long string of shops that leads from the low-lying Potomac shoreline all the way uphill to the town's towering Masonic Memorial.

At the foot of King Street, besides trendy shops and chic restaurants, is the city's famous torpedo-casings factory, built in 1918 and now the **Torpedo Factory Art Center.** In the 1970s, urban renovators eyed the unused cavernous space and realized that they could turn it into shops and studios for artists and craftsmen, some 165 of whom are now based here. *105 North Union Street; 703-838-4565.*

Two blocks up King, the past comes into focus at Alexandria's official visitors center, **Ramsay House,** with its shady, welcoming garden. The north end of this colonial clapboard cottage lays claim to being the oldest structure in Old Town, though it was built elsewhere and moved here after the town was established. *221 King Street; 703-838-4200.*

Another early building, the **Stabler-Leadbeater Apothecary,** one block south on Fairfax, has been returned to its late-18th-century appearance and now gleams with the glass bottles and paraphernalia it carried when it served as a major dispenser of pharmaceuticals from 1792 to 1933. *105–107 South Fairfax Street; 703-836-3713.*

If you keep walking down Fairfax and turn left onto Prince Street, you'll find yourself in **Gentry Row,** where stately 18th-century Georgian houses bristle with refinement. (Two of George Washington's physicians lived at Nos. 209 and 211.) If this block is a bit formal for your taste, wander down to the next one, locally known as **Captains' Row.** Here, there's a decided seaport-like feel to the way the small but winsome old cottages press against a street still paved with cobblestones. The cobblestones, by the way, probably came here as ballast in the holds of ships crossing the Atlantic.

The roots of the sternly simple **Old Presbyterian Meeting House** go back to 1772, when it was founded by Alexandria's burgeoning Scottish population. The church's hour of glory came in the winter of 1799, when George Washington died. A winter storm raged, so, "the walking being bad to the Episcopal Church" where Washington normally worshiped, the president's funeral service was held here. For four days, the bell in the church tower pealed out its mourning. In 1835 the old church was struck by lightning and virtually destroyed, but its congregation quickly rebuilt it. Today, its unpretentious clapboard uprightness continues to attract a devout following. The plain but compelling interior is open on weekdays, and services are held every Sunday.

On the waterfront in Alexandria.

Alexandria's Torpedo Factory.

The graveyard holds the stones of several prominent colonial Scots, including the church's builder, local entrepreneur John Carlyle. Beyond the graveyard stands the old manse, notable for both its age—it was built in 1787—and its peculiarly Alexandria-style architecture. This sort of half house is called a flounder because of its flat, windowless high side. About a score of these early-19th-century flounder houses are scattered throughout Old Town. *321 South Fairfax Street; 703-549-6670.*

The best place to get a taste of what socializing was like in early Alexandria is **Gadsby's Tavern Museum,** made up of a tavern dating from about 1785 and an adjoining hotel (1792). In the early days of Washington D.C. politics, this public house operated by John Gadsby was popular with the movers and shakers of government, including Washington, Jefferson, and John Quincy Adams. Its rooms recreate that early period, and not only can you still have a meal here in three of the tavern rooms, but you can also get a sense of what it was like to play a gentlemen's game of whist of an evening or attend a minuet gala in the ballroom upstairs. On the third floor, things are decidedly less lustrous. Here, overnight guests who wanted simple lodgings got them—as long as they were willing to share one of the small beds with a stranger or two. *134 North Royal Street; 703-838-4242.*

The imposing Georgian facade of the **Carlyle House** proves what a hardworking immigrant can attain. One of those early Scots merchants, John Carlyle came to Alexandria as a tobacco agent for an English concern, but he soon established his own business. No fool, he made a good marriage—to Sarah Fairfax, the daughter of one of Virginia's most respected families. By 1753 he was able to build himself the showiest house in town. The freestanding stone mansion attracted attention: in 1755 Gen. Edward Braddock held the now famous Governor's Council here, at which he exhorted five colonial governors to back the British in their fight against the French and the Indians. *121 North Fairfax Street; 703-549-2997.*

The **Alexandria Black History Resource Center,** focusing on the African-American experience, maintains an important collection of documents, videos, and periodicals. It also incorporates an important site in Alexandria's chapter of this continuing story. In 1939, a black lawyer named Samuel Tucker organized a sit-in at the Alexandria Free Library, which was closed to blacks. The city arrested the sitters but dropped the charges, so the case never went to trial. But in 1940, Alexandria built what was then called the Robinson Library for blacks, which was used until desegregation in the early 1960s and which is now an integral part of the center. The adjacent **Watson Reading Room** is a research repository named for Charles and Laura Watson, early black landowners in the city. *638 North Alfred Street; 703-838-4356.*

The Lyceum: Alexandria's History Museum betokened the coming of "culture" to Alexandria. Built in the late 1830s as a lecture hall-cum-museum-cum-library, the columned Greek Revival building once thundered with the oratory of such speechifiers as Daniel Webster. It continues to serve as a museum, with exhibits on state and local history. *201 South Washington Street; 703-838-4994.*

The serene walled grounds of historic **Christ Church** (1767–1773) offer a welcome break from the hustle of Washington Street. The beautifully proportioned little church, with its pepper-pot steeple and hourglass pulpit, is modeled after 18th-century English country churches. Washington worshiped here (and Lee was confirmed here), and every year, on the Sunday closest to Washington's birthday, the current president comes across the Potomac to sit in the first president's original pew and attend services. *118 North Washington Street; 703-549-1450.*

Alexandria also celebrates Washington's birthday with a big parade, but Old Town's most festive moment unquestionably comes during its Scottish Christmas Walk, held on the first Saturday in December. The day starts with a merry fife-

and-drum and bagpipe parade, with all the clans in their tartans, costumed living history reenactors, dog clubs, and antique cars. Afterwards, the musicians wander the streets, serenading as they go.

■ ALEXANDRIA'S LEE CONNECTION

As history, in its intricately flowing design, would have it, a few years after Virginia's first great hero, George Washington, died, the state's second great hero, Robert E. Lee, was born. Robert was himself the son of a Revolutionary War figure, "Lighthorse" Harry Lee, but by the time Robert was born, his father was an older man with a tarnished reputation. He was also on the verge of bankruptcy. In 1811 he moved his family from the Northern Neck to an Alexandria townhouse at 611 Cameron Street. A year later, he moved them again, to a nearby house at 617 Oronoco Street owned by his wife's relatives. And there, if the blunt truth be told, he left them.

Ostensibly on a trip to recover his health, Harry sailed for Barbados and died away from home. At the age of 6, Robert became the man of the house and the chief caregiver for his arthritic mother. Robert E. Lee's boyhood home, a graceful Federal townhouse, still stands on Oronoco Street, though it's now privately owned and not open to the public. Its walled garden has inspired a local tale that, even if apocryphal, is worth the telling. The story goes that some time after the Civil War, the owner of the house was sitting in his garden, when a distinguished, white-bearded head peered over the garden wall. It was Lee. "I just wanted to see if my mother's snowball bush was in bloom," the general explained.

(above) Robert E. Lee, taken by Matthew Brady.
(left) A spring day on King Street in Alexandria.

Lee's relatives owned so many houses in this vicinity that the corner of Oronoco and Washington Streets was called Lee Corners. Part of this legacy, the **Lee-Fendall House** is open for tours and furnished with fine early-19th-century antiques. It was also the home of labor leader John L. Lewis from 1937 to 1969. *614 Oronoco Street; 703-548-1789.*

■ OCCOQUAN   *map page 132, D-2*

This little 18th-century riverfront town ought to be on your itinerary. It's tucked away on the Occoquan River about 10 miles south of Alexandria, and few people know it's there. The name is a Dogue Indian word meaning "at the end of the water," but it feels like the end of the interstates, strip malls, and traffic lights.

The town was built at the highest point the Occoquan was navigable, and boats from these wharves took ice, grain, cordwood, flour, and fish to market. Later, they took Washington tourists and traveling shows, and in 1862, Gen. Wade Hampton and his men wintered here. The main north-south road ran through town, and this was the main delivery point for mail. As the century turned, Occoquan throve socially and culturally, with an opera house and the Lyric Theater. It survived a 1916 fire and Hurricane Agnes in 1972, and nowadays it's full of shops and galleries, antiques, boutiques, and restaurants (but nowhere to lay your head!).

The town's grid of streets is perfect for walking, and wherever you turn there are interesting houses, wonderful architecture, and something to catch the eye. **Rockledge** (410 Mill Street), a grand stone house now privately owned, dates from 1758 and was built with the help of William Buckland, who oversaw the interior construction at Gunston Hall. The **Mill House Museum** (413 Mill Street; 703-491-7525) operates in the only remaining part of the 18th-century gristmill. The Merchants' Association conducts evening Walking History and Ghost Tours (703-491-1736; reservations required) for small groups; the Prince William County Tourist Office (703-491-2168) is at 200 Mill Street. *Take I-95, Exit 160, to Route 123 north, to the third traffic light, and turn left where an inconspicuous sign says "To Occoquan."*

■ ARLINGTON   *map page 132, D-2*

Although Arlington and Alexandria are close neighbors, they have different characters and different pasts. They do have in common the fact that they were both part of the original national capital tract. In fact, what is now Arlington was part of the

At the Common Grounds Coffee Shop in Arlington.

County of Alexandria from 1846, when the whole parcel was retroceded to Virginia, until 1870. At that time the Virginia General Assembly passed a unique law that confuses all non-Virginians. It decreed that any city with a population of 5,000 or more would constitute a separate jurisdiction, completely independent of a county affiliation. And so Alexandria parted company with its rural northwestern half, which eventually became Arlington County, named in honor of its most obvious landmark, Arlington House, Robert E. Lee's home.

Throughout most of the 19th century, Arlington remained a rural farming community, but with the coming of World War I, its fields became fertile ground for war offices and commuters. The county's population growth through the 20th century accelerated steadily, yet Arlington still has a friendly, unpretentious feel. Fine old neighborhoods grace the northern side of the county, high-rise condominiums are scattered across its eastern half. In recent decades south Arlington has become a favored relocation spot for Hispanic and Asian immigrants.

Arlington has recently decided to bill itself as "the Virginia Side of the Nation's Capital," and its riverfront, threaded by the George Washington Memorial Parkway, does boast two national landmarks—the Pentagon and Arlington National Cemetery.

■ THE PENTAGON

The formidable five-sided fortress of the military establishment, the Pentagon sprawls beside the Potomac like an enormous starfish. Except for its location, there is nothing charming about the gargantuan low-slung structure, but its statistics are intriguing. The largest single-structure office building in the world, it covers 6.5 million square feet, each of its five sides is larger than the U.S. Capitol, and it was completed in just 16 months in 1941. Since the events of September 11, 2001, when terrorists hijacked an airplane and crashed it into the building, killing 182 people, guided tours of the interior are given only to school groups and people accompanied by one of the 20,000 Pentagon employees, not to individuals. *Pentagon exit off I-395; 703-697-1776.*

Aerial view of the Pentagon before September 11, 2001.

■ ARLINGTON NATIONAL CEMETERY

Within sight of the Pentagon, directly in front of Memorial Bridge, lies Arlington National Cemetery, a reminder, one hopes, of the human cost of war. For all the tragedies it recalls, the 624-acre cemetery, with its row after row of plain white headstones lined up and down grassy slopes, is an affecting, even beautiful place. More than 280,000 military personnel and their dependents are buried here, as are Robert Kennedy and John Fitzgerald Kennedy, whose simple grave is marked by an eternal flame. Smart-stepping guards attend the cemetery's Tomb of the Unknowns, which holds the remains of three unidentified soldiers, one from each of the world wars and one from the Korean War. An unknown soldier from the Vietnam War was also buried here until May 15, 1998, when, through DNA testing, the remains were identified as Lt. Michael Blassie and sent to his native Missouri to be buried beside his father. In September 2002, a marker was installed honoring those who died at the Pentagon on September 11, 2001.

Now solemn and honorable, Arlington National Cemetery got its start through an act of vengeance. Early in the Civil War, the Union took control of Arlington House, Lee's estate, and the Quartermaster General, Montgomery Meigs, decided that it would make a perfect burial ground for Union troops. He planted the first graves virtually in Lee's yard, to make certain that the Southern general would never feel comfortable living there again. A tourmobile will take you to the Lee mansion from the cemetery. *Memorial Drive, 703-235-1537.*

■ ARLINGTON HOUSE

Lee never did return here, but Arlington House, an imposing Greek Revival mansion, still stands in the middle of the cemetery atop a bluff overlooking Washington. The house was built between 1802 and 1817 by Lee's father-in-law, George Washington Parke Custis, George Washington's adopted grandson. Though this was really his wife's estate, Lee loved it, declaring that at Arlington House, his "affections and attachments are more strongly placed than at any other place in the world." During the 30 years following Lee's marriage to Mary Custis, Martha Washington's great-granddaughter, the couple spent as much time as possible here, while traveling back and forth to the different posts to which the aspiring young army engineer was sent. Six of their children were born here, and they thought of Arlington House as home.

(following pages) Arlington National Cemetery, with Arlington House in the background.

*FROM THE STORM-LASHED DECKS
OF THE MAYFLOWER
TO THE PRESENT HOUR,
WOMAN HAS STOOD LIKE A ROCK
FOR THE WELFARE AND THE GLORY
OF THE HISTORY OF THE COUNTRY
AND ONE MIGHT WELL ADD...
UNWRITTEN, UNREWARDED,
AND ALMOST UNRECOGNIZED.*

The Women in Military Service for America Memorial at Arlington National Cemetery was dedicated in 1997.

And it was to Arlington House that they repaired in April 1861, when war had become a certainty. Lee was still a U.S. officer, eminently respected. On April 20, he was called across the river to a meeting at Blair House and offered the command of Union forces. He returned torn and tormented. A fervent patriot, he nonetheless couldn't bring himself to fight against his home state. And so during that long night at Arlington House he made his fateful decision. With regret he resigned his commission. Two days later, he was on his way to Richmond to become commander of the Virginia forces. It would be another year before the South would give him the kind of sweeping command that he had turned down from the North.

Run by the National Park Service, Arlington House holds Lee memorabilia and poignant traces of the man's private life—rooms with his children's toys in them, his portrait as a dashing young officer, and one of his young wife. The mansion's wide portico with its Doric columns now overlooks the sweep of Washington and, just across the Potomac, the Lincoln Memorial. The view is not cruel coincidence. The Memorial Bridge between the house and the memorial was intended as a symbolic link, bridging the gulf for all time between the two great leaders, and consequently, between North and South. Equally in the spirit of reconciliation, a new exhibit on the enslaved families at Arlington House opened in 2002, the year of its bicentennial.

Arlington has one other, unexpected, inhabitant. Not only are Union soldiers buried in Lee's yard, but so is the capital's star-crossed designer—Pierre L'Enfant. This Frenchman came to America to fight for the Revolutionary cause, then stayed on after the battle was won. George Washington, impressed with his skills, hired him to lay out the new federal city, and L'Enfant set about designing an urban center on a sweeping scale, full of monuments, parks, broad avenues, and circles.

It is largely owing to L'Enfant that the capital is the beautiful city we see today, though the Frenchman got little credit in his lifetime. Obstreperous and arrogant, he offended the wrong people and was quickly removed from authority, taking his plans with him. All was not lost, however, because the plan was re-created from memory by Benjamin Banneker, a remarkable, self-taught black astronomer and mathematician who had assisted with the survey. The Frenchman spent the rest of his life railing against his ill-treatment. Finally, in 1909, L'Enfant got his just deserts, when his body was moved here and marked with a marble plaque incised with his city plan. He now enjoys a commanding vantage overlooking his "City of Magnificent Distances." *703-235-1537 or 703-235-1530.*

■ SUDDEN WILDERNESS

In the Potomac lies a memorial to another great man. **Theodore Roosevelt Island,** a sylvan little spot linked by a footbridge to the Virginia side of the river, serves as a monument to the nature-loving president. It's laced with forest paths that lead to views of Washington's Kennedy Center and Georgetown—it seems astonishing to be in the middle of the woods within spitting distance of the capital. In its heart lies a large fountained plaza with a statue of Roosevelt, hand upraised as though he were enthusiastically exhorting visitors to enjoy his little island. *Off the westbound side of the George Washington Memorial Parkway; 703-289-2500.*

SHENANDOAH VALLEY

Shenandoah, Daughter of the Stars, the native peoples are said to have called the river and the valley it watered—a romantic name for what must have been, even then, a romantic place. From the Blue Ridge vantage above the valley, you can look down on its broad, flat fertility and conjure the herds of buffalo and deer that grazed here centuries ago. Long after them came the Europeans—18th-century Irish, Scots, Germans—who knew a fertile field when they saw one.

Unquestionably, this swath of northwestern Virginia was, and still is, fertile. Watered by the Shenandoah River and the many brooks that weep their way out of the mountains, the Valley of Virginia smells like a farm, with the mixed aroma of just-mowed fields, turned earth, and pungent manure. Although the Blue Ridge defines its eastern extent and the higher, rougher Allegheny Mountains rise to its west, its north-south endpoints are a matter of some debate. In general, the valley begins somewhere in the vicinity of Winchester and ends somewhere below the initials George Washington carved in the impressively arching rock known as Natural Bridge. (And keep in mind that when people say "down the valley" they mean north, not south, because that's the way all the rivers in it flow.)

If the exact space the valley occupies is in dispute, its temperament is not. Like Don Quixote, it clings to the chivalry of the past as if it were a life raft able to buoy one above the irreverences, and irrelevancies, of modern life. Strung north to south along I-81 and U.S. 11, Winchester, Woodstock, Staunton, Lexington, and all the other valley towns wear their manners and their antebellum histories like badges of honor. True, burger chains and strip malls encircle many of their downtowns. But these enemy armies have been able to advance only so far. The center lines have held, and the main streets have kept their soda fountain–style drugstores, their homegrown restaurants, and their antiques shops with the consoling mustiness of memories. Here and there old stone mills by the river may have been gentrified into restaurants or shops, but their proprietors still greet you as if you were a kissing cousin whose citified ways they're willing to overlook.

White church steeples reach into blue heavens here, and residents, living amid such small-town grace, confer their own blessings on you. Pass strangers on the

A Shenandoah scene guaranteed to make a displaced Virginian homesick.

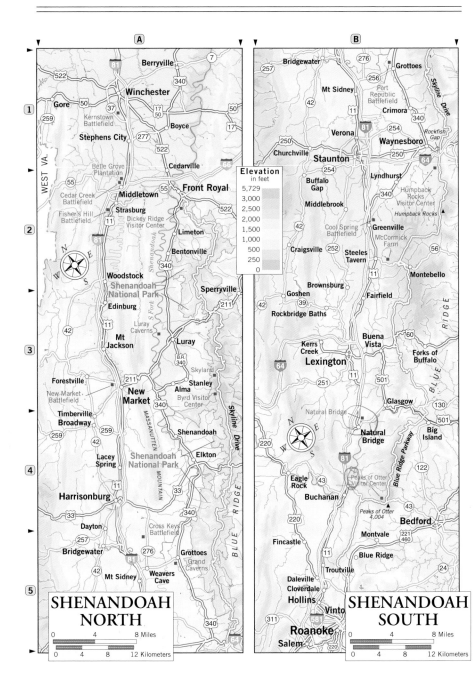

SHENANDOAH
NORTH

0   4   8 Miles

0   4   8   12 Kilometers

SHENANDOAH
SOUTH

0   4   8 Miles

0   4   8   12 Kilometers

street, and they almost always bestow a heartfelt "How you today?" They could be academics or students (the valley is full of small, well-heeled colleges); they could be farmers, merchants, horse breeders, fiddle players, or Mennonites. The valley has them all, as does the hovering Blue Ridge.

In spring the valley is petaled with dogwood and apple trees above the pale green of new grass. When summer comes, it drowses to the drone of cicadas and frogs and sun-slowed cows lowing in distant pastures. Then there is fall, when the sounds become more insistent and the land seems to rouse itself for a grand finale before the inevitability of winter. Autumn is a good time to head for the hills. The apples are ripe for the picking then, and at roadside stands lean-faced men in overalls sell baskets of them, as well as gallons of sweet cider, jars of honey, and homemade pickles.

You can shoot through the entire Shenandoah Valley in a matter of hours if you go nonstop on I-81. This old wagon route is the valley's main thoroughfare, and as such it's popular with multi-ton semis that shoulder down the road two abreast. Oddly enough, though, even the interstate has its upside. The views are glorious! The valley fans out from it, banked on the west by the Alleghenies and dissolving on the east into the soft, melancholy folds of the Blue Ridge. With a little imagination, you might believe that the Almighty had painted that long, low smear of gray-blue on the horizon—to keep the blended colors of Confederate and Union flying above this old battleground forever.

■ CIVIL WAR IN THE SHENANDOAH

For all its beauty, the valley has memories still painful to the touch. Maybe more than any place in the nation, this patch of earth was beaten beyond recognition during the Civil War. For the North, the valley meant two things: a back door to the Confederate capital in Richmond, and the fertile "breadbasket of the Confederacy"—something to be destroyed. And so, time and again, Northern troops shoved into the Valley of Virginia. And time and again, the South shoved them out.

This shoving began in earnest early in the war, with Stonewall Jackson's Valley Campaign in the spring of 1862. The summer before, Jackson's sangfroid at the First Battle of Manassas (or Bull Run) had earned him his famous sobriquet Stonewall. Beyond that designation, he remained just another obscure Southern officer, headquartered in Winchester with a force of only 8,000. It was events unfolding in Washington that would bring him fame. There, Union commander

CIVIL WAR TIME LINE

1861 **April:** Virginia secedes from the Union (following South Carolina, Mississippi, Florida, Alabama, Georgia, Louisiana, and Texas). Western counties of state remain loyal to Union and form West Virginia.

Col. Robert E. Lee, offered command of Union forces, resigns his commission to serve the South.

May: Richmond becomes the capital of the Confederacy.

July: Union forces are defeated at Battle of Manassas (Battle of Bull Run).

1862 **March:** Ironclads—the Union's *Monitor* and the Confederacy's *Virginia (Merrimac)*—duel in Hampton Roads.

Confederate Gen. Stonewall Jackson defeated at Kernstown, the opening conflict of the Shenandoah Valley Campaign.

May: Jackson wins at McDowell.

Confederates evacuate the Norfolk base, destroying the *Virginia* to prevent its capture.

August: Gen. Robert E. Lee is victorious at Second Battle of Manassas (Second Battle of Bull Run).

September: Union army under Gen. George McClellan halts Lee's attack on Washington in the Battle of Antietam, the bloodiest day of the war.

December: Union Gen. Ambrose Burnside's drive on Richmond fails at Fredericksburg.

1863 **January:** President Lincoln signs the Emancipation Proclamation.

March: Independent cavalry leader John Singleton Mosby captures Union's Gen. Edwin Stoughton at Fairfax Courthouse.

May: Lee defeats Gen. Joseph Hooker at Chancellorsville. Jackson is mortally wounded by his own men.

1864 **March:** Gen. Ulysses S. Grant named commander-in-chief of Union forces.

May–June: Grant pushes Lee's Army of Northern Virginia back toward Richmond in the Wilderness campaign. In an attempted surprise attack at Petersburg, command delays deny Grant victory, and the siege of Petersburg begins.

1865 **January:** U.S. House of Representatives passes the Thirteenth Amendment, abolishing slavery.

April: Confederates evacuate and burn Richmond.

Lee surrenders army to Grant at Appomattox.

President Lincoln shot dead at Ford's Theater in Washington.

May: President Andrew Johnson proclaims amnesty for citizens of the South.

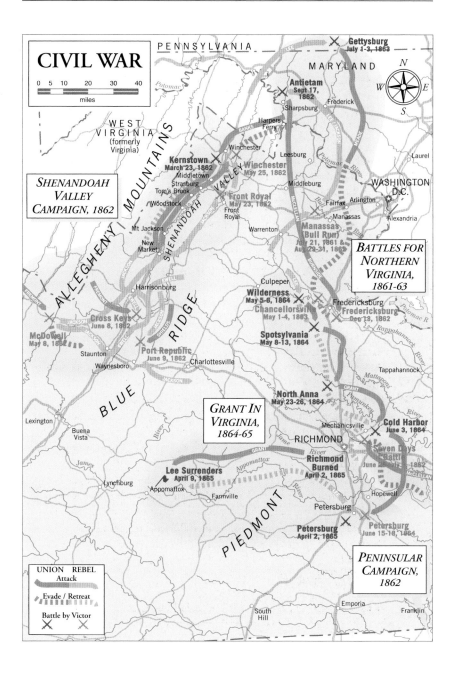

CIVIL WAR

0 5 10   20   30   40
miles

SHENANDOAH VALLEY CAMPAIGN, 1862

BATTLES FOR NORTHERN VIRGINIA, 1861-63

GRANT IN VIRGINIA, 1864-65

PENINSULAR CAMPAIGN, 1862

PENNSYLVANIA

MARYLAND

WEST VIRGINIA (formerly Virginia)

Gettysburg
July 1-3, 1863

Antietam
Sept 17, 1862
Sharpsburg   Frederick

Harpers Ferry
Winchester   Leesburg   Laurel

Kernstown
March 23, 1862
Middletown   **Winchester**   Middleburg   WASHINGTON D.C.
Strasburg   May 25, 1862
Tom's Brook   Fairfax Arlington
Woodstock   **Front Royal**   Manassas   Alexandria
May 23, 1862
Front Royal

Mt Jackson   Warrenton   **Manassas (Bull Run)**
July 21, 1861 &
New Market   Aug 29-31, 1862

Harrisonburg   Culpeper

Wilderness   Fredericksburg
May 5-6, 1864
Cross Keys   **Chancellorsville**   **Fredericksburg**
June 8, 1862   May 1-4, 1863   Dec 13, 1862

McDowell   **Spotsylvania**
May 8, 1862   May 8-13, 1864
Staunton
Waynesboro   Port Republic
June 9, 1862   Charlottesville   Tappahannock

North Anna
May 23-26, 1864
Lexington   **GRANT IN VIRGINIA, 1864-65**   Mechanicsville   **Cold Harbor**
June 3, 1864
Buena Vista   RICHMOND   **Seven Days Battle**
June 25-July 1, 1862
Lee Surrenders   **Richmond Burned**
April 9, 1865   April 2, 1865
Lynchburg   Appomattox   Hopewell
Farmville

Petersburg

Petersburg   **Petersburg**
April 2, 1865   June 15-18, 1864

South Hill   Emporia   Franklin

UNION REBEL
Attack

Evade / Retreat

Battle by Victor
✕

George McClellan was preparing to march a huge force up the Virginia Peninsula to attack Richmond. Once McClellan and his forces left Washington, President Lincoln became increasingly anxious that the federal capital was too exposed to attack. So he ordered additional forces into the outlying areas, into Fredericksburg and the Shenandoah.

First Battle of Kernstown

Jackson's position at the north end of the valley in early 1862 put him square in the path of history. On March 23 he tangled with Gen. James Shields at Kernstown, and there he suffered a tactical defeat. Still, he managed to shake the Union's confidence and apparently build his own. His brilliant Valley Campaign was under way.

Battle of McDowell

The second engagement came in May. Now reinforced with more men, Stonewall moved against a large enemy contingent under Gen. John C. Frémont, headed into the valley from the west. The Southern victory at McDowell forced the Yankees south up the valley. A couple of weeks later, the Stonewall Brigade thrust through a gap in Massanutten Mountain and surprised a Union garrison at **Front Royal,** two days later, overtaking the fleeing Northern forces at **Winchester.**

Strasburg to Port Republic

By now, Lincoln was convinced that the capital was at risk and poured reinforcements into the valley. To no avail. In early June, Jackson eluded three Union columns at Strasburg, while his compatriot Gen. Richard Ewell successfully took on General Frémont again, this time at **Cross Keys.** A day later, Jackson had also defeated Shields's men at Port Republic, and the Valley Campaign was at an end.

In little more than two months of fighting, Jackson had managed to push his self-proclaimed "foot cavalry" across 350 miles. Using the local gaps, ridges, and back roads to tactical advantage, he had bamboozled and surprised far superior Union forces for two months. His 18,500 men had defeated twice that number and had kept 50,000 Union troops too occupied to reinforce McClellan in his Peninsular Campaign to attack Richmond.

Second Battle of Winchester

A year later, Lee's second corps passed through the valley on its way to the debacle at Gettysburg, Pennsylvania. The Confederates under Ewell won a handy victory at the Second Battle of Winchester, and throughout the rest of 1863 and into the spring of 1864, the valley lay blessedly quiet.

Battle of New Market

Then, in May of 1864, the Union returned to the valley, intent on attacking Lee's rear and disrupting Confederate supply lines threatening the nation's capital. The first engagement, at the Battle of New Market, proved yet another Southern victory. Several weeks later the North's luck turned, when, at **Piedmont,** an overpowering Union division of 12,000 men routed a Confederate force of half that size that was defending the depot at Staunton.

Cool Spring and Second Kernstown

By the summer, Confederate general Jubal Early was in the valley, winning battles at Cool Spring and Kernstown. His victories were only a sad prelude to defeat.

Third Winchester

In Washington, Grant was now in charge, and at last Lincoln seemed to have a commander who knew how to win. Grant eyed the breadbasket of the Confederacy, then sent Philip Sheridan against it, telling him to "make of it a wasteland, so that even a crow flying over will have to carry its own provender." Sheridan moved cautiously into the valley, knowing that Jubal Early's men, though few, were war-hardened veterans. He managed to repulse them in the conflagration known as Third Winchester, although the fighting cost him 5,000 casualties. Troops sent in pursuit of the fleeing Early caught him three days later at **Fisher's Hill,** and again the Confederacy suffered defeat. When Confederate cavalry struck back at **Tom's Brook,** the Federals smashed them and sent them reeling south.

Cedar Creek

Now the valley lay open to Sheridan's devastating march. Though guerrilla fighters, including the daring Gray Ghost (John Mosby), harassed them, the Yankees burned barns, houses, mills, whatever lay in their path. By mid-October, Sheridan's army had proceeded as far as Cedar Creek, about 20 miles south of Winchester. Sheridan had headquartered at Belle Grove Plantation and, feeling that the situation was well in hand, made a brief visit to Washington. On his way back, he spent the night in Winchester.

(following pages) Vintage images of Civil War Virginia: African-American men, escaped slaves, in Culpeper, 1863 (top left). The Lincoln Gun guarding the mouth of the Chesapeake Bay, Fort Monroe, 1864 (bottom left). Secret Service men at Foller's House, Cumberland Landing, 1862 (top right). Captured Confederate encampment, Petersburg, 1864 (bottom right).

The following morning, with Sheridan absent, Early launched a surprise attack on the sleeping Northern army. The tactic appeared to work brilliantly, and by midday the bluecoats were in disorganized retreat. But Sheridan was on the way, dashing madly from Winchester to Cedar Creek. As he met his fleeing men on the road, he forced them back into battle. By late afternoon, the tables had been turned and the North snatched a decisive victory from near defeat. Early's mauled army never recovered. And Sheridan was free to continue his march through the valley.

■ **WINCHESTER** *map page 218, A-1*

At the northern end of the Shenandoah Valley and noted for something as innocent as apple blossoms, Winchester feels like old Virginia: Not overly stuffy, overly colonial, or unduly pretentious—just the Virginia of, say, 50 years ago, when the simple beauty of apple blossoms was something to celebrate. Unquestionably, Winchester, in the northwestern wedge of the state, sits in conservative country—once the home ground of Virginia's own apple grower–politician Harry Flood Byrd and his all-powerful Byrd machine. But the Byrd hegemony died with Harry nearly 40 years ago, leaving the town to evolve on its own. Byrd was only one of Winchester's luminaries. The writer Willa Cather came from Winchester, though she made her reputation describing the broad Nebraska prairie. Country singer Patsy Cline too was born and buried here. Her gravesite and a memorial to her lie south of town on Route 522.

But Winchester's roots go far deeper than this, back to the Shawnees and then to the Pennsylvania Quakers, the first whites to settle in the area, in the mid-1700s. The town today is a mix of many eras—from colonial past to post-yuppie present. Small streets twist by 18th-century stone buildings, gracious antebellum ones, antiques stores, and colonial-style restaurants. One small stone cabin, built in 1748 and now the **George Washington's Office Museum** (32 West Cork Street; 540-662-4412), served as his office in 1755 and 1756. Then a young surveyor, he was guarding Virginia's western frontier against the Indians and the French while overseeing the construction of Fort Loudoun.

One of the Quakers who came to Winchester was Abraham Hollingsworth, who hoped to establish a mill to augment his farming income. He built a log cabin on his 582-acre grant, and later began to build a limestone replacement, **Abram's Delight,** which was to house five generations of Hollingsworths and become

Downtown Winchester.

Winchester's oldest house. In 1753, his son Isaac hired a local builder to complete the house. One intriguing feature was an interior wall that could be raised on hinges and hooked up out of the way, so that the dining room and parlor could be converted into a Quaker meeting room, with ladies in the first and men in the second. The next generation, Jonah and his wife, Hannah, made many enlargements around 1800, and one of their 13 children, David, made more improvements around 1830. It's a treat to wander about this serene, foursquare place, with its furnishing from the 18th century—the quiet ways of the Quakers seem to pervade it still. *1340 South Pleasant Valley Road; 540-662-6519.*

Stonewall Jackson's Headquarters during the winter of 1861–62, just before he began his Valley Campaign, were in a Gothic Revival house lent to him and his wife by Lt. Col. Lewis T. Moore, the great-grandfather of Mary Tyler Moore. (The actress donated some of the house's beautifully reproduced wallpaper.) Jackson alternately suffered defeats and victories while here, and his departure did not ensure Winchester peace. *415 North Braddock Street; 540-667-3242.*

Throughout the war, this area at the head of the Shenandoah Valley was an endless battleground. Proof of that can be found in the approximately 7,500 soldiers that lie in peace here, about 4,500 of them Union men buried in Winchester National Cemetery and the remainder, Confederates, across Woodstock Lane in Stonewall Cemetery, which occupies a corner of Mount Hebron Cemetery. *Woodstock Lane, off Pleasant Valley Road.*

If you take a drive out east of Winchester, you'll see some lovely horse country and an interesting village or two no bigger than a wide place in the road. One of them, **White Post,** is distinguished by a white signpost at the center of the crossroads, first put there in 1750 by George Washington. Another drive-through is shady **Millwood,** where you can see the **Burwell-Morgan Mill** (15 Tannery Lane; 540-837-1799), which dates from the 1780s and was once owned by Gen. Daniel Morgan of Saratoga and Col. Nathaniel Burwell of Carter Hall. It ran until 1943; these days it is open for touring a few days a week from late spring to early fall.

Also in Millwood, on weekends from April through October, you can visit elegant **Long Branch,** built in 1811 by Robert Carter Burwell, with columns, a classical portico, and an exquisite, sweeping spiral stair. The estate had been owned by Lord Culpeper, Lord Fairfax (who in 1748 sent the teenage George Washington to survey his Shenandoah Valley estates), and Robert "King" Carter before Burwell. Long after him it was rescued by a Baltimore textile magnate, who added a superb collection of period furniture, hand-painted wallpapers, and gorgeous fabrics. Now a working horse farm, it is the site of many Clarke County festivities. *540-837-1856.*

Before leaving Clarke County, you should pay your respects to a venerable place of worship, the **Old Chapel,** built of stone in 1793 to replace an earlier log structure. In 1738 Lord Fairfax established Frederick Parish here, the first Episcopal parish west of the Blue Ridge, and in 1789 Col. Nathaniel Burwell (who was born at Carter's Grove Plantation outside Williamsburg in 1750) donated the land for the church. The simple interior has white plaster walls, a pulpit raised on high, and a small gallery across the back. "Old Chapel Sunday" services are held here at Easter and on the second Sunday in September. *Bishop Meade Road, between Millwood and Berryville; 540-837-1112.*

Patsy Cline *1932–1963*

Though her stardom lasted but three years, Patsy Cline left an indelible impression on country music. Known for her clear voice and haunting delivery, she was famous for "Walkin' After Midnight," "I Fall to Pieces," and other songs.

Born Virginia Hensley in Winchester, she won a tap-dancing contest at the age of 4. Family financial difficulties forced her to quit high school and work as a drugstore clerk, but she sang whenever she could, her hard life adding depth to her music.

At age 21, she married Gerald Cline and adopted the professional name Patsy Cline. She sought out every opportunity to perform, appearing on such regional radio and television shows as the *Louisiana Hayride,* the *Ozark Jubilee,* and the *Jimmy Dean Show.* In 1955 she got a recording contract with Four Star Records, but her big break came when she won the nationally televised *Arthur Godfrey's Talent Scouts* competition with "Walkin' After Midnight." The song was released immediately and sold a million copies.

Patsy's next recordings weren't as magical, and her career slowed. She divorced Cline and married Charlie Dick in 1957, then went into semiretirement for two years following the birth of her daughter. But in 1960 she accepted a spot as a regular on the *Grand Ole Opry* in Nashville and signed a recording contract with Decca. Her first release, "I Fall to Pieces," made No. 1, which she followed up with "Crazy," "She's Got You," "Leavin' on Your Mind," and other hits.

Then, in March of 1963, on the way back to Nashville from a benefit concert in Kansas City, she was killed in a plane crash along with fellow stars Hawkinshaw Hawkins and Cowboy Copas. Though her career ended there, her influence and popularity continue. The first female solo artist to be elected to the Country Music Hall of Fame (in 1973), she remains one of the best-loved country singers in history.

—Jessica Fisher

Belle Grove Plantation.

■ **BELLE GROVE PLANTATION** *map page 218, A-2*

Belle Grove Plantation sits in the middle of a rolling field below Middletown, 15 miles south of Winchester. Built in the late 1790s of limestone quarried on the property, the columned old house was the home of Maj. Isaac Hite Jr., James Madison's brother-in-law. Madison is said to have enlisted his friend Thomas Jefferson to help Hite with the design, and you can see Jeffersonian touches in Belle Grove's pavilions and its hidden staircase. Among the furnishings are several Madison family portraits by Charles Peale Polk and a linen press Hite ordered from a Winchester cabinetmaker. With two bedrooms and five rooms on the main floor, the house is not large, but considering that the valley was barely settled when it was built, you can see why it was once called "the most splendid building west of the Blue Ridge." In 1864, Belle Grove served as headquarters for the Union general Philip Sheridan and was in the thick of the Battle of Cedar Creek, Sheridan's decisive victory. *Route 11; 540-869-2028.*

(opposite) Antiquing is big in Strasburg, south of Middletown.

■ NEW MARKET BATTLEFIELD *map page 218, A-3*

In some ways, the Civil War still rages in the Valley of Virginia. Local buffs argue over exactly where battles took place, exactly who won them, and exactly who the true heroes were. One modern battleground is New Market Battlefield. For years, the Virginia Military Institute (VMI) has maintained the **New Market Battlefield State Historical Park** and the **Hall of Valor Civil War Museum,** which among other things extols the heroic contribution of its 247 teenage cadets to the 1864 Battle of New Market. Within the battlefield park, now beautiful and green and set off by split-rail fences, is the old Bushong farm, in whose orchard and pastures the battle took place. Its white clapboard house and nine reconstructed dependencies make a pastoral portrait most of the time, but every May the farm is the scene

VMI cadets at the Battle of New Market is the subject of Youth's Hour of Glory, *painted by Tom Lovell in 1964 and now hanging at the VMI Museum in Lexington.*

of renewed fighting, when latter-day Rebels and Yankees face off in a reenactment of the 1864 fray. *Route 305 (I-81, Exit 264); 540-740-3101.*

In recent years, however, another facility has opened nearby—the **New Market Battlefield Military Museum.** This columned roadside edifice displays some 2,500 artifacts from the Civil War era to the present, and it takes a somewhat different approach to the Battle of New Market. Its founder contends that the battlefield was actually on his property and hints that perhaps the role of the VMI cadets in the battle has been somewhat overplayed. In early 2003, the museum was for sale, and its future was somewhat in doubt, so call ahead before visiting. *Route 305; 540-740-8065.*

Perhaps you'll be able to take a look at both places and decide for yourself who is winning the new battle about the old battle of New Market. Most historians agree on these facts—that in May 1864, Confederate forces, reinforced by VMI cadets, bested Yankee troops that had entered the valley to disrupt Confederate supply and communication lines.

■ CAVERNS   *map page 218, A-3/5*

Of the many caverns that riddle central Virginia, **Luray Caverns** is the granddaddy of them all—and also very commercialized, drawing about half a million visitors a year. Its 64 underground acres of drip-castle stalactites, stalagmites, draperies, and flowstones do make for an awesome spectacle and have earned the caverns a Natural Landmark designation.

In 1878, an itinerant photographer and entrepreneur named Benton Stebbins, with the help of three local "partners," began exploring sinkholes in the region, thinking of the business possibilities of a cave. After weeks of searching, the Phantom Chasers, as locals called them, discovered a large one with promise—they could feel a stream of cool air blowing up from underground. Lowering themselves into it, they found themselves in the subterranean wonderland now called Luray Caverns. Recognizing the import of their discovery, the group kept quiet, and a month later bought the cave land at auction.

Within several months, Luray Caverns opened for business, and guided tours have been offered ever since. It's too bad, though, that the caverns aren't the way they were when the Phantom Chasers found them. Now a paved walkway interrupts the natural beauty, and glowing electric lights illuminate such spectacles as the Wishing Well, where coins sparkle. A wall of stalactites has even been turned

into pipes for the cavern's famous Great Stalactite Organ—nevertheless a fascinating contraption, invented by a Virginia mathematician in the 1950s. The guide on your tour may stop and serenade your group with a few notes.

The caverns are buried in a separate little pocket of land between the Blue Ridge and Massanutten Mountain. The latter, a wedge at the north end of the valley, cleaves the Shenandoah River into its North and South forks. Coming to Luray from the east or west on U.S. 211, you have some mountain roads to negotiate, though you can take Route 340 southwest from Front Royal. *I-81, Exit 264; 540-743-6551.*

If you continue south on Route 340, you'll come to **Grottoes.** Near the town a low formation called Cave Hill contains three caverns of note. Madison Cave, discovered around the time of the Revolution and described by Jefferson in his *Notes on the State of Virginia,* was visited—and autographed—by both Jefferson and Washington. Fountain Cave, found in 1835, was popular for some time, but today neither of these is open to the public. The best of all, and well worth a trip, is **Grand Caverns.**

In 1804 a young trapper named Bernard Weyer, seeking a trap that an animal had dragged off to an opening in the hill, found a staggeringly beautiful cavern. (The animal was variously reported to have been a groundhog, rabbit, skunk, muskrat, opossum, squirrel, bear, deer, raccoon, and porcupine.) This cavern was opened to the public in 1806, and articles and stories began to appear attesting to its beauty, its extent, and its fantastic features. Its large, gorgeous rooms with their high ceilings were often used for weddings and for church meetings complete with choir. In the 1830s an annual Great Illumination and Ball took place during the height of the season at the nearby mineral spring resorts, and the "Ball Room" filled with revelers, who ate and drank and danced to the music of a band by the light of 2,000 candles.

In the 1850s, David Hunter Strother, whose sketches and articles appeared in *Harper's Weekly* under the nom de plume of Porte Crayon, wrote:

> In the centre of this room hangs a mass of spar, which bears a fancied resemblance to a chandelier, while behind it rises the pulput, an elevated circular desk covered with the most graceful folds of white drapery. On the opposite side is a baldequin, enriched with glittering

The Double Column at Luray Caverns.

pendant crystals, and the whole ceiling is hung with stalactites dropping long points and broad wavy sheets, some of pure white…. These stone draperies are translucent and sonorous, emitting soft musical tones on being struck, and the heavier sheets which tapestry the side walls respond to the blows of the hand or foot with notes like deep-toned bells.

An article in *Parade* magazine published in 2002 named Grand the second-best caverns in the nation (after Carlsbad, New Mexico). The temperature is a steady 54 degrees, and in contrast to most caves, which are mainly "dead," having been touched and broken and too much visited, Grand Caverns remains 85 percent alive. The limestone-bearing water still seeps and drops, the formations slowly change, and in the hush of your visit you can imagine how it was eons ago. *I-81, Exit 235; 540-249-5705.*

■ **STAUNTON**   *map page 218, B-1*

Staunton (pronounced STANT-n)—along I-81 west of Charlottesville and north of Lexington—is a pretty place that doesn't try to define itself too narrowly. Though it was traditionally a farm town at the heart of agrarian Augusta County, it wasn't a backwater. In 1895, 35 trains a day passed through, downtown theaters offered 2,300 seats, and there were several schools and institutions. Nowadays, besides plenty of cap-wearing farmers driving pick-ups, its streets are alive with sophisticated retirees, teachers and students, and people involved in its burgeoning art and culture scene. The townsfolk here are particularly proud of their new Shakespeare theater—and of a bunch of local boys who made good, the Statler Brothers.

During the Civil War, five members of Staunton's Mountain Sax Band served in the Stonewall Brigade, and so the group later changed its name to the **Stonewall Brigade Band,** which is today the oldest publicly supported band in the nation. At the surrender at Appomattox, General Grant declined to confiscate the band's instruments as "spoils of war," a unifying gesture that bore the fruit of gratitude and good feelings and began a close relationship. The band played at Grant's inaugural parade in Washington and at his funeral and traveled to New York City to play at the dedication of his tomb. You can hear the band today in Gypsy Hill Park at the free concerts that take place on Mondays from June through August.

Around the old center of town, the hills are lined with Victorian houses and the creamy stuccoed buildings of **Mary Baldwin College,** a Southern girls' school in the haute tradition that has stepped into the 21st century without a tremor. Its offerings include the country's only all-female ROTC program, classes for exceptionally gifted children, and Shakespeare studies in collaboration with the Shenandoah Shakespeare company. *Frederick and North Coalter Streets.*

Across the street from Mary Baldwin stands the **Woodrow Wilson Birthplace.** Wilson, the son of a Presbyterian minister, was born here in 1856 but spent only 11 months in these genteel surroundings before his father was called to a church in Georgia. Nonetheless, Virginia seems to have held some claim on Wilson's soul. When he married his second wife, he chose to honeymoon at the Old Dominion's premier resort, the lavish Homestead. As he pulled up to its doors, the normally reserved Wilson could be heard singing "Oh, You Beautiful Doll" to his new bride.

Wilson's 1919 Pierce Arrow presidential limousine gleams in a glass-fronted garage that's even illuminated at night for drive-bys—but who can resist an up-close look? The museum just beyond the garage details his accomplishments as president and his vision of world peace. Park behind the house for the best view of the boxwood gardens that lead up to its rear porches. *18–24 North Coalter Street; 540-885-0897.*

The **Blackfriars Playhouse,** the home of Shenandoah Shakespeare, a highly regarded repertory group that specializes in producing Shakespeare's plays just as they would have been produced in Elizabethan times, has got people talking all over the valley. The company seamlessly transformed a building in downtown Staunton into an Elizabethan theater, a unique replica of Shakespeare's own indoor Blackfriars playhouse. Plays are performed here with the house lights on (in Shakespeare's time they weren't dimmed), and audience members can eat and drink at their seats. The actors perform on a central floor, and the audience surrounds it on three sides: at ground level, in raised tiers on the sides, and in the three-sided balcony. *10 South Market Street; 540-885-5588.*

Staunton has two wonderful B&Bs: the **Frederick House** (28 New Street; 540-885-4220), across from Mary Baldwin College, has rooms and suites in five restored houses that date from 1810 to 1910. The **Sampson-Eagon Inn** (238 East Beverley Street; 540-886-8200), across from the Woodrow Wilson Birthplace, is in a luxurious, antiques-filled antebellum mansion built in 1840.

At the southern edge of town, on the rambling grounds of the stellar **Frontier Culture Museum,** the state has re-created life on the farmsteads of Scots-Irish, American, German, and English settlers of the Shenandoah Valley. The museum

Shenandoah Shakespeare in action at the Blackfriars Playhouse.

did not reproduce these buildings, but actually transplanted them here, piece by piece—three from Europe and one from the valley itself. Wandering through them, you get a feel for the harsh realities of frontier life. The thatch-roofed, white-washed Scots-Irish cottage may look quaint, but imagine sharing it with your live-stock. Or consider the winter drafts that must have blown through the traditional American log house. *Route 250 (I-81, Exit 222); 540-332-7850.*

■ McCormick Farm   *map page 218, B-2*

Farther south, about halfway between Staunton and Lexington, standing in the shadow of the Blue Ridge, lie 634 acres that revolutionized agriculture. In 1831, a 22-year-old valley boy named Cyrus Hall McCormick, maybe tired of the laborious process of hand-reaping grain, figured out how to do it mechanically. McCormick's design for a horse-drawn mechanical reaper soon spread beyond the Valley of Virginia, opening up the country's vast western frontier with its simple technology and eventually benefiting the whole world.

McCormick's farm, also known as Walnut Grove, still holds the log workshop where young Cyrus tinkered. You can tour it and the blacksmith shop, museum, and grounds. The big overshot wheel of the family's stone mill turns picturesquely, and green fields stretch off around it. The farm, now a Shenandoah Valley Agricultural Research and Extension Center, a part of Virginia Tech, is the site of continuing research and education programs to improve agriculture and animal husbandry. *Route 606 (I-81, Exit 205); 540-377-2255.*

■ Lexington   *map page 218, B-3*

Of all Virginia's towns, this, in the end, may be the loveliest. About 30 miles south of Staunton off I-81, small, intimate Lexington stretches along a classic Main Street filled with the cafés, haberdasheries, and bookstores typical of a university town. Houses and public buildings from the early and mid-19th century line downtown and residential streets. Two redoubtable Virginia institutions overlook the town—Washington and Lee University and the Virginia Military Institute (VMI), each as essential to the state's identity as the dogwood.

The Maury River near Lexington.

■ WASHINGTON AND LEE UNIVERSITY

Washington and Lee stands amid stately oaks with perfectly articulated gentility. Begun in 1749 as Augusta Academy, a men's school, it was endowed by George Washington, whose name it now bears along with that of its most famous president, Robert E. Lee. Things have decidedly changed since Lee's time, because the school is now coed. Lee, the father of four daughters, no doubt would have approved.

Lee came here at war's end and never left. He is buried—and celebrated—in the campus's Victorian brick **Lee Chapel and Museum.** His office, on the lower level, remains intact, chairs still drawn up around a small conference table, and it's not hard to imagine the dignified, elderly Lee interviewing his students, explaining to them his simple code of behavior: "We have but one rule here...that every student must be a gentleman."

Down the hall from his office, in a family crypt, are Lee's remains and those of his wife, Mary. In the museum is the Washington-Custis-Lee collection of portraits, and in the chapel hang the famous Charles Willson Peale portrait of George Washington as a young man in uniform and the Theodore Pine portrait of Lee painted after Lee's death.

Behind the chapel sanctuary is a small room with the famous and beautiful white marble recumbent statue of Lee by the sculptor Edward Valentine. Uncle Robert, as his troops called him, lies with one hand on his chest, his features tranquil but craggy, like the terrain of an old battlefield. Outside the chapel, in a discreetly marked grave, are the remains of Lee's trusted horse, Traveller, reinterred here by the university in 1971.

The college was Lee's final home, when he had no other. He and his family came here virtually with nothing, and for the last five years of his life, from 1865 to 1870, he served as president. Those were taxing but apparently satisfying years. From here he exhorted his fellow Southerners to forget the past, become Americans again, and rebuild their dreams. He himself did that, turning this poor small college into a prestigious institution. Yet throughout those years Lee knew that at any moment he could be arrested and tried for treason. Instead, he was left in peace, and at age 63 he died of cerebral thrombosis in his home. The structure still stands on the campus, dignified, like the man himself. *Off Business Route 11; 540-458-8768 (chapel and museum).*

A statue of George Washington tops Washington Hall at Washington and Lee University.

The VMI Regimental Band plays in parades on post and around the world.

■ VIRGINIA MILITARY INSTITUTE

Virginia Military Institute butts right up against Washington and Lee, and entering its distinctly martial milieu causes an almost surreal mind shift. First-year cadets, called rats, chins tucked in and shoulders back, quickstep across the broad Parade Grounds in the shadow of turreted, Gothic military buildings. This bastion of soldierly male traditionalism, founded in 1839, lays claim to being the first state military college in the country. These days aspiring female candidates are allowed to join the cadet corps and are proving their mettle.

VMI is a place where nostalgia is thick on the ground, especially among alumni (who say "VMI is thicker than water"), and the institute venerates its heroes, two in particular. The **George C. Marshall Museum** (540-453-7103) traces the considerable contributions of this former cadet who went on to be army chief of staff, secretary of state, secretary of defense, and winner of the Nobel Peace Prize. A well-positioned statue and the **VMI Museum** commemorate the other hero, **Thomas Jonathan Jackson,** one of the school's 19th-century professors. Intensely private, devout, and so eccentric that his students called him "Tom Fool" Jackson, this unlikely soldier whose brilliance made him famous as "Stonewall" now stands forever surveying the comings and goings of cadets across the Parade Grounds. *Letcher Avenue off Business Route 11; 540-464-7334 (museum).*

■ STONEWALL JACKSON HOUSE

Jackson's simple brick town house, close to the VMI campus, mirrors in its modest but somewhat severe facade the character of the man himself. In the 1850s Jackson spent a happy interlude here, content to prepare his lectures on natural philosophy, read his Bible, dabble a bit in business, and listen to his wife, Mary Anna, play the piano in the parlor. The homey rooms are filled with Victorian furnishings and personal possessions that paint a softer, more intimate portrait of a man who, in war, was a martinet.

Jackson was 37 when he joined the Confederate cause. After his instant fame at the First Battle of Manassas, the newly christened Stonewall gradually became Lee's right hand. In his celebrated Valley Campaign, Jackson moved like no stone wall. Time and again he used daring, speed, and his knowledge of the terrain to evade or repulse Union troops that far outnumbered him.

He never lived to see the end of the war, dying in 1863 of complications suffered from a wound inadvertently inflicted by his own men. Even today, they say in the valley that if Stonewall had not fallen in the Battle of Chancellorsville, the war might have gone another way. *8 East Washington Street; 540-463-2552.*

Thomas Jonathan "Stonewall" Jackson.

Around the corner from Jackson's house is the **Willson-Walker House,** whose graceful porticos and classical pediment have adorned Main Street since 1820, by turns as a private residence, a meat market and grocery store, and student apartments. These days, it's an elegant restaurant, where you can find a good meal at lunch or dinner. *30 North Main Street; 540-463-3020.*

Stonewall Jackson lives on at Lexington's **Lime Kiln Theatre,** which every summer season presents *Stonewall Country* and other dramas in an appealing outdoor setting. The thick stone walls of the open-air, earth-floor theater are the remains of an old lime kiln—the setting alone is dramatic. Route 60W (I-81, Exit 188B); 540-463-3074.

■ **NATURAL BRIDGE** *map page 218, B-4*

Natural Bridge has been called many things: "Bridge of Gods" by the Monacan Indians; one of the Seven Wonders of the Natural World (who picks these wonders, anyway?); and "the most sublime of nature's works," by Thomas Jefferson. So impressed was he by this arc of rock measuring 215 feet high and 90 feet across that he purchased it and patented the surrounding 157 acres "for twenty shillings of good and lawful money." But even before Jefferson fell in love with it, George Washington had surveyed it and had, indeed, carved his initials in it.

The bridge rises sublimely above wooded Cedar Creek, its top traversed by Route 11. Still privately owned—though not by Jefferson's descendants—the bridge is operated as a public attraction. In other words, you have to pay a fee now to worship at the Bridge of Gods. Continue on the path past the bridge to the Monacan Indian Village, where interesting demonstrations of ancient skills and domestic tasks take place. *Route 11 and Route 130, about 15 miles southwest of Lexington; 540-291-2121.*

The approach to Natural Bridge is scarred by graffiti and roadside souvenir stands today, yet down below, some of the sylvan beauty portrayed in this 19th-century etching still remains.

Natural Bridge.

The Night I Stayed Too Late

When she was in her twenties, author Annie Dillard lived a year by Tinker Creek, in a valley in Virginia's Blue Ridge, observing nature, reading, and taking notes. Pilgrim at Tinker Creek, *the Pulitzer Prize–winning reflection on the natural world that took shape over those four seasons, has been compared to Thoreau's* Walden.

Where Tinker Creek flows under the sycamore log bridge to the tear-shaped island, it is slow and shallow, fringed thinly in cattail marsh. At this spot an astonishing bloom of life supports vast breeding populations of insects, fish, reptiles, birds, and mammals. On windless summer evenings I stalk along the creek bank or straddle the sycamore log in absolute stillness, watching for muskrats. The night I stayed too late I was hunched on the log staring spellbound at spreading, reflected stains of lilac on the water. A cloud in the sky suddenly lighted as if turned on by a switch; its reflection just as suddenly materialized on the water upstream, flat and floating, so that I couldn't see the creek bottom, or life in the water under the cloud. Downstream, away from the cloud on the water, water turtles smooth as beans were gliding down with the current in a series of easy, weightless push-offs, as men bound on the moon. I didn't know whether to trace the progress of one turtle I was sure of, risking sticking my face in one of the bridge's spider webs made invisible by the gathering dark, or take a chance on seeing the carp, or scan the mudbank in hope of seeing a muskrat, or follow the last of the swallows who caught at my heart and trailed it after them like streamers as they appeared from directly below, under the log, flying upstream with their tails forked, so fast.

—Annie Dillard, *Pilgrim at Tinker Creek,* 1974

■ SHENANDOAH NATIONAL PARK AND SKYLINE DRIVE
map page 218, A-2/4 and B-1

One of America's most popular parks, Shenandoah National Park is a gentle place, draped across the top of the Blue Ridge. Its quiet forests and deer-dotted meadows lie along the deservedly famous Skyline Drive. Meandering along the crest of the Blue Ridge, the drive runs from Front Royal south for 105 miles to Waynesboro, with ample places to pull over and gaze down on the serpentine course of the Shenandoah River or across a precipice into an intriguing hollow.

The hollows are unpeopled today, but it was not always so. Before the Skyline Drive was built, in the 1930s, this terrain was wild and remote, the home of mountaineers. Many made a hardscrabble living off the area's abundant chestnut trees, but the chestnut blight of the 1920s and 1930s put an end to that.

Change came first with an entrepreneur named George Pollock, who inherited a mountaintop near Luray and turned it into Skyland, a resort frequented by statesmen and presidents. The way up to Pollock's Skyland was rough in those days and the accommodations rustic, but that apparently was part of the appeal. Nightly entertainment centered around a campfire where live snakes were exhibited and Pollock showed off his marksmanship. Pollock's showmanship brought notice to the area, and in 1926 Congress authorized the establishment of Shenandoah National Park. Ten years later, Franklin D. Roosevelt sent the Civilian Conservation Corps in to build the Skyline Drive.

The park is mostly pristine mountain land, though it does have several developed areas with visitor facilities, including an updated version of Pollock's Skyland, where the entertainment is considerably milder. Many of the park's trails follow what were once the main roads through these gaps and hollows, and part of the **Appalachian Trail,** the Maine-to-Georgia hikers' highway, parallels the Skyline Drive through the park.

You can still find traces of the mountaineers' handiwork here and there. Close by a streambed, you may discover an old homestead, marked now only by a neatly chinked chimney or a stone fence. If you look closely, you're likely to see an apple tree or two at its edges and maybe the shoots of a hardy iris, planted who knows how long ago.

On a fine fall day, you can feel something of what the mountaineers had here in the Blue Ridge. Around you, invisible choruses of crickets ring out their year-end swan song; streams shush across moss-draped stones and past dark hemlock groves;

and any light breeze will set a blizzard of colored leaves falling. Above the canopy, crows croak reassuringly and wide-winged turkey buzzards wheel and dip. If you move quietly, you might see a deer or two gazing warily in your direction, their coats so blended with the forest that they recall poet Vachel Lindsay's "phantom deer" who arise with "all lost, wild America…shining in their eyes." *Off I-81; 540-999-3500.*

■ BLUE RIDGE PARKWAY   *map page 218, B-1–B-5*

The Blue Ridge Parkway continues south where the Skyline Drive leaves off. From Rockfish Gap, near Waynesboro, it follows the crest of the Blue Ridge through southwestern Virginia for a long, lovely 355 miles, then crosses into North Carolina and keeps going for another 114 miles. Part of the national park system, it contains the typical interpretive sites, lodges, and campgrounds, all done in classic Park Service style—professional but slightly homogenized. But if you hike half a mile off the road, you'll find terrain alive with possums, deer, and the occasional black bear, thickets of mountain laurel, and stands of oak and hemlock. From Rockfish Gap almost to Roanoke, the Appalachian Trail closely parallels the parkway, so walking the Blue Ridge is an option.

The scenic parkway is not the fast road to anywhere. The speed limit never exceeds 45 mph and is frequently less. Because you can get on and off the parkway at various points, many drivers choose to do a sort of Sunday drive, then return to the flatlands when they need to make time.

The parkway's northern section contains several sites worth a stop. At **Humpback Rocks** (Mile 6) a re-created mountain farmstead includes a windowless one-room log cabin, a weasel-proof chicken house, a barn, and other small outbuildings moved here from old farms in the area.

Down the road from the farmstead rise the 3,080-foot Humpback Rocks themselves, long a landmark along the old Howardsville Turnpike, a wagon trail through the mountains. Twisting through pleasant forests, the trail to the rocks climbs about 700 feet in just under a mile. School groups, young families, and fit seniors huff up the trail in determined hordes on any pretty weekend. At the top they're rewarded with a hawk's-eye view of the Shenandoah Valley to the west and the lower ranges rolling down into the Piedmont to the east. Even with the crowds, the sun-warmed slabs of rock make a fine place to lie back and enjoy the Virginia mountains.

Mountain laurel.

The James River Canal near the mouth of the North River was built by slaves and Irish immigrants.

Another 57 miles down the parkway, the character of the land changes briefly where the James River passes through on its way from the Appalachian hinterland to Tidewater and the Chesapeake Bay. Trees stand statuesque along grassy banks, while the river swirls sedately. As placid as it looks, however, it proved a cantankerous foe to the 19th-century canal builders who tried to tame it through here.

An old restored lock still stands just below the parkway, a remnant of the battle fought to make this river behave in accord with man's commercial agenda. Naturally, it was George Washington, the Great Canal Builder, who pressed for a canal system along the James to link the coast to the lucrative lands of the West. By the turn of the 19th century, the James River Canal had conquered the falls at Richmond, but the going was slow after that. Funds were hard to come by and control over what had become known as the James River and Kanawha Canal (after the Kanawha River in what is now West Virginia) passed back and forth between private owners and the state. The work of cutting a canal through mountain wilderness was backbreaking. Slave owners hired out their men for some of the work, but by the mid-1830s, two-thirds of the workers were Irish immigrants.

Blue Ridge Mountains.

Not until 1851 did the canal finally slice through the Blue Ridge, connecting Lynchburg with Buchanan. (John Marshall, chief justice of the U.S. Supreme Court, served as head of the project early in the 19th century.) After Buchanan, the builders pressed on, hoping to complete the system far into the West, where it would link with the Kanawha River, and thus the whole Ohio River system. But that never happened. A monumental war and the coming of the Iron Horse brought a slow death to the canal concept. By the 1880s, the James River and Kanawha Canal had become another relic of Virginia history.

From the James, one of the lowest elevations on the parkway, the road quickly climbs to its highest. At 3,950 feet, it's not exactly startling, but then the Blue Ridge is made up of old soft-sloping mountains, worn by the ages into a kind of gentle roundness. You can sense their time-taught patience particularly around the **Peaks of Otter** (540-586-1081), a managed area about 20 miles farther along at Milepost 86. Run by the Park Service, it has a pleasant lakeside lodge with spectacular views and a campground, boat rentals, and fishing—it's a place weekenders drive to for a mountain experience. The peaks rise above Abbott Lake on three sides, though it would be unforgivable hyperbole to say they hem it in.

World War II Veteran John Talton at the National D-Day Memorial overlooking Bedford. His Naval Combat Demolition Unit was in the first wave to hit Omaha Beach that day, June 6, 1944, and suffered 50 percent casualties.

The most famous of the peaks, **Sharp Top,** projects a stony crown into the sky, and busloads of tourists take the shuttle that winds to its summit. From here you can see, as the song says, for miles and miles and miles and miles. The 360-degree view even takes in the distant Alleghenies, pressed like shadows against the western horizon. **Flat Top,** at 4,004 feet the highest of the three peaks (elevation gain, 1,600 feet in 4.4 miles) is accessible by trail only, as is **Harkening Hill,** whose trail is designated "steep and strenuous."

The Blue Ridge Parkway begins near Shenandoah National Park (Mile Post 0); 828-271-4779.

The classic Virginia town of **Bedford** is nestled in the hills just below the peaks. If you're ready to get off the parkway, you can take Route 43 for 10 miles from the Peaks entrance down into this steepled, gracious little place.

There's a newly finished National D-Day Memorial here, honoring the veterans and dead. Bedford County suffered more losses on that momentous day than any other county in the nation. U.S. 460 and Route 43; 540-586-3329.

■ THE HOMESTEAD *map pages 264–265, E-2*

Over the past two centuries, the hills of Virginia have been home to dozens of spa resorts, where the weary, the ailing, or simply the self-indulgent came to soothe their aching bones in warm mineral waters and in all manner of sulfur springs, soda springs, and cold springs. Many of these resorts—especially those built on cold or smelly waters—burned down or closed their doors long ago. A few were retrofitted as nursing homes or retreats. Happily, though, the Homestead, the grande dame of them all, managed to survive into the present.

An immense and dignified brick edifice ensconced in the heart of the Alleghenies, the Homestead reigns over—or more precisely, is the raison d'être of—the little village of Hot Springs. Skirted by iridescent green golf courses, the resort was probably best described by President Lyndon Johnson, who declared something along the lines of "My God, what a spread!" In all, the Homestead covers 15,000 acres, and with tennis courts, swimming pools, stables, riding and carriage trails, skeet and trap fields, ski runs, mineral bath spas, and even wooded nature trails, there's always something to do. Three venerable golf courses include an 1892 original—the Old Course. The spirit of native Sam Snead, the "local boy" who became one of golf's greatest legends, is strong about the place.

For all its grandeur, the Homestead exhibits nary a trace of hauteur, retaining instead a down-home air. The veranda along the entrance feels like a front porch, complete with a line of rockers facing out to the grounds. The great hall, where tea and piano music are enjoyed every afternoon, stretches in a long double corridor overlooking the veranda, with groups of wing chairs, two fireplaces, and a row of Corinthian columns separating the strollers from the sitters.

Mineral springs, of course, spawned this living legend of a place. As far back as 7000 B.C., indigenous people had discovered the area's hot springs. Early in the 1700s, white explorers filtered into the area, but it was not until 1766 that a rustic guest lodge called the Homestead was put up. In 1832 Dr. Thomas Goode, from a well-established Virginia family, enlarged the hotel, built cabins and bathhouses, and began to attract people from as far away as Philadelphia, New York, and New Orleans.

During the Civil War the hotel never closed, and though records of those years have been lost, it probably was a place of recuperation for wounded soldiers. At war's end, the hotel saw a period of decline, but it slowly reestablished its reputation as a watering hole for the well-heeled, and by the 20th century, Vanderbilts,

Rockefellers, and Fords were entertaining here. In 1901, the old clapboard hotel burned to the ground, a fate that overtook so many hotels of the era. The new brick structure that began to go up within a year is still part of the hotel, with many additions and modifications, including its hallmark tower.

One remarkable feature that remains is the indoor tiled pool, where light pouring in from surrounding windows creates an ethereal atmosphere. The pool was built in 1903 in the 1892 spa structure, which survived the fire and now, beautifully restored, caters to guests with luxurious modern health and beauty treatments. *Main Street (U.S. 220), Hot Springs; 540-839-1766.*

■ **JEFFERSON POOLS** *map pages 264–265, E-2*
The historic Jefferson Pools, part of the Homestead, lie 5 miles north of the main complex in the hamlet of Warm Springs. Settled in 1727, it was a bustling little place by mid-century and by 1800 a sought-after resort. The mineral waters attracted all sorts of Virginians, including Thomas Jefferson, who once spent 22 days here and at the Homestead and emerged believing that his rheumatism had been not at all improved.

In those days, gentlemen and ladies took turns taking the waters, two hours for one, then two hours for the other. Today, there are separate bathhouses. For the modest, bathing suits are an option, as is the quaint costume called the Mother Hubbard romper suit. Provided to ladies free of charge, these short one-piece cover-ups recall the days when Mrs. Robert E. Lee came here to take the waters for her crippling arthritis. The chair in which they lowered her is on display inside the bathhouse.

About the bathhouses: These two white clapboard buildings charm with an aged beauty. The octagonal men's spa dates from 1761, and the women's, which is round, from 1836. Simple structures built above large mineral pools, they are filled with natural light streaming in from skylights to pierce the chest-deep water and highlight the colors of the stones lining the bottom. The water temperature here is a constant 98 degrees.

(opposite) Route 220 near Hot Springs.
(following pages) The Jefferson Pools at Warm Springs.

VIRGINIA HOSPITALITY

Jollity, the offspring of wisdom and good living!—Raleigh Tavern Motto

Virginians consider hospitality an art form, requiring a well-developed sense of the aesthetic. They will welcome you with heartfelt cordiality and a generous spirit, and some of them, particularly in the Tidewater and the Piedmont, will treat you to a taste of the fine old Virginia traditions—traditions that, sadly, are quickly passing into oblivion. After all, polishing heirloom silver and ironing heirloom linen (with little rolling irons so the hand-embroidery won't tear) are labor-intensive jobs. It's doubtful that such niceties will survive the post-historic high-tech world of the new century. So, for posterity, herewith are a few of the traditions that have made Virginia hospitality legendary.

First, the pineapple: This ancient symbol of fertility became a popular design element in 17th-century England, and in Virginia and other colonies the fruit came to symbolize hospitality. Its carved image was mounted over doorways and on furniture and hung outside inns.

At Christmas, the fruit makes a comeback, serving as a centerpiece on holiday tables. Christmas, being a season of both tradition and hospitality, is generally celebrated in high style. Pine garlands drape staircases, and magnolia, holly, boxwood, and cedar adorn doorways and mantels. Smithfield hams and their country cousins (raised and cured around Smithfield, Virginia) become the highlight of linen-draped buffet tables, the red meat carved paper thin and served with beaten biscuits. Polished pewter Jefferson cups (small, stemless, and handleless) gleam on sideboards, and punch bowls hold frothy, fumingly potent eggnog. Oysters too, scalloped or in thick, white stews, steam in bowls. Little dishes of salted Virginia peanuts are set about to keep appetites whetted and to dilute the effects of the before-dinner "bourbon and branch." (This last word derives from branch water. The name sticks, though these days Virginians do take the water from the tap—or even a bottle—rather than the stream out back.) After dinner, guests can expect classic Southern desserts—pecan or mincemeat pie and plum pudding.

In spring and summer, life becomes more casual and Virginians look to the Chesapeake Bay to supply the food for fish fries, clam bakes, and crab feasts. That exceptional gourmet treat, the sweet flesh of the blue crab, is best picked hot from the shell, dipped in butter, and eaten immediately by the picker. There are other ways to enjoy crab: in big, succulent crab cakes; as spicy deviled crab; as crab

Norfolk—backfin lump panned in butter; as crab imperial; and as delicately sautéed soft crabs. As for fish, there are flounder, spot, croaker, and in the fall, huge blues and rock fish. The fish usually come accompanied by homemade cornbread or custardy spoon bread, sliced tomatoes, cucumbers marinated in sugared vinegar, deviled eggs, fried okra, and robust potato salads.

Cookbooks abound with Virginia recipes, so even non-Virginians can attempt the culinary creations for which the state is justly famous. A few family favorites:

CORNBREAD

The secret to good cornbread is an iron skillet. Preheat your oven to 450 degrees and coat an iron skillet with 2 tsp. of vegetable oil. (Though hardly traditional, canola oil works well.) Put the skillet in the oven and let the oil heat as you continue.

Mix 2 eggs with 2 cups of nonfat buttermilk and a pinch of baking soda. Blend in 2 cups of white, self-rising cornmeal, and salt to taste. Pour batter into hot pan and bake about 20 minutes, until the top is slightly brown.

CRAB IMPERIAL

Pick through and remove any stray shell from 1 lb. of crabmeat (backfin preferable). Make a roux of 1 T. butter and 1 T. flour; add ½ cup milk and heat, stirring, till it bubbles and thickens. Add 1 tsp. minced onion, 1½ tsp. Worcestershire sauce, and 2 slices of white bread, cubed. Let cool. Stir in ½ cup mayonnaise, juice of half a lemon, ½ tsp. salt, and a few dashes of pepper.

In another pan, melt 2 T. butter and toss the crabmeat in it carefully, so the lumps don't break up. Gently combine crab with bread mixture and pour into a buttered baking dish or individual ramekins. Sprinkle with paprika, and bake in a preheated 450-degree oven for 10–15 minutes, till it bubbles and browns.

EGGNOG—FOR THE SPIRITED

Separate 6 eggs. Whip the yolks and slowly add to them 6 T. rum and 6 T. sugar. Set aside. Whip ½ pint whipping cream until it forms soft peaks and set aside. Whip the 6 egg whites until stiff. Gently fold the whipped cream into the egg yolk mixture, then the egg whites. Add to this ½ cup bourbon and about 1 pint of milk, to the desired consistency. Pour into a punch bowl and sprinkle the top with nutmeg. (If you worry about eating raw eggs, this may not be the beverage for you.)

WEST BY SOUTHWEST

From the rough scarp of the Alleghenies along Virginia's western flank to the Blue Ridge Highlands that roll south to North Carolina and Tennessee, this area is Virginia's hinterland. Nevertheless, a cross-section of people—coal miners, truckers, tobacco farmers, and small-town professionals—live and mind their own businesses here, apparently happy to remain undiscovered and left alone. Interstate 81 cuts a line through the quadrant, breaking its longtime isolation and paralleling Route 11, the modern-day name for the centuries-old "great wagon road" followed by Scots-Irish, Germans, and religious nonconformists who poured down the valley from Pennsylvania in the 18th and 19th centuries. Here and there a few picture-perfect towns sprout, but the genteel tone of the Shenandoah and the Piedmont is not the predominant voice.

Coal and railroads brought a quick prosperity to much of this area in the late 1800s, and although the boom was short-lived, mining and railroading remain economic backbones. And they've generated some compelling by-products— rough-and-tumble pockets of coal country with their own distinctive character, and a few urbane spots where the money of industry oils the local culture. Nowadays a new tourist trade, fueled by country music, is burgeoning.

If Virginia has an "empty quarter," it's the state's southwest corner, surrounded by Kentucky, West Virginia, Tennessee, and North Carolina. On leisurely Route 11 and the snaking back roads, you come upon pockets of classic hill country— images that stay with you: a stripy log cabin, its chimney serenely smoking in the mist, black-and-white cows grazing in the shadow of the Alleghenies; a small-time tobacco farm warped into a hillside, its weathered, earth-brown barns hung with bundles of the drying, burnished leaves. You share the twists and bends of these back roads with high-sided coal trucks that shuffle along like big dumb beasts. To them, cars are of no more consequence than an ant to an elephant. Be forewarned: The laws are a little different in these parts. The beasts have the right-of-way, no matter what the rules of the road say.

Falling Springs, Alleghany County, in May.

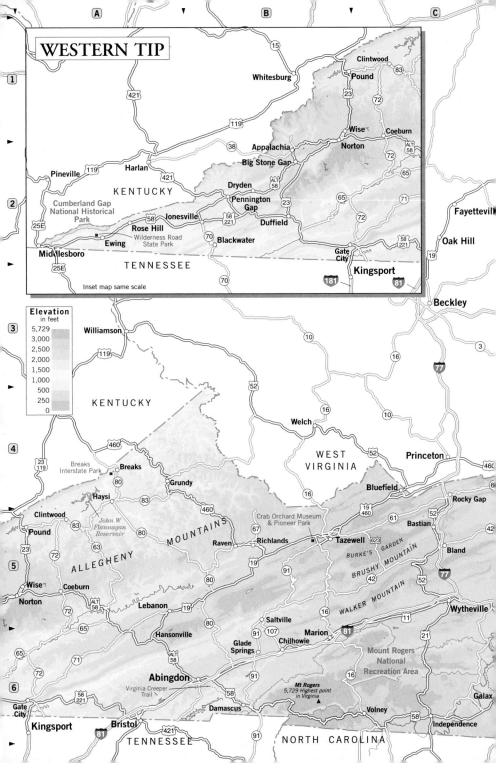

FIGHTING ON THE VIRGINIA FRONTIER

After attacks by the French and Indians on the Virginia frontier in 1755, the Virginia militia was in dire need of volunteers. Samuel Davies, a noted Presbyterian educator, made this appeal in 1758 and stimulated such a rush of recruits that some had to be turned away.

Ye young and hardy men, whose very faces seem to speak that God and nature formed you for soldiers, who are free from the encumbrance of families depending upon you for subsistence, and who are perhaps but of little service to society while at home, may I not speak for you and declare as your mouth, "Here we are, all ready to abandon our ease and rush into the glorious dangers of the field, in defense of our country?" Ye that love your country, enlist, for honor will follow you in life or death in such a cause. You that love your religion, enlist; for your religion is in danger. Can Protestant Christianity expect quarters from heathen savages and French Papists? Sure in such an alliance, the powers of hell make a third party. Ye that love your friends and relations, enlist; lest ye see them enslaved or butchered before your eyes. Ye that would catch at money, here is a proper bait for you—£10 for a few months' service, besides the usual pay of soldiers.

Perhaps some may object that should they enter the army their morals would be in danger of infection, and their virtue would be perpetually shocked with horrid scenes of vice....I wish I could remove it by giving you a universal assurance that the army is a school of religion and that soldiers, as they are more exposed to death than other men, are proportionably better prepared for it than others. But, alas! the reverse of this is too true; and the contagion of vice and irreligion is perhaps nowhere stronger than in the army; where, one would think, the Supreme Tribunal should be always in view, and it should be their chief care to prepare for eternity, on the slippery brink of which they stand every moment.

But, Gentlemen Officers, I must again appeal to you that, as for this company, you will not willingly allow any form of vice to be practised in it with impunity, but will always endeavor to recommend and enforce religion and good morals by your example and authority and to suppress the contrary.

—Rev. Samuel Davies, *The Curse of Cowardice*, 1758

Washington on His Mission to Ohio *during the French and Indian War. These early battles gave George Washington the experience necessary to fight the British army in the Revolution years later.*

■ BLUE RIDGE PARKWAY   *map pages 264–265, F-2–D-6*

You've left the Peaks of Otter behind and are meandering south on the Blue Ridge Parkway toward Roanoke, through the Jefferson National Forest. Before turning in to the city, though, take a short detour to see Virginia's **Explore Park** (Milepost 115; 540-427-1800), an outdoor living-history museum whose three areas are set up to illustrate early Native American life (1671), pre-Revolutionary frontier life (1740), and the rural mid–19th century. One exhibit explains the significance of batteaux, the flat cargo vessels used on rivers and canals. The batteau operators, many of them free black men but some of them slaves, were so important to the economy that special laws were passed to govern their travel and work. Besides taking in history at the park, you can also fish, hike, and mountain bike, and dine in a 19th-century tavern.

A little farther south on the parkway, you'll come to **Roanoke Mountain** and its scenic loop road. The Fishburn Parkway spur takes you into town, and on the way you can visit the **Mill Mountain Zoo** (Mill Mountain Park; 540-343-3241) and walk to the observation platform of the **Mill Mountain Star** (Mill Mountain Park; 540-342-6025), a huge neon-illuminated star visible all over Roanoke, from which you can see forever.

■ ROANOKE   *map pages 264–265, E-4*

Roanoke has a population of about 100,000 and a decidedly forward-looking focus. An upbeat, innovative old railroad town, the "Capital of the Blue Ridge" has transformed its downtown into an inviting mecca. Take Jefferson Street, the city's main stem, which tunnels through mid-century office buildings and storefronts, turn east on Campbell Avenue, and you're in the heart of the action at the vintage **Farmer's Market** (Campbell Avenue and Market Street; 540-342-2028), where from Monday through Saturday, vendors in outdoor stalls sell produce, jams, hams, flowers, honey, and crafts. Across the street, the city's old enclosed marketplace operates now as a food court and bevy of boutiques, where loose-fitting African- and Asian-print dresses flutter in shop windows.

The flavor of downtown Roanoke is distinctly artsy, thanks in large part to its pièce de résistance, **Center in the Square** (1 Market Square; 540-342-5700). Once a warehouse, the four-story L-shaped building was converted into an arts center in the early 1980s, and now a theater, several museums, and a garage make use of the space.

The Market Street area of downtown Roanoke at dusk.

The **Mill Mountain Theatre** serves up a theatrical smorgasbord—new and old dramas, comedies, musicals, Shakespeare, even experimental productions. *Center in the Square, Campbell Avenue; 540-342-5740*

The center's museum line-up includes the student-oriented **Science Museum of Western Virginia** (540-342-5726), on the fourth and fifth floors, which focuses on flora, fauna, ecology, computers, and the stars. The **Art Museum of Western Virginia** (540-342-5760), on the first and second floors, is a showcase for the works of up-and-coming artists in the southern Appalachians but also displays art from around the world. Exhibits at the third-floor **History Museum of Western Virginia** (540-342-5770) start with the region's Stone Age cultures, move through the days when the place was no more than a salt marsh crossroads called Big Lick, and then into the railroad heyday of the 19th century.

In 1882, railroad entrepreneur Frederick J. Kimball played out his dream of combining two railroads that crossed at Big Lick and starting a city at their junction. Largely because of the newly created Norfolk & Western, the junction soon grew into the city of Roanoke. Celebrating that heritage a few blocks northwest of Center on the Square in the former N&W freight station is the **Virginia Museum**

FARM FRESH
EGGS
1.75 dz.

WERTZ'S
Country Ham
Biscuit Slices

WERTZ'S
FULLY COOKED
COUNTRY HAM

WERTZ'S
FULLY COOKED
SLICED
COUNTRY HAM

WERTZ'S
Country Cured
Ham Hock

of Transportation. Exhibits here include old trucks, carriages, antique automobiles, a rocket, and planes. There's a model-train layout, a large collection of diesel engines, and a couple of first-class steam locomotives built in town. A permanent exhibit describes the role African-Americans played within the N&W from 1930 to 1970. Some of the rolling stock, displayed in the rail yard under a brand-new pavilion, can be boarded, so you can wander around in the old passenger cars and cabooses. *303 Norfolk Avenue; 540-342-5670.*

On a hill near the tracks, Kimball built a grand railroad hotel and, being a modest man, named it the **Hotel Roanoke,** not the Kimball. It was an immediate success, filled with businesspeople from all over, vacationers looking for cool mountain air, and local gentry attending meetings, parties, and dances. In the 1930s it acquired a distinctive, half-timbered Tudor-style facade. The hotel closed in 1989, but after a renovation and the addition of a conference center, it is once again open and *the* place to stay in town. *110 Shenandoah Avenue; 540-985-5900.*

The Center in the Square's latest project is the restoration of the Roanoke Passenger Station, across from the hotel and designed by Raymond Loewy in the 1940s. It will become the **O. Winston Link Museum,** dedicated to the works of the man who photographed the Norfolk & Western Railway, and should be open by early 2004, sharing space with the Roanoke Convention and Visitors Bureau. *209 Shenandoah Avenue.*

About 1.5 miles to the southwest—take Campbell Avenue SW to Fifth Street SW—in the **Old Southwest Historic District,** you can get a clear picture of the prosperity the railroads spawned. Columned, turreted, verandaed mansions dignify the streets of this part of town, listed in the Virginia Landmarks Register and the National Register of Historic Places.

At the other end of town, on the ground floor of the first black public high school in western Virginia, is the **Harrison Museum of African American Culture,** which celebrates the achievements of African-Americans, particularly of this region, and surveys African-American culture in general. Memorabilia, photographs, and artifacts are on exhibit, and the museum periodically sponsors festivals and other special events. *523 Harrison Avenue NW; 540-345-4818.*

(opposite) Roanoke's Farmer's Market has been in continuous operation since 1882.

■ FINCASTLE *map pages 264–265, E-4*

Before you leave the Roanoke area, take a drive north on U.S. 220 to historic Fincastle, the seat of Botetourt County (pronounced BOTTA-tot) and a virtual museum of architecture. This colonial town, incorporated in 1772, and the county, established two years earlier, were named for English lords who were, respectively, lieutenant governor and governor general of Virginia. At the time, Botetourt County was a vast tract comprising present-day Kentucky, much of West Virginia, Ohio, Indiana, and Illinois, and part of Wisconsin—territory then inhabited mainly by animals and Indians. At the **Botetourt County Museum,** in the old courthouse complex, a group of charming brick buildings shaded by huge trees, you can see a wonderful collection of articles owned over the last 250 years by local people and learn some of the town's history. Get a walking-tour map, which will guide you to all the interesting 18th- and 19th-century houses and shops in town, many of them log buildings later covered with clapboard or shingles. *Courthouse Square; 540-473-8394.*

■ BOOKER T. WASHINGTON NATIONAL MONUMENT
map pages 264–265, E-5

The Booker T. Washington National Monument stands in stark contrast to urbane Roanoke. Here, in the countryside 20 miles south of the city (take Route 116 to Route 122), tumbling meadowlands ripple off into forests that sweeten the air. The air must have smelled even sweeter in Booker Taliaferro Washington's day, but the air would have been all that was sweet for this boy slave. When you visit his birthplace, the old Burroughs tobacco farm, you are struck by the poverty and yearning that must have shaped this great man's early life. Born into slavery in 1856, he lived out his first nine years here, sharing a tiny one-room cabin with his mother and siblings. Laws barred him from being educated at all, but the boy had a yearning to learn: "From the time that I can remember having any thoughts about anything, I recall that I had an intense longing to learn to read." Happily for Washington, he was born on the cusp of change, and when the Emancipation Proclamation was finally read to area slaves in 1865, Booker and his family found themselves free.

They migrated to Malden, West Virginia, and the boy took work in local salt and coal mines and managed to attend school as well. One day, he overheard miners describing a school devoted to black education in Hampton, Virginia, and the young Washington "resolved at once to go to that school." And so at 16, he took an eastbound stagecoach, heading in the general direction of Virginia. But early in his pilgrimage he ran out of money and took to walking and "begging rides" all the way to Richmond. Here, hungry and penniless, he took work as a dockhand loading pig iron onto an outgoing ship. To save money, he slept underneath the board sidewalk, something he recalled years later when he was feted in Richmond as a celebrity.

When he finally made it to the doors of the Hampton Normal and Agricultural Institute, he looked, according to his own description, like a tramp. The head teacher apparently had serious doubts about admitting him, and so she set him to cleaning the school's recitation room. This he did—dusting and sweeping it several times before asking her to inspect it. She was impressed enough with his thoroughness to admit him, and he became what he had dreamed of becoming—a student.

In his autobiography, *Up From Slavery,* Washington recounts with humor and grace those hard early years, relating heartfelt stories of slave life and of his new life in Hampton. So different was the one from the other that he confessed he didn't even know how to sleep correctly at the institute. "The sheets were quite a puzzle to me," he recalled. "The first night I slept under both of them, and the second night I slept on top of both of them."

Once finished with his studies in Hampton, he returned to Malden to teach, then went on for more schooling at the Wayland Institute in Washington, D.C. In 1879, his mentor in Hampton, Samuel Armstrong, called him back to help in the institute's experiment in educating American Indians. After two years, Armstrong approached Washington with another project. A new black school was being established in Tuskegee, Alabama, and the search was on to find someone to head it. Would Washington like to be considered?

Tuskegee Institute became Booker T. Washington's life work. Over the course of more than 30 years, he took it from a place where classes were held in a "shanty" to a distinguished institution. In the process, he established his reputation as a leading educator and social thinker. Washington was often criticized for being too conservative, for conceding too much to segregationists, and for conciliating powerful whites, but in later life he seems to have shifted his thinking, for he spoke out against racism and joined ranks with his former critics, moving away from some of his earlier policies. As much as his life and accomplishments have been written

CHILDHOOD IN THE SLAVE QUARTERS

Of my ancestry I know almost nothing. In the slave quarters, and even later, I heard whispered conversations among the coloured people of the tortures which the slaves, including, no doubt, my ancestors on my mother's side, suffered in the middle passage of the slave ship while being conveyed from Africa to America. I have been unsuccessful in securing any information that would throw any accurate light upon the history of my family beyond my mother. She, I remember, had a half-brother and a half-sister. In the days of slavery not very much attention was given to family history and family records—that is, black family records. My mother, I suppose, attracted the attention of a purchaser who was afterward my owner and hers. Her addition to the slave family attracted about as much attention as the purchase of a new horse or cow. Of my father I know even less than of my mother. I do not even known his name. I have heard reports to the effect that he was a white man who lived on one of the near-by plantations. Whoever he was, I never heard of his taking the least interest in me or providing in any way for my rearing. But I do not find especial fault with him. He was simply another unfortunate victim of the institution which the Nation unhappily had engrafted upon it at that time.

The cabin was not only our living-place, but was also used as the kitchen for the plantation. My mother was the plantation cook. The cabin was without glass windows; it had only openings in the side which let in the light, and also the cold, chilly air of winter. There was a door to the cabin—that is, something that was called a door—but the uncertain hinges by which it was hung, and the large cracks in it, to say nothing of the fact that it was too small, made the room a very uncomfortable one. In addition to these openings there was, in the lower right-hand corner of the room, the "cat-hole,"—a contrivance which almost every mansion or cabin in Virginia possessed during the ante-bellum period. The "cat-hole" was a square opening, about seven by eight inches, provided for the purpose of letting the cat pass in and out of the house at will during the night. In the case of our particular cabin I could never understand the necessity for this convenience, since there were at least a half-dozen other places in the cabin that would have accommodated the cats. There was no wooden floor in our cabin, the naked earth being used as a floor. In the centre of the earthen floor there was a large, deep opening covered with boards, which was used as a place in which to store sweet potatoes during the winter. An impression of this potato-hole is very distinctly engraved upon my memory, because I recall that during the process of putting the potatoes in and taking them out I would often come into possession of one or two, which I roasted and thoroughly enjoyed. There was no cooking-stove on our plantation, and all the cooking for the whites and slaves my mother had to do over an open fireplace, mostly in pots and "skillets." While the poorly built cabin caused us to suffer with cold in the winter, the heat from the open fireplace in summer was equally trying.

The early years of my life, which were spent in the little cabin, were not very different from those of thousands of other slaves. My mother, of course, had little time in which to give attention to the train-ing of her children during the day. She snatched a few moments for our care in the early morning before her work began, and at night after the day's work was done. One of

Booker T. Washington in a portrait taken between 1890 and 1900.

my earliest recollections is that of my mother cooking a chicken late at night, and awakening her children for the purpose of feeding them. How or where she got it I do not know. I presume, however, it was procured from our owner's farm. Some peo-ple may call this theft. If such a thing were to happen now, I should condemn it as theft myself. But taking place at the time it did, and for the reason that it did, no one could ever make me believe that my mother was guilty of thieving. She was simply a victim of the system of slavery. I cannot remember having slept in a bed until after our family was declared free by the Emancipation Proclamation. Three children—John, my older brother, Amanda, my sister, and myself—had a pallet on the dirt floor, or, to be more correct, we slept in and on a bundle of filthy rags laid upon the dirt floor.

—Booker T. Washington, *Up From Slavery,* 1901

about and recorded, nothing leaves quite such a lasting impression of the man as a trip to his birthplace.

The monument, like most National Park Service projects, is faithful to the facts. Split-rail fences bound the pastures where the Burroughs family once farmed and where Washington lived as an impoverished slave. This was a modest tobacco farm of 206 acres, and the owners too lived in a small house whose foundations have been outlined in stone. A re-creation of the chinked-log Washington cabin is situated nearby, dirt-floored and grimly dark inside. Off below the houses stands a horse barn and livestock area, and the Park Service also maintains a vegetable and tobacco plot. Inside the small visitors center, a slide presentation affectingly chronicles the life of this exemplary Virginian. *12130 Booker T. Washington Highway, Hardy; 540-721-2094.*

■ SMITH MOUNTAIN LAKE STATE PARK
   map pages 264–265, F-5

While you're in the neighborhood, take a look at Smith Mountain Lake, one of the fastest-growing areas in Virginia, drawing retirees and boomers, vacationers and weekenders. The lake was formed when the Roanoke River was dammed in 1966, and the waters now lap on the shores of three counties, providing a summer playground for swimming, fishing, golf, sailing, houseboating, and just messing around in the water. *Off Route 626; 540-297-6066.*

■ SMITHFIELD PLANTATION   *map pages 264–265, D-4*

It is a surprise to find in this backcountry land of log cabins and pioneers a colonial plantation house built in 1773 in the elegant eastern-Virginia style. Snug up against the Virginia Tech campus in Blacksburg, Smithfield, the home of the Preston family for nearly 200 years, was initially protected from Indians and Tory neighbors by a high stockade fence. The builder, William Preston, died in 1783 leaving a wife, Susanna, and 10 children, and over the next 40 years, she ran the place alone, doubling the plantation's value. It stayed in the family until 1959, when a descendant gave it to the Association for the Preservation of Virginia Antiquities to restore and maintain. Costumed guides give tours (except in winter),

Puckett Cabin, at Milepost 189.9 of the Blue Ridge Parkway, was the home of the legendary "Aunt" Orelena Puckett (1837–1939), a midwife who delivered more than 1,000 babies.

and special events are held here, in the house and in the restored 18th-century garden. *1000 Smithfield Plantation Road, Blacksburg; 540-231-3947.*

■ FLOYD   *map pages 264–265, D-5*

This is a two-bit town with something to say—and it says it every Friday night at the **Country Store** (540-745-4563). You come to this emporium one block past the only traffic light in Floyd County, and if you pay your admission ($3, and apologies are given for the inflation that raised the price from $2), from 6:30 to 7:30 you'll hear gospel music played by anybody and everybody who wants to make a joyful noise unto the Lord. After 7:30, the place becomes a hoedown. Group after group is announced, takes its place, and strikes up, and everybody dances. Everybody, that is, except the old folks, kids, dogs, shy people, out-of-towners, or those with two left feet. They sit in rows of chairs or, in summer, hang around the edges as the music and dancing spill out into the street, drinking and eating and visiting with relatives and friends. Everybody has a ball!

Some seem to hope that Floyd will become another Galax, home of the famous Old Fiddlers' Convention, and that much money will be made. Others hope the place won't change. Whatever happens, Floyd will go its own way, having been for generations a pocket of resistance. According to one historian, during the Civil War this county had the highest number of deserters and "Unionists" of any in the South—Floyd men eased on home at the slightest chance—not out of fear or laziness, but to live out their lives of hardship and hard work with nobody telling them what to do. After the war, they saw that it would be to everybody's benefit to give their black neighbors land to farm.

Floyd's feisty citizenry includes plenty of old-time Christians and few nine-to-fivers; this town goes in for the counterculture, for communes and crafts. It was 1948 before Floyd County got electricity, and when the phone companies dragged their feet, it started its own Citizens' Telephone Co-op (which now has broadband). Today the county is fighting a proposed gas pipeline from West Virginia.

Maybe the hoedown's fame will spread and the world will beat a path to Floyd's door; maybe **Oddfella's Cantina** (540-745-3463) will get a stylish chef and doll up its comfy old booths—it might even come to pass that Floyd will have to get another stoplight. But don't bet on it.

Winter scene near Maggie, off Route 42, northwest of Roanoke.

If you continue south on the Blue Ridge Parkway, you can see **Mabry Mill** (Milepost 176, 540-745-9662), one of the most photographed spots in the state. Here you can watch demonstrations in a beautiful old mill complex and black-smith shop and buy water-ground grits or cornmeal to take home. In nearby **Meadows of Dan,** there's the Meadows of Dan campground (2182 Jeb Stuart Highway; 276-952-2292), with luxurious new cabins in an unspoiled spot, and Primland Resort (4621 Busted Rock Road; 276-251-8012), with mountaintop chalets, fly-fishing, riding, shooting, and golf.

But if you're making time on the interstate, take a short detour to the **Wilderness Road Regional Museum,** in the tiny town of Newbern, all of which is on the National Register of Historic Places. In this, the first county seat of Pulaski County, building lots were laid out along the road in 1810, with the requirement that each buyer build "a hewed log house at least one and a half stories high, with a shingle roof, brick or stone chimney, seams filled with lime mortar, two glass windows with twelve lights each." It made for a pretty town. Two of the early houses combined, furnished as of the period, with half a dozen outbuildings, make up the museum, which also provides brochures to lead you on a self-guided tour of town. *Route 611 off I-81, Exit 98; 540-674-4835.*

Paralleling this part of I-81 flows the New River, a history-rich waterway that rises in North Carolina and runs through Tennessee and Virginia and on to the Ohio River. It's one of the world's oldest rivers and a rare one that flows north for much of its length. The **New River Trail State Park** (276-699-6778), snakes along its banks for 57 miles, from Galax and Fries to Pulaski, along an abandoned stretch of N&W Railway tracks. It's a beautiful park, much used by bikers, hikers and riders.

About midway along this stretch of the New River, you come to **Shot Tower Historic State Park.** Thomas Jackson, a local businessman and part owner of the lead mines in nearby Austinville, finished building the 75-foot tower, which was used to make ammunition, in 1807. The thick limestone walls, slightly sloped, rise squarely from a 20-foot-square base, below which a shaft drops another 75 feet to the level of the river. From a kettle over a furnace at the top of the tower, molten lead was poured through sieves of different sizes, forming itself into round shot during the long fall into a kettle of water below. The shot were removed via a hori-zontal tunnel leading to the riverbank. When Jackson died in 1824, the tower went out of business, but it was reopened briefly during the Civil War and was attacked twice by Union troops.

It's a spooky, leafy green place, and you get glimpses of the river through the trees. A trail leads down to the river, and a wooden staircase leads up to the top, where you can see the kettle and the pouring apparatus and go out on a small balcony perched high in the trees. *On Route 52 off I-77, Exit 24; 276-699-1791.*

■ **BURKE'S GARDEN**   *map pages 264–265, C-5*

The Appalachian Trail goes right by this little valley high in the Alleghenies, but if you're not on foot, you can get here anyway, from I-77. Take Route 61 west toward Tazewell to Route 623 south, and the road will switchback over the mountain wall that surrounds Burke's Garden and down into what looks like paradise. They call it God's Thumbprint, and this oval hollow, at 3,100 feet, is the highest valley east of the Rockies. People wondered for years whether it was the depression left by an asteroid or the cone of a volcano that had imploded, but the most recent geological thinking is that it's a collapsed earth dome that once roofed over a 10-mile-long cavern.

When James Burke, a member of a surveying team led by Col. William Preston, the builder of Smithfield Plantation, discovered this bowl in 1748, he announced to the others that he'd found the Garden of Eden. The party returned to survey the bowl, but were forced by a storm to break camp and leave. Burke buried some potato peelings to conceal the campsite from Indians, and the next year when the party returned, they found a flourishing potato patch where the peelings had been buried. "Not the garden of Eden," said the men, "but Burke's garden!"

The 280 people who live here today grow all sorts of vegetables and fruit, and raise pigs and cattle, and sheep and chickens. Some are craftspeople, many run farm stands—on the honor system—it really feels a bit like the Land of Oz. In 1880, George Washington Vanderbilt thought so too. He tried to buy the garden, but nobody would sell, so he had to build his famous Biltmore in Asheville, North Carolina. Burke's Garden has 14 miles of paved roads for biking, a Lutheran church, and the smallest telephone company in the state. But come nightfall, you'll have to rest your head elsewhere, since the only amenity is the **General Store** (276-988-5091), which provides light snacks but no beds.

The **Crab Orchard Museum and Pioneer Park** sits right beside U.S. 19/460, 3 miles southwest of Tazewell. Yet another cluster of log buildings dedicated to explaining the life of Virginia's early white settlers, this site does have a compelling twist. It's located on a prehistoric hunting ground frequented 10,500 years ago by

Pioneer-era structures at the Crab Orchard Museum and Pioneer Park.

the ancestors of the Cherokee and Shawnee Indians. Archaeological digs across the road have turned up their stone tools and other artifacts. At the museum there's a pioneer village of log and stone buildings brought here from the surrounding area that depict the life of the early settlers. Reenactments, craft shows, workshops, and Pickin' on the Porches—bluegrass jam sessions—liven things up throughout the year. *U.S. 19/460 at Crab Orchard Road; 276-988-6755.*

■ **SALTVILLE** *map pages 264–265, B-5*

In 1782 a Col. Arthur Campbell was digging a well for saltmaking here when he came across some "bones of uncommon size"; he gave them to his friend Thomas Jefferson, who mentioned them in his *Notes on the State of Virginia.* That was the first recorded find of the woolly mammoth, mastodon, giant sloth, musk ox, and other beasts that roamed North America many millennia ago. Their bones are still being uncovered at the annual archaeological digs conducted here by the Museum of the Middle Appalachians.

After the animals came the early Native Americans, and since that time, people have always lived here. Salt is a mighty magnet, and in 1753 a land grant was issued in the name of King George II, although the town was not incorporated until 1896. Two Civil War battles were fought here when the Union tried to stop the Southern production of salt.

Saltville, at the end of Route 107, off I-81's Exit 35, is a tiny town, and all of its sights are on West Main Street, downtown on the square. The **Madame Russell House** is a replica of one built in 1788 by William Russell for his wife, Elizabeth, a sister of Patrick Henry who helped establish Methodism in the area. Another of Henry's sisters, Susanna, who had married James Madison's cousin, lived across the valley, and she could call to Elizabeth across the gap. Jeb Stuart's widow lived in William King's old house, now the **King-Stuart House,** and established a grammar school in the 1795 structure. The general's brother W. A. Stuart built another house around 1840 that was later occupied by Robert Porterfield, the founder of Abingdon's Barter Theatre.

Salt here was not dug out of the earth but pumped out as brine, and at **Salt Park** you can see a walking-beam salt-well pump and the original kettles where the brine was evaporated. The prominent Preston family manufactured salt here for several generations and was influential throughout the South.

The remarkable **Museum of the Middle Appalachians** contains displays of prehistoric bones, including a full-size replica of a mastodon skeleton; Woodland Indian artifacts; Civil War exhibits; a scale model of the valley; and geological and fossil collections. You can visit the archaeological digs and see the huge photographic collection that documents Saltville since the 1800s. *123 Palmer Avenue; 276-496-3633.*

■ MOUNT ROGERS NATIONAL RECREATION AREA
map pages 264–265, B/C-6

Mount Rogers National Recreation Area sprawls across the southeast side of I-81, encompassing 117,000 acres and enclosing Virginia's highest peak, 5,729-foot Mount Rogers. This wooded land welcomes loggers, hunters, and cattlemen, as well as hikers, skiers, fishermen, and campers—though there are three pristine and protected wilderness areas. The Appalachian Trail corkscrews through the area and across the shoulder of Mount Rogers, with a spur trail leading off to its wooded summit. The 33.4-mile rail-to-trail Virginia Creeper Trail creeps through the southern end of the area from White Top (5,520 feet) to Abingdon by way of Damascus, so the hiking options are enticing. Among the roads lacing the area, graveled and twisting Routes 689 and 80, in the south-central region, lead up to Elk Garden and views of Rogers. *U.S. Forest Service headquarters, Route 16, south I-81's Marion Exit; 276-783-5196.*

■ BREAKS INTERSTATE PARK *map pages 264–265, A-4*

Buried high in the heart of the Alleghenies off U.S. 460 is a jewel of a place called Breaks Interstate Park. With a liberal dash of hyperbole, it bears the designation Grand Canyon of the South, but at 1,600 feet deep and 5 miles long, the Breaks Canyon does rank as the largest gorge east of the Mississippi.

It's called an interstate park because the canyon cleaves Pine Mountain as it angles between Virginia and Kentucky. Though parklands lie in both states, all the facilities—the pleasant little restaurant and lodge rooms overlooking the gorge, the visitors center, campgrounds, and a small recreational lake—are in Virginia.

Down in the gorge, the **Russell Fork River** riffles desultorily along, patiently cutting its way through the soft shale of Pine Mountain, forming the eponymous breaks; but on October weekends, water released from the John Flannagan Reservoir creates Class 5 rapids for whitewater rafting. Erosion has produced fantastic formations, like the sandstone-capped Towers and the Chimney, both rising sentinel-like from the canyon floor. Before the gorge became parkland, it served the railroads, and if you stand at one of the several overlooks, you can see the track laid by the Clinchfield Railroad in 1915. It clings to a low bench just above the Russell Fork River and still serves passing coal trains treading this mining country.

The Virginia cliffs above the canyon are hardly the wild place they were when moonshiners hid out here or when the West Virginia Hatfields and Kentucky McCoys carried their blood feud across the border into this area. The seasons move gracefully above the canyon. In early spring the redbuds and dogwood dapple the forest, giving way as the season progresses to thickets of white and pink mountain laurel and rhododendron. In fall, the forests blaze orange and gold, and winter brings a blanket of snow. *Route 80, 8 miles north of Haysi; 276-865-4413.*

Breaks Interstate Park, on the Virginia-Kentucky border.

■ **ABINGDON** *map pages 264–265, B-6*

After you have wandered Virginia's southwest backcountry, stumbling into Abingdon feels like discovering an oasis. On U.S. 58, off I-81, Abingdon is compact and cultured, with a few broad tree-lined streets graced by big well-kept houses. It was incorporated in 1778, part of a 1750 land grant from George II to the explorer and surveyor Dr. Thomas Walker, a neighbor of Thomas Jefferson's in Albemarle County. Around the beautiful old Washington County Courthouse, which has a double cupola, antiques shops, restaurants, craft shops, and a few galleries proclaim this to be a town with taste as well as history.

Many residents attribute Abingdon's good breeding to its most famous feature—the old **Barter Theatre.** In a renovated red brick building that was a Presbyterian church, then a Temperance hall, and later an opera house, the theater has been going strong for 70 years. The Barter counts among its past players Gregory Peck, Hume Cronyn, Ned Beatty, Patricia Neal, Ernest Borgnine, and Kevin Spacey.

It began out of necessity. In 1933, in the midst of the Depression, an aspiring actor and native of southwest Virginia named Robert Porterfield found himself in New York City, out of work and hungry. So why not, he reasoned, open a theater in a rural area where food was plentiful, and instead of selling tickets to cash-poor local farmers, let them barter produce to attend plays? To try out his idea, Porterfield chose Abingdon. At the time, New York's old Empire Theater was being torn down, and Porterfield was offered its plush seats, sconces, and gilded plaques if he could carry them home. The transport was managed, and the theater proved a roaring success.

Over the years, such luminaries as Noel Coward, Thornton Wilder, George Bernard Shaw, and Tennessee Williams have exchanged their playwriting royalties for spinach and Virginia hams, and theatergoers from every continent have come to attend performances at this, the official state theater of Virginia. Payment is now by cash or credit card, but about three times a year, the theater revives the old tradition and accepts food in exchange for tickets. Productions in the old hall, and in a smaller theater, Barter Stage II, opened in an 1829 building across the street in the 1960s, range from traditional classics to contemporary dramas. *133 West Main Street; 276-628-3991.*

Close by both Barter theaters rises another Abingdon landmark, **Camberley's Martha Washington Inn** (150 West Main Street; 276-628-3161). The grand old

The Barter Theatre in Abingdon has fostered the career of many famous actors and actresses.

antebellum mansion, affectionately known as the Martha, has enjoyed a number of incarnations. The Preston family built it in 1832 and lived in it until 1858, when the building was transformed into Martha Washington College, a fashionable school for women. The school never closed during the Civil War, although it became at times a makeshift hospital, with the young women doing the nursing. The college fell on hard times and closed in 1932, but the Martha reopened a few years later as a stylish hotel. Since then, under various owners, it has lodged and fed presidents and celebrities. In the mid-1980s it was renovated and modernized, without compromising its genteel grace.

Another charming place to stay, just a few blocks east, is the **Crooked Cabin,** built in 1780. The six-room log cabin, rented as a single unit, sits right on Main Street in the historic district, with a walled patio garden in back. *303 East Main Street; 276-628-9583.*

On a hill at the west end of town, the **William King Regional Arts Center** (415 Academy Drive; 276-628-5005) overlooks downtown Abingdon. The building was one of the earliest schools in the region and today is an affiliate of the Virginia Museum of Fine Arts. Its galleries show the arts of the region and of other cultures—primitive and contemporary—including painting, sculpture, textile art, and decorative arts. You can also visit resident artists in their studios or take classes.

When you leave, stop at Depot Square to see more artists at work at the **Arts Depot,** the renovated former train station, and have a bite at the **Starving Artist Café** (134 Wall Street; 726-628-8445), where you can also have a leisurely look at more art on display. (Set aside plenty of time; the place is always jammed, for good reason, and you'll probably have to wait on the bench outside.)

At the east end of Abingdon you might visit the **Tavern** (222 East Main Street; 276-628-1118), not just for the food, but to see the oldest building in town (1779), where King Louis Philippe of France, Henry Clay, and Andrew Jackson dined. It has been a private house, bakery, post office (the old mail slot can be seen from the street), and a Civil War hospital (the charcoaled numbers of soldiers' beds are still on the wall on the third floor).

On lower Pecan Street you can pick up the western end of the **Virginia Creeper Trail,** a footpath that winds 34 miles from here to Damascus, passing through serene pastures and deep forests, and crossing bridges above stone-laced riverbeds. The trail follows an old Indian trace that became a railroad bed through the mountains. Because the steam trains traveling this line had a long, slow pull through rough terrain, they were known as Virginia creepers, after the vine of the same name. In the 1980s, Norfolk & Western Railway sold this right-of-way, and the old roadbed entered the postindustrial area of the recreationist. Now hikers, bikers, joggers, and horse lovers steam along the old path.

■ CUMBERLAND GAP   *map pages 264–265, A-2*

In some ways it's ironic that this area has lapsed back into isolation, because it was through here that the westward ho–ing settlers poured on their way to Kentucky and the far wilderness. The Cumberland Gap is the only natural break in the formidable wall of the Appalachians as they stretch from Maine to Georgia. This pass was used farther back in time than history records, first by the buffalo and deer in search of salt and, long before white settlers set foot here, by Native Americans in search of game and of each other—the gap lay along the famous Warrior's Path, which ran from the Potomac River to the Ohio.

In 1750, Dr. Thomas Walker explored this break in the mountains. Others came after him—fur traders, hunters, cattlemen, and pioneer farmers—but most notable among them was Daniel Boone, a Pennsylvania-born boy with a taste for the wilderness, who left his home in North Carolina to explore this region. No great flood of humanity poured through the gap, though, until the 1775 Treaty of Sycamore Shoals brought about peace with hostile tribes. Boone was hired to build the **Wilderness Road** through the gap and into western Virginia, now Kentucky. In three weeks, he and 30 woodsmen had blazed the 208-mile footpath that would later be widened to accommodate pioneer wagons, livestock, and the nation's dreams of expansion.

The Wilderness Road actually was a continuation of the old **Great Wagon Road,** which led from Pennsylvania down the Shenandoah Valley, opening the area to the floods of Scots-Irish, Germans, Mennonites, and Quakers who settled southwestern Virginia, giving it its hardworking, religious flavor.

As the western lands were settled, the Wilderness Road also became a route for goods and produce moving east. By the 1820s and '30s, though, traffic along the gap declined as newly built canals and steamboats offered easier passage.

Today the **Cumberland Gap National Historical Park** comprises a long narrow strip along Virginia's border with Kentucky and Tennessee. Traffic moving westward along present-day Route 58 meets U.S. 25E, a superhighway, in Tennessee and is funneled into the Cumberland Gap Tunnel, opened in 1996, to the park visitors center in Kentucky (606-248-2817).

Meanwhile, the old trails of the Wilderness Road are being restored to their 1780–1810 natural contours and landscape. If you're set on traveling through the gap itself, you can still do it the old-fashioned way—on foot. In fact, most of the 200,000 acres of high, green wilderness are accessible only on foot. Otherwise, you can make the snaking, 4-mile drive up to the 2,440-foot **Pinnacle Peak.** From here, the Alleghenies seem to roll off in waves toward the horizon. You might also climb the 1.2-mile trail to **Tri-State Peak** and stand (or lie) simultaneously in Virginia, Kentucky, and Tennessee.

(following pages) View off Route 58, the Wilderness Road, en route to Cumberland Gap.

PRACTICAL INFORMATION

■ AREA CODES AND TIME ZONE

The area code for Richmond and vicinity is 804. In the Virginia suburbs of Washington, D.C., including Alexandria and Arlington, the area code is 703 or 571; elsewhere in northern and western Virginia (Winchester, Roanoke, Fredericksburg), 540. In southwestern Virginia, including Abingdon, 276; in the central part of the state (Lynchburg and Charlottesville), 434; in the southeast corner, including Norfolk, Williamsburg, and the Eastern Shore, 757. Virginia is in the Eastern time zone.

■ METRIC CONVERSIONS

1 foot = .305 meters
1 mile = 1.6 kilometers
Centigrade = Fahrenheit temperature minus 32, divided by 1.8
1 pound = .45 kilograms

■ CLIMATE

The weather in Virginia is relatively temperate and predictable. The greatest shock to travelers here is the humidity, which makes summers feel hotter and winters colder than the temperature warrants. The humidity is, generally, higher in coastal areas, though the Tidewater flatlands and the mountains too tend to be plenty moist. The moderating effects of the ocean and the Chesapeake Bay make winters milder along the coast.

Spring and fall are the optimal seasons, though heavy rains can occur in either. Summers are unrelentingly hot, winters unpredictable—in some years the state gets several serious snowfalls and extremely low temperatures; in other years winters are quite moderate. The mountains get more snow and colder weather than the rest of the state.

In general, daytime temperatures average as follows. Winter: 30 degrees F to low 40s; spring: 60 degrees to low 80s; summer: 80s and 90s; fall: 50s to low 70s.

■ GETTING THERE AND AROUND

■ BY AIR

Richmond International Airport (RIC), gateway to central Virginia, is 7 miles southeast of the city. It is served by most major U.S. airlines and Air Canada. *I-64, Exit 197A (Airport Drive), or I-295, Exit 31 (Airport Drive); 804-226 3000; www.flyrichmond.com.*

Norfolk International Airport (ORF) serves southeastern Virginia and the Greater Hampton Roads area. *757-857-3351; www.norfolkairport.com.*

Ronald Reagan Washington National Airport (DCA), 3 miles south of downtown Washington, D.C., between Arlington and Alexandria, serves Washington and northern Virginia with flights on all major domestic carriers. *I-395, Exit 10 (George Washington Parkway South); 703-417-8000; www.mwaa.com/national.*

Dulles International Airport (IAD), 26 miles northwest of Washington, D.C., is served by domestic and international carriers. *Route 28 off I-66; 703-572-2700; www.mwaa.com/dulles.*

■ BY CAR

Interstate 95 runs north-south through Virginia. At Richmond it intersects I-64, which runs east-west—east toward Williamsburg, Hampton Roads, the Chesapeake Bay Bridge-Tunnel, and Virginia's Eastern Shore, and west toward Charlottesville and the Shenandoah Valley. At Staunton, I-64 intersects I-81, which runs northeast-southwest, down the entire Valley of Virginia. Route 29 leaves Washington on its southwest route through the state, running along east of the Blue Ridge Mountains, through Warrenton and Charlottesville, all the way to Danville, near the North Carolina line. Route 58 runs east-west, across southern Virginia, connecting the ocean to the Cumberland Gap. Route 460 roughly parallels it about 50 miles north, connecting Suffolk, Petersburg, and Lynchburg to Roanoke and Blacksburg.

Scenic drives include the 105-mile Skyline Drive, a spectacular route along the spine of the Blue Ridge Mountains from Front Royal to Waynesboro, and the 469-mile Blue Ridge Parkway, which continues through mountain splendor from Waynesboro south into North Carolina.

■ BY TRAIN

Amtrak operates daily north-south service along the Eastern Seaboard, stopping in Virginia in Alexandria, Quantico, Fredericksburg, Richmond, and Petersburg. Two trains a day branch off at Richmond, to Williamsburg and Newport News (a connecting bus takes you on to Norfolk and Virginia Beach). Trains from New York to New Orleans stop at Alexandria, Manassas, Culpeper, Charlottesville, Lynchburg, and Danville. East-west trains between Washington and Chicago stop in Alexandria, Manassas, Culpeper, Charlottesville, Staunton, and Clifton Forge. *800-872-7245; www.amtrak.com.*

■ BY BUS

Greyhound Lines serves many towns. Trailways, affiliated with Greyhound, also serves the state. *800-231-2222; www.greyhound.com.*

■ FOOD

Seafood is Virginia's forte, and almost every restaurant offers some kind of fish or shellfish, but some people never order seafood when they're more than 100 miles from the Chesapeake Bay—west of the fall line they stick to steak. In rural areas you'll find southern fare: grits and greens and red-eye gravy, but only in refined dining rooms can you sample Smithfield, or "country," ham and delicacies like batter bread (called spoon bread too). What the state is not noted for is its diversity of authentic ethnic cuisines, although gradually the ethnic horizon is broadening. Most towns have the American version of Italian and Chinese eateries, and true Asian, Mediterranean, and Latin American restaurants are turning up in some surprising places.

■ LODGING

Virginia has the typical collection of roadside motels and chain hotels. In addition, the state—particularly in the northwest, the Shenandoah Valley, and parts of Tidewater—offers an impressive collection of bed-and-breakfasts and small inns. Most of these are truly charming, and many are in historic buildings. Antique furnishings and Virginia hospitality predominate.

Metrorail commuters in the Pentagon station, Arlington. Operated by the Washington Metropolitan Area Transit Authority, Metrorail can take you from the nation's capital and Ronald Reagan Washington National Airport to various sites in northern Virginia.

■ **RESERVATIONS SERVICES**

Bed and Breakfast Association of Virginia. *888-660-2228; www.innvirginia.com.*
Virginia Hospitality and Travel Association. *www.vhta.org.*
Virginia Tourism Office. *202-872-0523 or 800-934-9184; www.virginia.org.*

■ **HOTEL AND MOTEL CHAINS**

Best Western. *800-528-1234; www.bestwestern.com.*
Comfort Inn. *800-228-5150; www.comfortinn.com.*
Days Inn. *800-325-2525; www.daysinn.com.*
Doubletree. *800-222-8733; www.doubletree.com.*
Econo Lodge. *800-446-6900; www.econolodge.com.*
Embassy Suites. *800-362-2779; www.embassysuites.com.*
Hilton Hotels. *800-445-8667; www.hilton.com.*
Holiday Inn. *800-465-4329; www.6c.com.*
Hyatt Hotels. *800-233-1234; www.hyatt.com.*
Marriott Hotels. *800-228-9290; www.marriott.com.*
Omni. *800-843-6664; www.omnihotels.com.*
Quality Inns. *800-228-5151; www.qualityinn.com.*
Radisson. *800-333-3333; www.radisson.com.*
Ramada Inns. *800-272-6232; www.ramada.com.*
Sheraton. *800-325-3535; www.sheraton.com.*
Travelodge. *800-255-3050; www.travelodge.com.*
Westin Hotels. *800-228-3000; www.westin.com.*

■ **CAMPING**

National Park Service. *800-365-2267; reservations.nps.gov.*
National Recreation Reservation Service (for facilities managed by the U.S. Forest
Service and Army Corps of Engineers). *877-444-6777; www.reserveusa.com.*
Recreation.gov (for sites managed by the Bureau of Land Management and other
federal agencies). *www.recreation.gov.*
Virginia State Parks. *800-933-7275; www.dcr.state.va.us/parks.*

■ OFFICIAL TOURISM INFORMATION

Virginia. *804-786-4484 or 800-932-5827; www.virginia.org.*

Abingdon. *276-676-2282 or 800-435-3440; www.abingdon.com/tourism.*

Alexandria. *800-388-9119; www.funside.com.*

Arlington. *800-677-6267; www.stayarlington.com.*

Charlottesville/Albemarle County. *434-293-6789 or 877-386-1102; www.charlottesvilletourism.org.*

Chincoteague. *757-336-6161; www.chincoteaguechamber.com.*

Eastern Shore. *757-787-2460; www.esvatourism.org.*

Fairfax County. *703-550-2450 or 800-732-4732; www.visitfairfax.org.*

Floyd County. *540-745-4407; www.visitfloyd.org.*

Fredericksburg. *540-373-1776 or 800-678-4748; www.fredericksburgvirginia.net.*

Gloucester County. *804-693-0014; www.co.gloucester.va.us/pr/tourism.htm.*

Hampton. *757-722-1222 or 800-487-8778; www.hamptoncvb.com.*

Lynchburg. *434-847-1811 or 800-732-5821; www.lynchburgchamber.org.*

Manassas. *877-848-3018; www.visitmanassas.org.*

Newport News. *757-886-7777 or 888-493-7386; www.newport-news.org.*

Norfolk. *757-664-6620 or 800-368-3097; www.norfolkcvb.com.*

Petersburg. *804-733-2300; www.petersburg-va.org.*

Historic Petersburg. *804-732-2096; www.historicpetersburg.org.*

Portsmouth. *800-767-8782; www.portsmouth.va.us.*

Richmond. *804-782-2777 or 800-370-9004; www.richmondva.org.*

Roanoke Valley. *540-342-6025 or 800-635-5535; www.visitroanokeva.com.*

Shenandoah Valley. *540-740-3132; www.svta.org.*

Staunton. *540-332-3865 or 800-342-7982; www.stauntonva.org.*

Virginia Beach. *757-437-4888 or 800-822-3224; www.vbfun.com.*

Williamsburg. *757-253-0192 or 800-368-6511; www.visitwilliamsburg.com.*

Colonial Williamsburg. *800-447-8679; www.history.org.*

Winchester/Frederick County. *800-662-1360; www.visitwinchesterva.com.*

Yorktown. *757-890-3300; www.yorkcounty.gov/tourism.*

■ USEFUL WEB SITES

Association for the Preservation of Virginia Antiquities. Owns and maintains historic properties. *www.apva.org/apva/index.html.*

Civil War Preservation Trust. Preserves endangered Civil War battlefield sites. *www.civilwar.org.*

Historic Garden Week in Virginia. Annual spring event bills itself as "America's oldest and largest house and garden tour program." *www.vagardenweek.org.*

Jamestown 1607–2007. Countdown to the 400th anniversary of the first permanent English settlement in America. *www.jamestown2007.org.*

My Virginia. Official Commonwealth of Virginia site. *www.vipnet.org/cmsportal.*

Richmond Times-Dispatch. Daily newspaper. *www.timesdispatch.com.*

Shenandoah at War. Information about valley battlefields. *www.shenandoahatwar.org.*

Virginia Civil War Trails. Information on war sites throughout the state; includes maps for driving tours. *www.civilwartraveler.com/virginia.*

Virginia Department of Game and Inland Fisheries. Information about hunting, fishing, boating, and wildlife. *www.dgif.state.va.us.*

Virginia Department of Historic Resources. A listing of historic properties. *state.vipnet.org/dhr/home.htm.*

■ FESTIVALS AND EVENTS

■ FEBRUARY

George Washington Birthday Celebration, Alexandria. Colonial costume parties, a ball, a parade, and other activities. *703-838-5005 or 703-838-4200.*

■ MARCH

Highland Maple Festival, Monterey. A celebration of maple syrup the second and third weekends—watch it being made, and then pour it over pancakes. *540-468-2550.*

■ APRIL

Easter Decoy and Art Festival, Chincoteague. Local and national artists display their work. Seafood and down-home cooking too. *757-336-6161.*

Historic Garden Week. Historic private homes and gardens statewide open their doors and gates. *804-644-7776.*

International Azalea Festival, Norfolk. Weeklong festivities celebrating the city's role in NATO. *757-622-2312.*

Strawberry Hill Races, Richmond. Major steeplechase race, plus a tailgate competition and a carriage promenade through city streets. *804-228-3200.*

■ MAY

Afr'Am Fest, Norfolk. Celebration of African-American culture—soulful cuisine, arts and crafts, live music. *757-456-1743.*

Roanoke Festival in the Park. Art and craft shows, parades, sports competitions, performing arts, and food. *540-342-2640.*

Shenandoah Apple Blossom Festival, Winchester. Parade and entertainment presided over by apple-blossom queen and her court. *540-662-3863.*

Virginia Arts Festival, Norfolk and other waterfront cities. A month of dance, theater, classical music, and jazz, plus the Virginia International Tattoo. *757-282-2800.*

Virginia Gold Cup, The Plains. One of the country's premier steeplechase events. Seven races are held in the heart of hunt country. *540-347-2612.*

■ JUNE

Hampton Jazz Festival, Hampton. Three-day fest attracts musicians from all over the country. *757-838-4203.*

Harborfest, Norfolk. Seafood, soul food, tall ships, water and air shows, military demonstrations, and parades of sail. *757-627-5329.*

James River Batteau Festival, Lynchburg to Maidens Adventure. Traditional boats head downriver on an 8-day trip toward the capital. *434-528-3950.*

Vintage Virginia, The Plains. The state's wineries offer samples. Also jazz, blues, and reggae bands and arts and crafts purveyors. *800-277-2075.*

■ JULY

Pony Swim, Chincoteague. The wild ponies of Assateague Island are rounded up and swim to Chincoteague Island, where the foals are sold at auction. *757-336-6161.*

■ **August**
Old Fiddler's Convention, Galax. Country and mountain musicians compete. *276-236-8541.*
Virginia Wine Festival, The Plains. State's oldest wine festival, with wine tasting, food, and music. *800-520-9670.*

■ **September**
Harvest Jubilee, Danville. Celebrates tobacco, the crops' farmers, and auctioneers. Music, crafts, sports, and farm exhibits. *434-799-5200.*
Neptune Festival, Virginia Beach. Oceanfront festivities include a sand castle contest, surfing, sailing, arts and crafts, and an air show. *757-498-0215.*

■ **October**
Oyster Festival, Chincoteague. All-you-can-eat picnic draws a crowd, so best to bring your own folding chairs, tables, or blanket. *757-336-6161.*
Virginia Film Festival, Charlottesville. Gaining in stature, with screenings of important new films and appearances by stars. *800-882-3378.*
Waterford Homes Tour and Crafts Exhibit, Waterford. One of the largest juried crafts shows in the East, in a historic town. *540-882-3018.*

■ **November**
Waterfowl Week, Assateague Island. Migratory birds arrive at the Chincoteague National Wildlife Refuge, and roads normally closed to traffic open so visitors can get a better view. *757-336-6122.*

■ **December**
Grand Illumination, Williamsburg. Candlelight and 18th century–style decorations brighten the historic area, along with caroling, fife-and-drum corps music, and fireworks. *800-447-8679.*
Scottish Christmas Walk, Alexandria. Bagpipers and bands parade through streets decorated for Christmas. House tours, arts and crafts, Christmas greenery, food. *703-838-5005 or 703-549-0111.*

RECOMMENDED READING

■ History

Allen, Thomas B. *The Blue and the Gray.* Washington, D.C.: National Geographic Society, 1993.

Barden, Thomas E., ed. *Virginia Folk Legends.* Charlottesville: University of Virginia Press, 1991.

Bowers, John. *Stonewall Jackson: Portrait of a Soldier.* New York: William Morrow, 1989.

Brodie, Fawn. *Thomas Jefferson, An Intimate History.* New York: W.W. Norton, 1998.

Dabney, Virginius. *Virginia, The New Dominion: A History from 1607 to the Present.* Charlottesville: University of Virginia Press, 1983.

Ellis, Joseph J. *American Sphinx: The Character of Thomas Jefferson.* New York: Vintage Books, 1998.

Foote, Shelby. *The Civil War.* 3 Vols. New York: Vintage, 1986.

Fox, James. *Five Sisters: The Langhornes of Virginia.* New York: Simon and Schuster, 2000.

Freeman, Douglas Southall. *R. E. Lee, A Biography.* 4 Vols. San Diego: Simon Publications, 2001.

Gordon-Reed, Annette. *Thomas Jefferson and Sally Hemings: An American Controversy.* Charlottesville: University of Virginia Press, 1997.

Janney, Werner L. and Asa Moore. *John Jay Janney's Virginia: An American Farm Lad's Life in the Early 19th Century.* McLean, Va.: EPM Publishing, Inc., 1978.

Jones, Katharine M., ed. *Heroines of Dixie.* New York: Ballantine Books, 1955.

Loth, Calder, ed. *Virginia Landmarks of Black History.* Charlottesville: University of Virginia Press, 1995.

National Park Service. *Appomattox Court House.* Washington, D.C.: United States Department of the Interior, 1980.

Reeder, Carolyn and Jack Reeder. *Shenandoah Vestiges: What the Mountain People Left Behind.* Washington, D.C.: Potomac Appalachian Trail Club, 1995.

Robertson, James I. Jr. *Civil War Virginia: Battleground for a Nation.* Charlottesville: University of Virginia Press, 1991.

Rouse, Parke Jr. *The James: Where a Nation Began.* Richmond: Dietz, 1991.

Salmon, John S. *The Official Virginia Civil War Battlefield Guide.* Mechanicsburg, Pa.: Stackpole Books, 2001.

Thomas, David Hurst, et al. *The Native Americans: An Illustrated History.* Atlanta: Turner Publishing, 1993.

Washington, Booker T. *Up from Slavery: An Autobiography.* New York: Modern Library, 1999.

Whitehead, John Hurt III. *The Watermen of the Chesapeake Bay.* 2nd ed. Centerville, Md.: Tidewater Publishing, 1987.

Wilson, Charles Reagan and William Ferris, eds. *Encyclopedia of Southern Culture.* Chapel Hill: University of North Carolina Press, 1989.

■ FICTION AND NON-FICTION

Davids, Richard C. *The Man Who Moved a Mountain.* Minneapolis: Fortress Press, 1986.

de Hart, Allen. *The Trails of Virginia: Hiking the Old Dominion.* Chapel Hill: University of North Carolina Press, 1995.

Dillard, Annie. *Pilgrim at Tinker Creek.* New York: HarperCollins, 1998.

Glasgow, Ellen. *Vein of Iron.* Charlottesville: University of Virginia Press, 1995.

———. *The Sheltered Life.* Charlottesville: University of Virginia Press, 1994.

Koch, Adrienne and William Peden, eds. *The Life and Selected Writings of Thomas Jefferson.* New York: Modern Library, 1993.

Styron, William. *The Confessions of Nat Turner.* New York: Vintage, 1992.

———. *Lie Down in Darkness.* New York: Vintage, 1992.

———. *Tidewater Morning.* New York: Vintage, 1994.

Thom, James Alexander. *Follow the River.* New York: Ballantine Books, 1986.

I N D E X

COMPASS AMERICAN GUIDES

Alaska

American Southwest

Arizona

Boston

Chicago

Coastal California

Colorado

Connecticut & Rhode Island

Florida

Georgia

Gulf South

Hawaii

Idaho

Kentucky

Las Vegas

Maine

Manhattan

Massachusetts

Michigan

Minnesota

Montana

Nevada

New Hampshire

New Mexico

New Orleans

North Carolina

Oregon

Pacific Northwest

Pennsylvania

San Francisco

Santa Fe

South Carolina

South Dakota

Tennessee

Texas

Utah

Vermont

Virginia

Wine Country

Wisconsin

Wyoming

Compass American Guides are available at special discounts for bulk purchases for sales promotions or premiums. Special editions, including personalized covers, excerpts of existing guides, and corporate imprints, can be created in large quantities for special needs. For more information, contact your local bookseller or write to Special Markets, Fodor's Travel Publications, 1745 Broadway, New York, NY 10019. Inquiries from Canada should be directed to your local Canadian bookseller or sent to Random House of Canada, Ltd., Marketing Department, 2775 Matheson Boulevard East, Mississauga, Ontario L4W 4P7. Inquiries from the United Kingdom should be sent to Fodor's Travel Publications, 20 Vauxhall Bridge Road, London, England SW1V 2SA.

COMPASS AMERICAN GUIDES

Critics, booksellers, and travelers all agree: you're lost without a Compass.

"This splendid series provides exactly the sort of historical and cultural detail about North American destinations that curious-minded travelers need."
—*Washington Post*

"This is a series that constantly stuns us...no guide with photos this good should have writing this good. But it does." —*New York Daily News*

"Of the many guidebooks on the market, few are as visually stimulating, as thoroughly researched, or as lively written as the Compass American Guide series."
—*Chicago Tribune*

"Good to read ahead of time, then take along so you don't miss anything."
—*San Diego Magazine*

"Magnificent photography. First rate."—*Money*

"Written by longtime residents of each destination...these handsome and literate guides are strong on history and culture, and illustrated with gorgeous photos."
—*San Francisco Chronicle*

"The color photographs sparkle, the archival illustrations illuminate windows to the past, and the writing is usually of the utmost caliber." —*Michigan Tribune*

"Class acts, worth reading and shelving for keeps even if you're not a traveler. "
—*New Orleans Times-Picayune*

"Beautiful photographs and literate writing are the hallmarks of the Compass guides." —*Nashville Tennessean*

"History, geography, and wanderlust converge in these well-conceived books."
—*Raleigh News & Observer*

"Oh, my goodness! What a gorgeous series this is."—*Booklist*

ACKNOWLEDGMENTS

■ FROM THE AUTHOR

From K.M. Kostyal for the original edition: Heartfelt appreciation goes first to the many public affairs people at visitors centers, museums, and historic homes across the state. The Virginia Tourism Corporation also offered endless information and guidance, as did the Library of Virginia, the Arlington libraries, and the Lloyd House historical library in Alexandria. My thanks also to the editor of this book's original edition, Kit Duane, who appreciates the subtleties of the Virginia psyche. Thanks also to Tobias Steed for his consummate professionalism and understanding of the writer's world. For leading me down the esoteric paths of grammatical finesse, and for his fine literary sensibilities, my thanks to Werner Janney. Finally, I want to thank my husband, Buzz, for his support and patience. And to my son, Will, a thanks for simply being himself.

Many thanks to convention and visitors bureau staff members for their help: Sam Martinette at Norfolk, Janene Charbeneau at Richmond, and Sergei Troubetzkoy at Staunton. I'm also grateful to David Mitchell at Stratford. Thanks also to Mary Sanders and John Hoover at the Homestead, M. McKay-Smith Abeles of Buttonwood, Katharine F. Heath of Carysbrook, Richard Caden at Montrose House, Nat and Sherry Morison of Welbourne, and many other innkeepers all over Virginia.

■ FROM THE PUBLISHER

Compass American Guides would like to thank Joan Keener for copyediting the manuscript of this book and Ellen Klages for proofreading it. Compass American Guides would also like to thank the following individuals or institutions for the use of their illustrations or photographs on the pages noted below. All other photographs in the book are by David M. Doody.

Overview
Page 12 top, Richard T. Nowitz

History
Page 20, Library of Virginia
Page 23, Library of Congress

Piedmont

Northern Virginia

Shenandoah Valley

Page 224 top, Timothy H. O'Sullivan, ©David M. Doody, Image Alchemy
    Collection
Page 224 bottom, ©David M. Doody, Image Alchemy Collection
Page 225 top, James F. Gibson, ©David M. Doody, Image Alchemy Collection
Page 225 bottom, Timothy H. O'Sullivan, ©David M. Doody, Image Alchemy
    Collection
Page 229, Hulton Archive/Getty Images
Page 232, VMI Museum
Page 234, Luray Caverns
Pages 238–239, Shenandoah Shakespeare
Page 244, Virginia Military Institute
Page 245, Stonewall Jackson Foundation
Page 246, Library of Congress
Page 247, Virginia Tourism Corporation
Page 252, The New-York Historical Society

West by Southwest

Page 267, Library of Virginia
Page 270, Roanoke Valley Convention & Visitors Bureau
Page 275, Library of Congress, Prints and Photographs Division (LC-USZ62-
    119897)
Page 287, Virginia Tourism Corporation

ABOUT THE AUTHOR

Born and raised in coastal Virginia, K.M. Kostyal earned a graduate degree in social anthropology from the University of Virginia. In 1976, she joined the staff of the National Geographic Society. Initially involved in its book publications, she later became a contributing editor for the Society's *National Geographic Traveler* magazine. She has also twice won the Society of American Travel Writers Lowell Thomas Award. Ms. Kostyal is the author of *Stonewall Jackson: A Life Portrait* and *Art of the State: Virginia.*

CONTRIBUTOR

Conrad Little Paulus, who revised this edition, was a senior editor at Fodor's in the early 1990s and before that a copy editor at *Travel & Leisure* and *Seventeen* magazines. Born in Norfolk and raised in Richmond, she is a transplanted Virginian who considers her home base to be New York—where she went to college, worked, raised her children, and currently lives. But she returns often to Virginia, visiting family and friends in Virginia Beach, Arlington, Norfolk, and Petersburg.

ABOUT THE PHOTOGRAPHER

As the Colonial Williamsburg Foundation's photographic services manager, David M. Doody produces much of the photography seen in Colonial Williamsburg's books, brochures, calendars, and post cards, and on its Web site. A resident of Virginia since 1984, he is also an active freelancer, and his assignments have given him an intimate knowledge of the state. His work has appeared in major American newspapers and magazines, as well as in the *Colonial Williamsburg Journal,* a quarterly focusing on Colonial American life. Among his book credits are *Animals of Colonial Williamsburg,* his latest, published in 2003, and *Where Banners Flew* (1997), an aerial view of Virginia history.